Masculine Jealousy and Contemporary Cinema

Masculine Jealousy and Contemporary Cinema

Candida Yates

palgrave
macmillan

First published 2007 by
PALGRAVE MACMILLAN
Houndmills, Basingstoke, Hampshire RG21 6XS and
175 Fifth Avenue, New York, N.Y. 10010
Companies and representatives throughout the world

PALGRAVE MACMILLAN is the global academic imprint of the Palgrave Macmillan division of St. Martin's Press, LLC and of Palgrave Macmillan Ltd. Macmillan® is a registered trademark in the United States, United Kingdom and other countries. Palgrave is a registered trademark in the European Union and other countries.

ISBN 13: 978–1–4039–8621–4
ISBN 10: 1–4039–8621–5

This book is printed on paper suitable for recycling and made from fully managed and sustained forest sources. Logging, pulping and manufacturing processes are expected to conform to the environmental regulations of the country of origin.

A catalogue record for this book is available from the British Library.

Library of Congress Cataloging-in-Publication Data

Yates, Candida, 1959–
    Masculine jealousy and contemporary cinema / Candida Yates.
        p. cm.
    Includes bibliographical references and index.
    ISBN 1–4039–8621–5 (alk. paper)
    1. Men in motion pictures. 2. Masculinity in motion pictures. 3. Jealousy in motion pictures. I. Title.
    PN1995.9.M46Y38 2007
    791.43'653–dc22   2007016447

Transfrred to Digital Printing 2008

This book is dedicated to the memory of my mother,
Juliet (Jill) Yates (1929–2007)

Contents

Acknowledgements

This book was written with the encouragement and support of a number of colleagues, friends and institutions. Acknowledgement should go to the British Film Institute Library Reading Room, London, and the librarians there for their helpful assistance and advice in obtaining archive film material and publicity. Thanks also to librarian Robin Stinson at the University of East London. My warmest thanks to my friend and colleague Dr Caroline Bainbridge for her unqualified enthusiasm and generosity regarding the writing of this book and for her insightful comments on draft chapters. My thanks also to Professor Shelley Day Sclater for her helpful comments on earlier draft chapters, and to my Psychosocial Studies colleagues and students at The University of East London who have supported my work on this book with enthusiasm – and Dr Heather Price and Dr David Jones deserve special thanks here. I also want to thank Professor Barry Richards, Dr Corinne Squire, Dr Amal Treacher and Dr Susannah Radstone, who were involved in the earlier stages of my research into masculine jealousy and cinema.

I would like to express gratitude to Penny Simmons at Password Publishing for her advice and support in the formatting and copy editing of the manuscript and to Jill Lake and Melanie Blair at Palgrave Macmillan for their support in the development of the book. My thanks to Nicholas Wolfson for his generosity in allowing me to reproduce his painting 'Jealousy' (1973) on the cover of this book see: (www.nicholaswolfson.com).

The following parts have peen published elsewhere: a modified version of Chapter 7 has been published in the Journal For Cultural Research, 10(3), July 2006, pp. 219–235, and some parts of Chapter 2 were published in a modified form in Psychoanalytic Studies, 2(1), 2000, pp. 77–88.

I want to thank my family for their support in getting the book written, and last but not least, its completion owes much to the warm encouragement, love and support of Lindsay Wells.

1
Setting the Scene: Masculinity, Jealousy and Contemporary Culture

This book offers a new understanding of the relationships between masculinity and male jealousy. Its focus is the representation of jealousy in contemporary cinema as a marker of the relationships between masculinity, fantasy and cultural change. Jealousy has played a key role in the shaping of masculine identities and provides a useful focus to explore the tensions and contradictions of Western masculinities, within the shifting and uncertain terrain of late modern culture.[1] Historically, male jealousy and its relationship to the shaping of men and masculinities remains under-researched within cultural and psychosocial studies. The main debates around jealousy tend to unfold with reference to either psychology or sociology. Psychologically, jealousy is closely related to envy, but whereas envy involves two people, jealousy involves three. Sociologically, the emphasis generally distinguishes between envy and jealousy. As sociologist Van Sommers suggests, 'Envy concerns what you would like to have but don't possess, jealousy ... concerns what you have and don't wish to lose' (1988: 1). This book carves out a space in which to consider the psycho-cultural manifestations of heterosexual jealousy by exploring key images of its themes of loss and anxiety as well as its emotional significance.

The insecurities that underpin male jealousy can be discussed in the context of recent discussions about the alleged 'crisis' of masculinity (Coward, 1999a; Segal, 1990). The psychosocial and cultural meanings of this crisis and whether it signifies a shift towards more positive reflexive masculinities have also been the subject of debate. On the one hand, some suggest that changes in contemporary culture have, in a positive fashion, opened up new cultural spaces for the emergence of more fluid, less defensive masculinities (Minsky, 1998; Segal, 1990). On the other hand, it is often argued that the changes and uncertainties of contemporary culture have provoked a more defensive response in the media, and that new so-called 'feminized' images of men, have contributed to a paranoid cultural 'backlash' against both feminism and new masculinities (Faludi, 1991, 1999).

This book applies cultural, social and psychoanalytic theories to engage with these debates through the study of masculine jealousy and its representation in Hollywood films. It challenges the binary model of theorizing masculinities as being either positive or negative, to argue that contemporary representations of masculinity often contain different elements of both these positions. This ambiguity reflects the doubts and fears about the loss of male entitlement more generally and a new cultural awareness of the contradictions and costs of more traditional definitions of masculinity (Bainbridge and Yates, 2005).[2] Such feelings may also reflect an acceptance of a more nuanced vision of masculinity as a psychological, social and cultural construction.

Jealousy is a useful lens through which to explore such dilemmas as it tests the ability to cope with complex emotions and affects that arise in relation to wounded narcissism and feelings of loss.[3] Socially and culturally, the rules governing the codes of masculine jealousy have played a significant role in guarding the social and emotional boundaries of Western men and masculinities (Stearns, 1989). Male jealousies are shaped by historical factors and the cultural contexts in which they are symbolized and expressed. It is commonly argued that male jealousy has not fared well in the modern Western history of the emotions (Clanton, 1996; Mullen, 1991; Stearns, 1989). Before the twentieth century, jealousy was regarded in social rather than psychological terms and as an appropriate defensive response to a man's wounded social pride and honour (Baumgart, 1990; Van Sommers, 1988). Male jealousy was sanctioned as a male prerogative, and as a way to defend against the adultery of women and the threat of the 'cuckoo in the nest' (Moi, 1987: 136). But this is no longer the case. The rules of entitlement and possession have changed and male jealousy is now often pathologized as a sick and dangerous emotion (Mullen, 1991). As numerous self-help books on jealousy imply, jealousy often signifies emotional immaturity, over-dependency and a refusal to respect the territorial space of one's partner.[4] At worst, male jealousy has become associated with the excesses of chauvinistic possessiveness, and violent misogyny (Mathes, 1992). Arguably, this diminished figure of the modern-day jealous man can be seen as iconic for the anxieties about masculinity and contemporary cultural change. However, it is possible now to point to the emergence of more positive representations of male jealousy within contemporary culture. One can link this to the 'emotionalization' of masculine identities (Lupton, 1998), and by way of a backlash against feminism, to jealousy's popular cultural appeal as a signifier of old-fashioned manly passion in the face of an increasingly feminized world. As this book explores, the depiction of masculine jealousy in mainstream cinema reflects these contradictions, where hegemonic meanings of masculinity and emotions such as jealousy are continually contested, negotiated and remade.

Masculinities in popular culture and Hollywood cinema

Hollwood has long dominated mainstream film and can be seen as 'dominant cinema'.[5] As such, it acts as a useful barometer of popular attitudes and values, including those surrounding emotion. This book uses this assumption to explore the link between masculinity and jealousy and its representations in popular culture. Hollywood cinema continues to be commercially, politically and psychosocially significant as a popular cultural site of mass entertainment and pleasure and there are many more diverse images of masculinity available than previously. Films both affect and reflect society and provide a means through which to analyse the relationship between subjectivity and culture. The meanings of a film are created in the interface between the audience and the film text. From the perspective of the viewer, the reading of the film is derived from their positioning; first, as an unconscious spectator, and second, as part of a broader social audience, where socio-cultural influences come into play, and shape the meaning of the text (Austin, 2002; Kuhn, 1994). Thus films act as a meeting point where cultural myths and ideologies, unconscious fantasies and desires are expressed and played out (Lebeau, 2001).

Since the 1970s, and in particular since the pioneering work of Laura Mulvey (1975), film has been a key site of psychoanalytic theorizing about gender and culture. Following the approach taken by psychoanalytic feminists in film and cultural studies, the view is that Hollywood cinema contributes to the 'ubiquitous and routine testing of masculinity by means of which patriarchal masculinity continues to maintain itself' (Radstone, 1995a: 115). However, recent research suggests that cultural spaces of male ambiguity that have a potential for something new and different may be emerging within mainstream cinema (Kirkham and Thumim, 1995; Lehman, 2001). One can apply Winnicott's (1971) description of 'transitional space' to these cultural forms to suggest that they point to a shift in the representation of masculinity and the kinds of identifications that are being opened up for audiences (Bainbridge and Yates, 2005). In contrast to the rigid narratives of the fetishized and voyeuristic 'looks' that have hitherto characterized much of the dominant Hollywood cinema, new representations of men have emerged over the last decade that suggest modes of masculinity that are less narcissistic, more nuanced and complex (Bainbridge and Yates, 2005). Such images point to more fluid spaces being opened up for audiences and the imaginative work that that can take place in relation to film.

Representations of male jealousy have always played a central role in Hollywood narratives and this continues to be the case in contemporary cinema. A number of films in mainstream cinema over the last two decades have used the cultural trope of 'masculinity in crisis' and male jealousy has played a significant role in the narrative: *Basic Instinct* (1992), *The English Patient* (1996), *Nil By Mouth* (1997), *Boogie Nights* (1997), *Lolita* (1997), *High Fidelity* (2000), *Memento* (2000), *Closer* (2004), *Brokeback Mountain* (2005), *Basic Instinct 2* (2006). Images of jealousy in films such as these arguably reflect the cultural lack of faith in the traditional fictions and narratives of masculinity more generally (Butler, 2000). Perhaps the possessive gaze of the hero and the emotional and moral outcomes of jealous triangles are less certain than in previous years; the object of jealousy is less passive and more able to challenge the power and possession of the masculine jealous subject.

The film *A Perfect Murder* (1998) provides an example of this.[6] The film stars Michael Douglas as the cuckolded husband and his interpretation of the role recalls the ruthless masculinity of his earlier role 'Ghekko' in the film *Wall Street* (1987). Yet his vulnerability is also signalled visually through the depiction of his aging and emotionally expressive jealous body. His character decides to punish his wife (played by Gwyneth Paltrow) for having an affair by teaming up with her lover and planning her murder. But the plan goes wrong and when she finally discovers her husband's murderous plot, she kills him and escapes punishment, thus signalling a shift in law as a symbol of patriarchal masculinity. The film is a remake of Hitchcock's *Dial M for Murder* (1954), when the desires of the wife (played by Grace Kelly) were given less narrative expression than in the 1998 film, in which the wife has both a career and a sexual identity, thus reflecting the cultural changes that have occurred since the 1950s. Yet in the contemporary version, the agency of the wife as the object of jealousy is counteracted by her passive positioning in relation to contemporary strategies of narrative and *mise-en-scène*.[7] Thus, hegemonic masculinity is reasserted, counteracting the symbolic depletion of the husband's masculine status as cuckold in relation to the revenge of the trophy wife.

One of the main comparisons between *A Perfect Murder* and *Dial M For Murder* is the heightened emotionalism of the jealous protagonist in the contemporary film. Douglas's high-octane performance relates, perhaps, to the emotionalization of cultural masculinities more generally (Lupton, 1998). The powerful depiction of male jealousy and its relationship to issues of rivalry and sexual difference can be found in films such as *Closer* (2004), in which the rivalry of the two leading male protagonists (played by Jude Law and Clive Owen) is central to the jealous narrative. At the beginning of the film the hostility between the two men is interwoven with their (unintentional) desire that comes about as a result of their internet correspondence using false names (and genders). However, this desire then turns to jealous antagonism and a desire to possess the independent and often elusive female characters (played by Julia Roberts and Natalie Portman). Films such as these show how masculinity is largely shaped in relation to difference and the impossible desire to possess the (feminine) other. Yet the 'other' in this context of male jealousy does not only refer to the otherness of Woman; it also refers to the difficulty of tolerating the differences of masculinity and the rivalries which may arise as a defence against the possibilities of homoerotic desire.

This book takes up these themes by examining five case studies of films released over the last two decades, where the depiction of male jealousy plays a central role in the narrative and where the male star represents a culturally significant and historically salient type of masculinity. The case studies are of the following films: *Taxi Driver* (M. Scorsese, USA, 1976/1996); *A Perfect Murder* (A. Davis, USA, 1998); *The End of The Affair* (N. Jordan, UK/USA, 1999); *The Piano* (J. Campion, Australia/New Zealand/France, 1993) and *Unfaithful* (A. Lyne, USA, 2002). Whilst they cannot be defined as popular 'blockbuster' hits, these films were all commercially successful in the United Kingdom and the United States. *Taxi Driver, The Piano* and *The End Of The Affair* were also critically acclaimed.[8] Using these films, their stars and related publicity, this book analyses these representations of masculine jealousy to explore the possibilities of, and for, more fluid and less narcissistic formations of masculinity within contemporary culture. The book moves beyond a discussion of the jealous sensibility of some men to explore the overly defended and jealous nature of masculinity itself as a cultural formation and how that defensiveness is symbolized in certain films today.

There are of course, different forms of male jealousy and the professional jealousies between men in work settings have been a recurring
theme of the cinema in the late twentieth and early twenty-first centuries. In films such as *Wall Street* (1987), *In The Company of Men* (1997)
and *Boiler Room* (2000), the dog-eat-dog culture of the executive world
provides the ruthless setting for male rivalry and the narcissistic struggle for masculine dominance. Epitomized perhaps in the film *American
Psycho* (2000), such jealousies often appear to be rooted more in narcissism and the envy of material possessions than in the rivalrous desire
with another man for the possession of a woman. Yet it is often the
case that even in films where women are not immediately visible as the
focus of antagonism, the violent struggles between men also contain
misogyny when, as in *In The Company Of Men*, a vulnerable female
character is caught up as an unwitting object of rivalrous exchange
between two ruthless male colleagues.

The erotic possession of women is often a feature of 'rescue' narratives where the hero 'saves' the woman from an evil rival. This scenario
can be found in 'action' films such as *Mission Impossible II* (2000) where
the hero 'Ethan' (Tom Cruise) fights his 'evil' rival 'Sean Ambrose'
(Dougray Scott) to rescue both the woman, 'Nyhal' (Thandi Newton),
and the world from a deadly chemical virus, or as in *Taxi Driver*
(1976/1996), where 'Travis Bickle' (Robert De Niro) wants to save both
the prostitute, 'Iris' (Jodie Foster), and New York from the 'evil' of vice
and corruption.[9]

Of course, the boundaries between different forms of male jealousy
often overlap. However, this book focuses mainly on formations of male
sexual jealousy, defined as 'reactions to intrusions upon a sexual attachment' (Van Sommers, 1988: 1).[10] The terms *male* and *masculine* jealousy
are by necessity sometimes used interchangeably, however, the term *masculine* jealousy is preferred, as it highlights the relationship between masculinity and jealousy as a psychosocial and cultural construction that
changes over time.[11] The theoretical model used in this book is 'psycho-
cultural', as it focuses on the interrelations among social, cultural and
psychical spheres of analysis, in which masculine jealousy is seen as the
outcome of social, cultural and unconscious forces. The different aspects
of this approach to subjectivity and culture are outlined below.

Masculinity, jealousy and the unconscious

Psychoanalytic theory provides a rich language to explore the complexities of gendered subjectivities and their relationship to culture and

the production of fantasy. It allows space for the contradictions and paradoxes that arise in relation to unconscious psychic processes that other theories of culture and identity ignore. Using a psychoanalytic perspective, one can argue that the shaping of gendered subjectivities is always de-centred by the psychic forces of the unconscious (Minsky, 1996). The workings of the unconscious can be traced back to the earliest years of life and shape our early relationships to objects in our internal and external worlds. The unconscious finds symbolic expression individually and culturally through the fantasies, projections and identifications which continually mediate the discourses, representations and practices of everyday life (Bainbridge, Radstone, Rustin and Yates, 2007). The acquisition of a gender identity plays a central role in this process. The subject's psychic entry into the symbolic sphere of culture and relations of sexual difference means that its cultural identity is also a gendered identity (Benvenuto and Kennedy, 1986).

Psychoanalysis can help us understand the psychic forces that underpin the binary cultural construction of gender, where femininity becomes the psychic and cultural other of masculinity. Psychoanalytic explanations of sexual difference point to a powerful psychic investment in maintaining this opposition.[12] Psychoanalytic theories of masculinity relate such anxieties to the defensive psychic processes that influence the shaping of masculinities. This work implies that psychologically, male subjectivities are shaped defensively and reactively in relation to a series of Oedipal struggles and anxieties related to parental figures. These psychoanalytic accounts often reinforce a negative picture of men and masculinities in contemporary culture as being overly defended and precarious.[13] Such explanations of masculinity also have pessimistic implications for the kind of male jealousies that may be experienced as a result, with the suggestion that these are likely to be narcissistic and overly possessive.

However, I apply the language of the British psychoanalyst D. W. Winnicott to present the possibility of less 'reactionary' psychic formations of what I term 'a good enough' masculinity.[14] This model acknowledges the potential ambiguities and complexities of masculinity and uses the term 'good enough' to mean a non-idealizing acceptance of masculinity and its limits in the face of uncertainty and cultural change. This less defensive model of masculinity also has implications for the kind of jealousies that may accompany it. Such a model presents a more positive picture of masculinity that suggests the possibility of tolerating the complexity of social relations and the triangular dilemmas of jealousy and its related fantasies.

Hegemonic masculinities, jealousy and cultural change

Alongside the unconscious psychic forces that shape masculinities, there are also socio-political and cultural dimensions. Gendered subjectivities are not fixed, but subject to contestation and change; they are shaped in a complex interrelation of social, cultural and psychical forces, and historically specific social and cultural discourses (Segal, 1990; Yates, 2000). Following the model of patriarchal masculinity first developed by the sociologist R. W. Connell (1995), one can argue that gender constitutes a site of struggle, and is always in process and subject to change at conscious and unconscious levels of experience. Within everyday discourses, competing definitions of gender jostle for position within a number of discursive sites, within the patriarchal hierarchy of what Connell names the 'gender order'. Connell argues that gendered struggle not only occurs between men and women, but also between men as they compete for dominance, a struggle that is played out in the cultural sphere for definitions of masculinity.

Hegemonic gender struggles take place in different areas of life within the Western developed world. Connell argues that ideological discourses and practices interact to reproduce, in historically specific ways, the gender order, which in turn contribute to the ongoing formation of other social structures such as class, race and ethnicity (1995: 74). The hegemonic values associated with patriarchal masculinity have a social and political reality, because they legitimate real relations of power between men and women, as represented by the discourses of our everyday lives. These discourses operate and are constantly negotiated in the stories we tell and the narratives by which we make sense of our world (Yates and Day Sclater, 2000). In the past, these narratives often reinforced cultural binary divisions of gender and the cultural marginalization of femininity, including the omission of alternative heroes embodying less narcissistic and more 'feminized' visions of masculinity.

Yet the shifting social and economic realities, together with the challenges presented by feminism, have challenged those boundaries and divisions. Against this backdrop, the figure of the jealous man may be viewed as emblematic of the cuckolded status of masculinity more generally. However, in order to provide a context for that discussion of the male cuckold as symbolized in film, it is necessary to set the scene for the discussion of masculine jealousy by turning to the relationship between masculinities, the alleged feminization of Western societies and popular culture.

The crisis of masculinities and the feminization of culture and society

It is often argued that recent changes in Western masculinities are related to the 'feminization' of society and its values (Segal, 1999; Wilkinson and Mulgan, 1995). How this process of feminization is defined, and whether or not it is viewed as a good thing, depends upon the political perspective and theoretical framework of the writer. Broadly speaking, the argument refers to an increased blurring of boundaries between masculinity and femininity, in which the values, practices and traits associated with the signifier 'femininity' have now extended to men and have become increasingly dominant throughout contemporary Western societies. Cultural commentators point to the relationship between the feminization of culture and a postmodern scepticism towards the old patriarchal grand narratives as having contributed to the undermining of authority (Owens, 1985) and having found widespread representation in popular culture more generally (Bainbridge and Yates, 2005). Thus, cinematic images depicting the loss of male authority and the unreliability of masculine narratives have been a recurrent cinematic theme of the late twentieth and early twenty-first centuries. For example, the depiction of psychological trauma and male confusion were foregrounded in films such as *Forrest Gump* (1994), *The Game* (1997), *Fight Club* (1999), *Magnolia* (1999), *Memento* (2000), *Mystic River* (2003) and *Eternal Sunshine of the Spotless Mind* (2004). In these films, the fallibility of memory and history as recorded through the personal narratives of the male protagonists were highlighted, thus emphasizing the instability of masculinity and its fictions more generally.

The feminization of masculinity is also associated with the 'emotionalization' of society and popular culture and the greater propensity of men to express their emotions (Lupton, 1998; Yates, 2001). Men have always expressed 'emotions', but now it is argued that the traditional division of emotional labour, in which women have traditionally been perceived as the caring, nurturing sex, is being challenged (Hochschild, 1983; Lupton. 1998). Gill, Henwood and McLean argue that second-wave feminism with its critique of masculinity and patriarchal social relations was a key influence in the emergence of 'new masculinities' (2000: 210), and the feminist notion of 'the personal is political' was also enormously influential in highlighting the value of subjective, emotional experience. Today, for example, sociologists argue that men are adopting more feminized modes of relating and (following women) are more likely to adopt a 'reflexive' narrative of the 'emotional self' to express themselves

(Giddens, 1992; Lupton, 1998). Throughout the 1990s, confessional first-person narratives of men were used in films to convey an authentic sense of masculinity and its emotional dilemmas. Comedies starring Hugh Grant in films such as *Notting Hill* (1999) and *About a Boy* (2002) which used his voice-over to chart a particular (English) version of confused masculinity were an example of this genre, and also historical dramas such as *The End Of The Affair* (1999), included a (male) first-person diary narrative, which began with Ralph Fiennes's character telling us 'I am a jealous man'.

From a sociological perspective, the feminization of society refers to the changes in family patterns that have accompanied the expansion of the female workforce (Day Sclater, 2000; Muncie and Wetherell, 1995). Sociologists point to the increase in lone-parent families, usually headed by women, and men are taking on many of the family tasks traditionally associated with 'mothering' (Bainham, Day Sclater and Richards, 1999). These dilemmas about fatherhood and the family have been a recurring theme in popular culture and there have been a number of popular novels about the joys and problems of new-man fatherhood; for example, Parsons's *Man and Boy* (1999) and Hornby's *About a Boy* (2000). Hornby's book was adapted and released as a film and the importance of fatherhood has been a constant theme of the mainstream cinema (Bruzzi, 2005). Films such as *Shine* (1996), *Quiz Show* (1994), *The Full Monty* (1997), *Magnolia* (1999), *Billy Elliott* (2000), *The Weather Man* (2005) and *The Ballad of Jack and Rose* (2005) are good examples of films where the poignant relationship between fathers and their children were central to the narrative.[15]

Throughout the 1980s and 1990s, the absence or inadequacy of 'career' mothers was also a strong theme in films such as *Three Men and a Baby* (1987) and *Three Men and A Little Lady* (1990). The backlash against mothers and feminism articulates, perhaps, a particular narcissistic fantasy which engages with the possibility of families without mothers, and possibly points to an envious colonization of the maternal role and the creativity it represents. A more overt example of this envious hostility towards mothers and their legal parental rights, are the campaigning rightwing 'pro-family' men's groups in the United States and the United Kingdom (Collier, 1996: 26).[16] More recently, however, a new kind of fatherhood has been portrayed through the films *Brokeback Mountain* (2005) and *Broken Flowers* (2005), where the fallibility and vulnerability of fatherhood is acknowledged. The character played by Bill Murray in *Broken Flowers* depicts an aging Lothario coming to terms with loss in relation to his life as a single man living without children. One day he receives an unsigned letter from an old girl-friend who tells him that he has a son who is looking for him. After an initial reluctance, the film shows his journey searching for this lost son and, in doing so, discovering that he has a desire for fatherhood after all. The film's representation of masculinity and the frustrated desire and curiosity regarding his son, point to a mode of masculinity that acknowledges the ambivalence of desire and the fallibility of fatherhood which contrasts with the manic discourses of fatherhood as articulated though certain sections of the men's movement.

Consumer culture, the objectification of male bodies and a backlash to feminization and change

Commentators often relate the feminization of society to the practices and values of consumer culture (Bocock, 1993; Lury, 1996). The spectacle and adornment of the male body in contemporary consumer culture has been seen as a contributory factor in the feminization of men. Just as women have traditionally been targeted by advertisers as objects of the 'look', men are now increasingly invited to identify narcissistically with the images in consumer culture (Faludi, 1999; Gill, Henwood and Richards, 2000).[17] However, the cultural preoccupation with the body in consumer culture has arguably created new sets of insecurities about measuring up to the male body images on offer. As Faludi argues: 'The gaze that hounds men is the very gaze that women have been trying to escape' (1999: 5).[18] Faludi believes that these anxieties about the persecutory female gaze were symbolically played out in the United Kingdom and the United States particularly on the pages of the 'lad' magazines of the 1990s (1999: 528). Faludi argues that it is easier for men to believe they are being belittled by the recognizable scapegoat of demanding women and the female gaze than by the less tangible, impersonal forces of late-modern capitalism and the broader social changes associated with corporate culture.

Researchers have highlighted the anxieties of those men who feel threatened by the feminization of society and the socio-economic changes associated with it (Collier, 1996). Such anxiety provides the context for what Faludi (1991) has described as a 'backlash' against feminism, in cultural, social and political spheres of life. This point has relevance for the later discussions of film case studies. As those chapters explore, the negative 'backlash' response to cultural change was a recurring theme of the dominant cinema of the late twentieth and early twenty-first centuries (Creed, 1993; Harwood, 1997). Glenn Close's portrayal of the psychotically jealous mistress in the film *Fatal Attraction* (1987) is often cited as a good example of this (Coward: 1999b: 11). As we have seen, representations of fathers replacing neglectful career mothers also provide an example of this cultural backlash. Annette Bening's performance as the neurotic and materialist career-driven wife and mother in *American Beauty* (1999) is apt here. The implication was that while her husband's mid-life crisis was an appropriate emotional response to the alienating and false world of consumer capitalism, she remained greedily seduced by its vacuous aspirations, thus reinforcing the perception of the close relationship between femininity and the superficiality of consumerism.

A different cultural response: the new 'emotional man' and the plurality of masculinities

However, it is not the case that the feminization of culture is always linked negatively to a male 'crisis of identity'. As Segal argues, 'Men can and do change' (1990: xii). She reminds us that many men have also welcomed the less polarized visions of masculinity and femininity associated with the feminization of society and she cautions against placing all men together in the same reactionary grouping. Segal argues that just as there are different femininities, there are also different masculinities, which challenge each other, including more progressive voices which struggle to be heard in the face of more defensive narratives of what it means to be a man.

Certain contemporary male journalists have spoken out against those who complain about the plight of men today and have emphasized the benefits men experience from a more feminized society. Drawing on a study of British men by a communications agency, it was reported that 'most (British) men are "overwhelmingly optimistic" about life and are happy to be on an equal footing with women' (Summerskill, 2002: 6). Subordinate and marginalized masculinities that challenge more traditional forms are now finding new voices in popular culture and examples of more sensitive, feelingful masculinities can also be found in Hollywood cinema, where since the early 1990s, there are many more diverse representations of masculine subjectivities than in previous decades (Bainbridge and Yates, 2005). As Jeffords has argued in relation to representations of Hollywood masculinities and the male body:

> More film time is devoted to explorations of their ethical dilemmas, emotional traumas, and psychological goals, and less to their skill

with weapons, their athletic abilities, or their gutsy showdowns of opponents.

(1993: 245)

Such men are often portrayed as having so-called 'feminine' qualities associated with sensitive soul-searching, emotional vulnerability, or even personal confusion. These qualities are often embodied in the particular style of male film stars, who bring a particular set of meanings to the roles they play as a consequence of their star personas and the publicity that surrounds them more generally (Dyer, 1998a; Kirkham and Thumim, 1995). The images of masculinity embodied by these male stars, often portray the complex ambiguities of masculinity and what it means to be a man. One can cite examples here of male stars who are portrayed as having deep and complex interior lives, as for instance, Ralph Fiennes in *The End Of the Affair,* (1999) and *The Constant Gardener* (2005), or Robert Downey Jr. and Sean Penn who, on and off screen, appear prone to suffer from melodramatic bouts of neurotic vulnerability. Press reports tell us of Denzel Washington's 'huge capacity to feel. Everything he does is filled with raw emotion' (Lley, 2006: 15), and Brad Pitt, whose scarred body in *Fight Club* (1999) conveys a scarred and tortured soul underneath. Pitt's most recent public incarnation as the father to Angelina Jolie's children, represents perhaps a new development in the shaping of his public image as a sensitive masculine heart-throb. It is arguably significant that Daniel Craig's interpretation of James Bond in *Casino Royale* (2006) conveys a more psychologically complex personality than previous Bonds, whose machismo is matched by a capacity for wounded vulnerability and a history of disappointed love.

It is important to emphasize that the representation of emotional masculinities in Hollywood (and popular culture more generally) is nothing new. Male melodramas of the 1950s, such as *Rebel Without a Cause* (1955) and *East of Eden* (1955) provide examples of this, where the intensely emotional roles played by James Dean exemplify images of tortured masculinity. Representations of emotional masculinities are specific to the broader socio-political and cultural context of their consumption and provide clues about the shaping of male subjectivities in that setting. In the past, Hollywood representations of masculinity have invoked narcissistic modes of identification to defend the male psyche against the unpleasures of loss (Mulvey, 1975). However, contemporary cinematic images of masculinity now invite a more diverse set of identifications and represent a different set of losses and risks for male audiences.

Feminist debates about emotional masculinities and cinema

These changing images of masculinity, which potentially facilitate new modes of male fantasy and masculine spectatorship, also have implications for the destabilization of masculinity within contemporary culture and the breakdown of cultural binary oppositions more generally. However, some argue that the 'pathos' of new masculinities in contemporary films is often achieved at the expense of women and the female protagonists in the films themselves (Rowe, 1995). Citing actors such as Woody Allen, Rowe argues that in such films, male protagonists often adopt emotional traits culturally associated with femininity, so as to appear twice as sensitive as the female (1995: 185).[19] In particular, Rowe cites the genre of melodrama as an ideological narrative form that has traditionally 'spoken' to women, but which is now increasingly being appropriated by men to articulate the suffering of male protagonists.[20] Rowe argues that the 'melancholic man' takes on aspects of loss and lack associated with femininity, and that these aspects are used to signify the suffering and unhappiness of men at the expense of representations of women, in which sensitive men are portrayed as noble victims of powerful phallic women (1995: 186). Thus, from this sceptical perspective, images of the sensitive, feminized man do not mean that patriarchal masculinity is now being divested of power. Instead, it suggests that the opposite is the case, as images of the sensitive, emotional man can reinforce male narcissism.[21]

The depiction of the boyfriend 'Nate' (Adrian Grenier) in the film *The Devil Wears Prada* (2006) provides a case in point. In that film, and in contrast to his girlfriend 'Andy' (Anne Hathaway), he takes on the traditional feminine role of the nurturing, sensitive partner who cooks for a living and who is linked symbolically to a domestic sphere of social relations, rather than the phallic corporate sphere of fashion, celebrity and money. The film's heroine 'Andy' (who has to sell her soul in order to 'make it' in the fashion world) becomes aligned with ambition, superficiality and excess, whilst he inherits the values once associated with 'caring' femininity.

Radstone (1995a: 155) takes up the theme of emotional masculinities at the cinema in her analysis of Al Pacino and the particular qualities of vulnerability he exudes. She argues that the blurring of gender boundaries exemplified by feminized images of men in popular cinema may signify 'patriarchy adapting itself to incorporate the feminine'. Here, Radstone reminds us that popular culture constitutes a site of hegemonic struggle, where definitions of masculinity are fought out. She argues that it is through this process that 'cracks' in masculinity are discovered and 'mended'. But as she goes on to say, 'cracks do not necessarily imply collapse' (Radstone, 1995a).

Debates about the representation of emotional masculinities are significant when applied to the representation of jealousy at the movies, where throughout the late twentieth and early twenty-first centuries, the 'plight' of the jealous man has often been depicted in melodramatic and tragic terms. For example, one can cite Jeremy Irons's interpretation of Humbert Humbert in the recent version of *Lolita* (1997), whose jealousy is depicted as tragic, if foolish; or Sam Neill as the sensitive husband in *The Piano* (1993), whose sexual jealousy nearly destroys him and his wife. Richard Gere's portrayal of the jealous husband in *Unfaithful* (2002) also provides an interesting take on the theme of tragic male jealousy and its consequences. In that film, the sense of tragedy is articulated less in relation to the violent murder of the youthful lover (Oliver Martinez), and more in terms of the emotional catastrophe of marital infidelity and the disillusionment of coming to terms with an unfaithful wife.

The 1995 film adaptation of *Othello* is also interesting to explore in this context. In contrast to previous cinematic versions, it emphasizes the 'tragedy' of Othello's jealous predicament, rather than Desdemona's tragic end at the hands of her jealous husband.[22] *Othello* provides a useful case study to examine the ways in which representations of jealousy may be used defensively to shore up notions of hegemonic masculinity and its hierarchies. Interestingly, in that film, Othello's jealousy is depicted as being part of a medical condition of epilepsy. Fishburne is the first black actor to play the role of Othello in a major big-budget film and as a number of critics argue, he is represented as more emotionally vulnerable and naive than previous cinematic interpretations of the role.[23] His performance has clear implications for images of black masculinity as defined as a wounded condition. Fishburne's tearful and naive Othello also appears less culpable for his actions (and by implication less bad) than the character of Iago played by Kenneth Branagh. Branagh's performance emphasizes the misogyny of Iago and he also conveys a strong homoerotic component to his love and hatred of Othello.

Thus, in this instance, the otherness of jealousy as a deviant and uncivilized passion is conveyed less through Fishburne's interpretation of Othello's tearful vulnerability, than through Iago's ambiguous sexuality, invoking the traditional defences in Hollywood cinema against homoerotic desire (Neale, 1983).[24] This link was made in the press reviews of *Othello*, when the terms 'cuckoldry' and 'sexual jealousy' were mostly applied not to Fishburne's Othello, but to Branagh's Iago: 'Iago's sexual jealousy is stung by the Moor's success in bed' (Curtis, 1996: 13).[25]

This brief analysis of *Othello* shows that whilst the experience of jealousy may be an intensely personal emotion, it is also shaped historically by social and cultural practices, and the fantasy settings of cinema, stardom and related popular texts also contribute to this process.

These themes are revisited throughout the course of the book, which is divided into two parts. Part I discusses the psycho-cultural shaping of masculine jealousy and its relationship to issues of representation of masculinity in film, male fantasy and film spectatorship. Chapter 2 includes an extensive discussion of psychoanalytic accounts of masculinity and jealousy and Chapters 3 and 4 develop the psycho-cultural studies methodology used in this book. Such an approach combines theories of culture, society and the unconscious to explore the nuances of film narratives as emotional texts and also issues related to the processes of affective spectatorship, masculinities and the male gaze.

The analysis of film reviews is an under-utilized resource in film and cultural studies and the book presents an interdisciplinary method through which to explore the psycho-cultural meanings of the film texts as well as those of the reviews and related publicity. In contrast to film studies methodologies which in the past have tended to ignore the role of emotion or which have only focused on the film text or audience response, I argue that the fantasies of male jealousy evoked by the film's mode of address are also present in the film reviews and can be seen as an indication of broader socio-cultural anxieties about masculinity. The psycho-cultural method taken here suggests that reviewers occupy a liminal space between the viewing public and the film institution and points to the interrelatedness of the fantasies of masculine jealousy across those spheres of cultural analysis.

Part II (Chapters 5 to 9) examines the five films mentioned earlier by means of case studies: *Taxi Driver* (1976/1996), *A Perfect Murder* (1998); *The End of The Affair* (1999); *The Piano* (1993) and *Unfaithful* (2002). There are synopses for each of these films in the appendices at the end of the book. Synopses and related images and reviews for these, and all other films cited, can be accessed at http://www.imdb.com/.[26] Chapter 10 concludes by reflecting on the implications of the case studies, returning to the questions of masculine jealousy and cinema, and the possibilities for 'good enough' masculinities in contemporary culture.

Part I
The Psycho-Cultural Shaping of Masculine Jealousy

2
Psychoanalytic Understandings of Masculinity and Jealousy

> Jealousy is based on love and aims at the possession of the love object and the removal of the rival. It pertains to a triangular relationship and therefore to a time of life when objects are clearly recognized and differentiated from one another.
>
> (Segal, 1988: 40).

Introduction

Psychoanalysis, with its emphasis on the unconscious and the unpredictable aspects of human behaviour, offers a useful set of theories to explore the tensions and contradictions of masculine jealousy. It also provides a valuable framework for the analysis of gender and cinema. This chapter explores the psychoanalytic approach to jealousy by bringing together issues of jealousy, masculinity and sexual difference.

In contrast to psychiatric clinical discourses that have routinely pathologized the disorder of passionate and conflictual feelings such as jealousy,[1] psychoanalytic discourse argues that jealousy is a fact of life, and a painful, 'normal unhappiness' that has to be endured (Fenichel, 1946; Freud, 1922).[2] Yet jealousy remains a relatively under-researched topic in psychoanalysis, and the few texts that have explicitly addressed it have tended to dwell on its neurotic and paranoid forms.[3] Moreover, the relationship between masculinity and jealousy has received little attention. This is surprising because, as classical psychoanalytic theory reminds us, jealousy plays a significant role in the shaping of gendered subjectivities and in helping the subject to come to terms with the losses and compromises associated with the Oedipus complex (Laplanche and Pontalis, 1988: 282–7).

Psychoanalytic writers on gender often present a pessimistic picture of contemporary masculinities (Maguire, 1995; Minsky, 1998). I want to argue that given the negative explanations of the male psyche as being either an outcome of castration anxiety or maternal envy, then overly possessive, neurotic jealousy would seem to be the most likely outcome. However, it is possible to explore a more positive, 'good enough' psychoanalytic model of masculinity that has different implications for male jealousy. Whilst extreme jealousies may fall into the realm of pathology, I would like to extend the use of this terminology when considering the ordinary jealousies which, as Freud (1922) argues, may occur as part of the range of feeling states experienced in everyday life. A good enough jealousy in this context does not stem purely from a need to bolster up a fragile self, but rather, signifies a capacity for love and attachment and implies a more fluid and less defensive mode of gendered experience. This should not be seen as a conservative romanticization of male jealousy. Instead, it signifies a capacity to cope with the disappointments of difference and separation, and the social and cultural uncertainties of contemporary life more generally, without resorting to destructive narcissistic subject positions as a defence.

Jealousy as love and hate: the ambivalent feeling subject

Jealousy is one of the most ambiguous emotions because it contains hate *and* love, and perhaps for this reason it has been notoriously difficult to define and analyse (Shepherd, 1961; Stearns, 1988). In the past, this contradiction has been resolved by psychiatrists and clinical psychologists by splitting jealousy into models of rational and irrational types (Chrichton, 1996; Martin, 1998), thus ignoring the irrational components of the emotion that cut across even apparently 'normal' forms of everyday jealousy. However, Freud (1922: 197) argues that all jealousy has an irrational component to it, because of its relationship to the unconscious.

The analysis of internal conflictual feelings has always been central to psychoanalysis. For Freud, the dominant narrative here is around the conflicts of bisexuality and the dilemmas of identification that are stirred up around the parental objects during the Oedipus crisis and the castration complex (Laplanche and Pontalis, 1988: 26–8). By contrast, Melanie Klein argues that the central conflict is the struggle between love and hate in the 'depressive position' (Hinshelwood, 1991: 218).[4] Jealousy occupies a central place in these tensions of the ambivalent subject.

Certain forms of good enough jealous feelings suggest the ability to cope with emotional ambivalence and so may be a sign that one is able to tolerate the kind of internal conflict which constitutes the relative 'precariousness' of gendered identities (Minsky, 1998: 8–15). More extreme and overly possessive forms of jealousy, or indeed the denial of jealousy altogether, may be read as symptomatic of a destructive narcissistic defence against some imagined threat to the self and of a fragile over-precarious identity. In short, destructive forms of jealousy derive from an *inability* to cope with emotional ambivalence. Psychoanalysis theorizes jealousy from a number of perspectives found in the work of Freud, Jones, Lacan, Klein and other contemporary psychoanalytic writers in the field, as the next section will explore. It is interesting to apply these ideas to different psychoanalytic models of the construction of masculine subjectivities and to think through the relevance of this material for an understanding of cinematic representations.

Freud's account of 'normal' Oedipal jealousy

Jealousy is one of those affective states, like grief, that may be described as normal. If anyone appears to be without it, the inference is justified that it has undergone severe repression and consequently plays all the greater part in his unconscious mental life.

(Freud, 1922: 197).

Jealousy and related themes occupy a central place in Freud's work, though he only explicitly addressed it once in his 1922 paper 'Some Neurotic Mechanisms in Jealousy, Paranoia and Homosexuality'. Before Freud, psychiatric studies of jealousy carried out at the turn of the twentieth century tended to ignore the concept of normal jealousy and instead focused on the causes of delusional jealousy (Van Sommers, 1988). The recurring theme of this work was the relationship between alcoholism and jealousy. These studies were mainly descriptive and while pathologizing the emotion, had little to say as to how jealousy might be overcome or cured (Baumgart, 1990).

Freud's (1922) paper provides some useful and even compassionate insights into the experience of 'normal' jealousy that are worth returning to for an understanding of non-reactive, good enough jealousy.[5] He outlines three layers of jealousy: normal, projected and delusional, which may overlap in different instances. Freud traces the unconscious mechanisms and feelings that lie behind jealousy back to the Oedipus complex and says that while jealousy is not innate, it is normal and everyone experiences it at some point in their lives.[6] He likens jealousy to a form of mourning or grief, which accompanies the 'imagined loss of the love object' (Freud, 1922: 197). Second, he points to feelings of rejection, which leave the jealous subject humiliated and narciss-istically wounded. Third, he says that normal jealousy provokes aggres-sive feelings and hostility towards the rival, and fourth, the jealous person will blame himself for the loss and become self-critical. Finally, Freud argues that so called 'normal' heterosexual jealousy may, at an unconscious level, be experienced bisexually. As the marital therapist Baumgart argues, jealous grief about a wife's infidelity and the loss of her love to a male rival, may also be reversed, and instead the jealous subject may experience loss about 'an unconsciously loved man' and a loathing for the female partner who, as a rival, has succeeded in taking away 'the possible love object' (1990: 150).

Freud suggests that the different affects associated with normal jeal-ousy feed into his other two layers, which are neurotic and morbid jealousy. These signify an inability to cope with unresolved Oedipal conflicts and dilemmas. In the second layer of 'projective jealousy', the jealous subject projects his wish to be unfaithful on to the beloved (Freud, 1922: 198). In the third layer of morbid or paranoid jealousy, the jealous subject projects his repressed or unresolved 'homosexual' desires on to the beloved. Here, it is as if the jealous subject says, 'I do not wish to be unfaithful with him, she does!'.

Neurotic guilt and wishful jealousies

From a Freudian perspective, desire is limitless and projected jealousy can provide a 'safety valve' for the guilty subject who wishes to fend off the guilt surrounding his bisexuality and the desire for infidelity (Freud, 1922: 199).[7] Freud says that the more a person 'denies these temptations in himself', and the internalized guilt that accompanies them, then the more likely they are to gain some relief from projecting their guilty desires on to their partner (1922: 198). The wish to relieve guilt through the mechanism of projective jealousy illustrates the way in which there may be some unconscious 'secondary gains' for the subject experiencing jealousy (Downing, 1977: 76). The relationship between jealousy and Oedipal guilt is raised by Freud in an earlier paper 'A Special Object Choice Made By Men' (1910). In this paper, he argues that a man's guilt about competing with his father for the mother may manifest itself in choosing women who, like the mother, are already attached to another. The presence of a third party means that the guilt can be projected elsewhere. The aggression towards the rival and the hurt at the betrayal of the beloved can feed into the jealous subject's own tragic narrative of unrequited love. Taking into account the psychic bisexuality of the Freudian jealous subject, one can also argue that such a scenario also becomes the means of retaining the father as a love object.

Seidenberg later discusses the pleasures of these triangular scenarios for the jealous man who creates them to work out unresolved Oedipal conflicts. He names this 'aspect' of neurotic jealousy 'the jealous wish' because of 'the wish and gratification, which the mechanism of jealousy fulfils' (Seidenberg, 1952: 346). A theme of Seidenberg's (1952) and Freud's (1910) work is the way in which the male rival functions as a narcissistic mirror for the jealous subject, who feels the need to project his forbidden Oedipal desires on to a rivalrous third party. In projecting those desires on to the rival, the jealous man becomes the subject and object of his own gaze and the jealousy becomes all the more circular and tortuous. As Morel (2000) argues, the masquerading jealous subject (who sets up jealousy scenarios in order to relive early Oedipal fantasies) has been a recurrent theme of literature and narrative. The jealous lover Bendrix in Graham Greene's (1951) book *The End Of The Affair* (later adapted for cinema) provides a good example of the masquerading jealous subject in action. In that story, Bendrix takes a perverse pleasure in hearing about his mistress's indiscretions from a private detective and, despite the jealous pain, feels strangely compelled to imagine her life with her husband Henry. In the film *Indecent Proposal* (1993), the extreme reaction of the husband (Woody Harrelson) to his wife's infidelity provides another example of the 'jealous wish'. In that film, the wife (Demi Moore) is positioned as an object of financial exchange between the poor husband and the rich lover/businessman (Robert Redford), who offers to pay the husband a million dollars for a night of 'passion' with his wife. The film's focus on the husband's despair invites the audience to sympathize with his point of view and to collude with his agonized, yet fascinated jealous gaze as she leaves him to make love with another man. From the perspective of the French psychoanalyst, Lacan, the perverse pleasures of jealousy in such scenarios may produce an ecstasy of suffering, 'a *jouissance* that is tortuous pain endlessly feeding off itself' (Morel, 2000: 158). Central to this tortuous experience is the seemingly endless imaginative process of thinking about the possible scenarios between the lover and the rival.

A Lacanian perspective on jealousy

For Jacques Lacan (1901–1981), jealousy stems from the 'mirror phase' (as explained below), and is underpinned by the desire for the lost object (*objet petit a*), which is always related to the jealous subject's own emptiness and lack (Lacan, 1991: 115–16). Lacan suggests that jealousy includes a powerful envious aggression towards the rivalrous third party, who becomes a narcissistic mirror 'ideal image' for the jealous subject, and who also appears to possess everything that the jealous subject lacks. For Lacan, narcissism is always a fact that underpins the construction of human identities and so jealousy is always over-determined by narcissism and its related insecurities ([1958] 1977). He argues that the notion of a coherent 'self' is a fiction and that the ego is based on a process of narcissistic identification and mis-recognition. Lacan says that this process takes place during what he calls the 'mirror phase', and places this 'pre-Oedipal' occurrence at the heart of his account about the construction of subjectivity.

The 'mirror phase' occurs at around 6–10 months, when the infant is held by another/mother in front of a mirror and experiences a delight in the co-ordination and wholeness of its image which, in terms of its own motor co-ordination, it has not yet achieved (Lacan, [1949] 1977: 1–7).[8] The infant then identifies with the image and internalizes it. This identification is formed in a moment of mis-recognition because the infant is anticipating and attributing to itself something it has yet to achieve. Lacan ([1958] 1977) argues that the mirror phase institutes within the subject a gap or a sense of lack, which the subject forever tries to fill and overcome. However, from this perspective, the unconscious memories of our initial helpless state continue to haunt us.[9]

Lacan suggests that during the mirror phase, the infant is 'drawn, enthralled and captivated by the gaze of the other' (Benvenuto and Kennedy, 1986: 58). However, this narcissistic moment may also be infused with feelings of envy, rivalry and mistrust. The infant may envy the perfect reflection of its own image (the imaginary other), and experience a rivalry towards this narcissistic image which seems so contained, perfect and unobtainable (Houzel, 2001: 131). This experience of aggressive rivalry is not surprising as, in Lacanian terms, the organized image, which masks the disorganization of the subject, occupies a symbolic place between life and death and the existential possibility of psychic survival and psychic disintegration. According to Lacan, the experience of the mirror phase influences all future spatial identifications and relationships with others (Benvenuto and Kennedy,

1986: 57–8). Lacan provides an example of this in his now often quoted description (taken from St. Augustine) of the child's envious stare at his brother at the breast of his mother (1991: 116). Lacan does not define the boy's resentment here as jealousy, but as envy, because he argues that the boy does not actually want or need the breast, but instead merely wants to possess it for possession's sake:

> Everyone knows that envy is usually aroused by the possession of goods which would be of no use to the person who is envious of them, and about the true nature of which he does not have the least idea.
>
> (1991: 116)

The sight of the brother may remind the boy of his own narcissistic fragility, something that provokes envy of the other's apparent completeness; there is jealousy contained in the scene. This is because both the mother and the brother appear to be enjoying each other at the expense of the third young jealous onlooker, who is excluded from the loving intimacy between mother and son. The jealousy experienced here is bound up with the different narcissistic identifications of the mirror stage, which in Lacan's narrative of subjectivity, sets up an unconscious ontological split and a sense of undefined longing within the subject, that can never fully be resolved.

Narcissistic jealousies as a sign of hate

The relationship between narcissistic aggression and jealousy examined by Lacan, is explored in an earlier paper by the psychoanalyst Ernest Jones (1929). Jones develops Freud's ideas about the relationship between neurotic jealousy and excessive Oedipal ambivalence. Whereas Freud argues that the different feelings of jealousy are rooted in the loss and search for love, Jones argues that neurotic jealousy is in fact, a sign of hate and self-loathing.

In his paper 'Jealousy' (1929), he emphasizes the narcissistic roots of jealousy and the ways in which these are played out in overly dependent narcissistic love attachments. Jones argues that narcissistic love signifies a refusal to acknowledge the otherness of the person and has its roots in defensive hateful aggression, and the kind of jealousy that is likely to emerge from this will be particularly aggressive. Jones argues that this is because jealousy is not related to the wish to defend a love based on attachment, but rather, manifests itself as part of a broader armoury of psychic defences designed to bolster the fragile ego of the male subject.

The kind of person Jones is describing is someone who is so insecure that he is ruled by a defensive need to be loved and a compulsion to retain exclusive possession and control of the (love) object. The loss of a woman creates a huge crisis for a man like this, because his very sense of selfhood is maintained through the mirror of her desire. This form of narcissistic jealousy is represented in *The Piano* when, following the discovery of his wife's infidelity, the husband (Sam Neill) boards up the house so that the wife (Holly Hunter) cannot escape. According to Jones, people who are unable to deal with the disappointments of object love and loss have an unhealthy 'ambivalent attitude towards the idea of being loved' (1929: 337). On the one hand, they have 'a craving for it' and on the other, 'a dread of it'. This ambivalence makes them particularly vulnerable to jealousy because the terrors of being abandoned may also lead them to invent a rivalrous third party, or they may, through flirting or actual infidelity, create a rival to make the partner jealous.

As with Freud, Jones makes a link between flirting and jealousy. However, whereas Freud sees flirting as a harmless and even a useful outlet for the desires that might otherwise find expression in projective jealousy, Jones takes a far more negative view of what he refers to in rather theatrical terms as the flirtatious 'Don Juan'. Jones argues that flirting does not so much prevent and provide an outlet for jealousy, but instead creates it (1929: 330). He argues that flirting is motivated by a need to make one's partner jealous. Thus for Jones, the reason that flirts don't get jealous is because they make other people jealous instead. He argues that the flirtatious 'Don Juans of this world' are the worst in this respect, because their exaggerated charm implies that they have the most to hide. Thus, from this perspective, flirtation is not always harmless, but rather an example of an attempt to deal with loss by the sadistic mastery of the object. Mitchell takes up this theme in her discussion of the jealous male hysteric, who wards off his own jealous madness by projecting it into others. Mitchell illustrates this with the story of *Don Giovanni*, which was adapted from *Don Juan*:

> The key theme in *Don Giovanni* is jealousy. Don Giovanni is driven by the need to make others jealous so as not to be tormented by jealousy itself. Compulsively, desperately, he makes Masetto the bridegroom jealous by seducing his bride-to-be, and he makes every woman jealous of the other.

(2000: 260)

John Malkovich's character 'Vicomte Sebastian de Valmont' in the film *Dangerous Liaisons* (1988) also provides an interesting illustration of the flirtatious *Don Juan* at work.[10] Dedicated to a life of seduction and sexual conquest, Valmont's flirtatious sensibility appears to be influenced as much by narcissism as it is by the pleasure of sexual conquest. The film is underscored throughout by the themes of jealousy and revenge as Valmont and his lover, the ruthless 'Marquise Isabelle de Merteuil' (Glenn Close), engage in a battle of sexual and psychological one-upmanship. The cynicism of their game playing is countered by scenes of mutual sexual flirtation and intense jealous mistrust, in which the couple's love for one another is also accompanied by the fear of intimacy implied by such jealous desire. In the end, Valmont falls in love with another woman 'Madame de Tourvel' (Michelle Pfeiffer), breaks her heart and then dies in a duel. Whereas the 'tragedy' of his ending perhaps goes some way towards restoring his masculinity, Glenn Close's character 'the Marquise' is publicly shamed, and as with the women in the *Don Giovanni* story, she is left carrying the jealousy of the other.

Jealousy and homosexuality

Mullen (1991) argues that the feminization and pathologization of male jealousy has been a feature of the twentieth-century medical and psychiatric discourses about jealousy.[11] The relationship between homosexuality and jealousy is, for instance, a recurrent theme in classical psychoanalytic accounts of jealousy. For example, Jones (1929) makes a link between narcissism, homosexuality and jealousy. However, some of Jones's homophobic assumptions make uncomfortable reading for the modern reader. A central underlying theme of Jones's paper is that jealousy is a weak and cowardly emotion and incompatible with traditional moral values and the characteristics of heterosexual masculinity. In relating neurotic jealousy to narcissism and so-called 'pre-genital' modes of sexual fantasy, he argues that it is symptomatic of repressed homosexuality and a failure to identify with the father in an appropriate way. For Jones, a jealous man appears to have all the negative traits associated with weak, 'narcissistic' femininity. Jealousy is therefore a perversion of what he considers to be appropriate genital attachment. Jones argues that jealousy not only masks hate, but it also 'masks repressed homosexuality' (1929: 329). Thus, he rather dramatically claimed that 'the jealous man' is also the 'masked homosexual man'.[12] As a result of this, boys grow up pretending to be what they are not (the masked homosexual), and later project their guilt and their desires on to their partners whom they accuse of infidelity. Jones argues that this would explain why certain men are far more interested in attacking the male rival than the woman herself.

As the title of the 1922 paper 'Some Neurotic Mechanisms in Jealousy, Paranoia and Homosexuality' suggests, Freud also relates his theory of jealousy to paranoia and homosexuality. Freud's attitudes towards homosexuality were not without ambiguity (1924: 24) and one can place his theory of paranoid jealousy in this pathologizing context.[13] As Maguire points out,

> Freud stressed the continuity between heterosexual and homosexual love, saying that he had never conducted a single psychoanalysis without 'having to take into account a considerable current of homosexuality'.
>
> (1995: 195)

Freud suggests that humans are all born with a bisexual predisposition (1924; 1925). However, he argues that young children learn to channel or 'swerve' their desires away from what society deems perverse, and instead take up a heterosexual orientation.[14] Nevertheless, Freud also says that the Oedipus complex is never finally resolved, as we carry the traces of our repressed loves and desires with us throughout our lives (Mitchell, 1975, 2000). The homoerotic component of male rivalry can be seen in Hollywood film epics such as *Ben Hur* (1959), *Spartacus* (1960) and more recently *Gladiator* (2000), where the rivalrous battles of the male protagonists are both infused with an erotic physicality, yet also a show of violence to counter the image of male intimacy displayed through combat in the gladiator ring.[15] Such homoeroticism is more explicitly dealt with in the film *Beau Travail* (1998), which explores the homoerotic undercurrents of love and jealousy between men in the French Foreign Legion. Against a backdrop of harsh military routines and the asceticism of army life in a colonial desert outpost, the tough sergeant major 'Galoup' (Dennis Lavent) develops a desire for the officer father figure 'Forestier' (Michel Subor) and suffers a poignant and intense, murderous jealousy because of Forestier's interest in the handsome recruit 'Sentain' (Grégoire Colin).

But Lagache reminds us that extreme forms of jealousy and homosexuality are not always related. He warns his readers against making generalizations and points to the contradictions that often arise between 'theory and clinical experience'. This is especially the case, given the discourses that continue to pathologize homosexuality as a perversion of some 'true' heterosexual condition:

> Jealousy has other functions besides that of a defence against homosexuality; it has other roots, genital and above all pre-genital. And moreover, the significance of the term 'homosexual' is not unambiguous. It is used to denote not only a form of behaviour, but also motivation, that is, the instigating force of behaviour, which may be latent, and in appearance inactive. In individual cases homosexual behaviour and its motivations do not always correspond.
>
> (Lagache, 1949: 24)

Oral jealousy

A number of psychoanalytic writers have commented that certain forms of jealousy have a 'devouring' quality about them (Klein, 1957; Riviere, 1932; Schmideberg, 1953). For example, the greedy narcissistic lover may cause their partner to feel as though they are being sucked dry and consumed by their possessive attentions (Baumgart, 1990: 203). Jealousy such as this has its roots in the early oral phase of development in which the insatiable greedy baby described by Freud (1933) lives in a world governed by the narcissistic wish for immediate gratification. The infantile wish for oral gratification is theoretically elaborated by the psychoanalysts Melanie Klein (1882–1960) and her followers, who emphasize the destructive potential in the first infantile relationship at the breast, placing it at the centre of their psychoanalytic narrative of the ambivalent feeling subject (Klein, 1957; Riviere, 1932). However, Klein also argues that it is possible to experience a reparative jealousy, and I now turn to her work to explore this further.

Reparative and envious jealousies

Klein presents her most developed analysis of the relationship between jealousy and envy in her 1957 paper 'Envy and Gratitude'.[16] In contrast to Freud, Klein argues that the foundation of jealousy lies in the pre-Oedipal level of paranoid envy at the breast. Although this envious relationship does not involve three live people, it does involve a subject and two imaginary objects, and the psychic meanings that become attached to those objects may become displaced on to later jealousy situations. Klein distinguishes between envy, jealousy and greed in the following ways:

Envy is the angry feeling that another person possesses and enjoys something desirable – the envious impulse being to take it away or to spoil it ... envy implies the subject's relation to one person only and goes back to the earliest exclusive relation with the mother. *Jealousy* is based on envy, but involves a relation to at least two people; it is mainly concerned with love that the subject feels is his due and has been taken away, or is in danger of being taken away, from him by his rival. In the everyday conception of jealousy, a man or a woman feels deprived of the loved person by someone else. *Greed* is the impetuous and insatiable craving, exceeding what the subject needs and what the object is able to give. At the unconscious level, greed aims primarily at completely scooping out, sucking dry and devouring the breast: that is to say, its aim is destructive introjection.

(1957: 181)

Klein (1957) argues that jealousy demonstrates a capacity to love and to acknowledge loss, she says it can act as a positive means to work through the persecutory feelings inherent in an encounter with a rejecting or withholding object. For Klein, the Oedipus complex occurs at a much earlier time than in Freud's account (Klein, 1928, 1945). She argues that it coincides with the paranoid-schizoid position, when the infant lives in an imaginary world of ideal or persecutory part objects. Klein suggests that the Oedipal feelings that emerge at this time are characterized by oral aggression, which leads to persecutory phantasies.[17] Most importantly, these feelings are suffused with envy of the withholding breast. In her theory of the combined parent, Klein says that the maternal object contains all that is desirable in her body, including the penis, and the maternal part objects and the penis are envied for having each other (1945, 1952). The infant has phantasies of robbing this plentiful phallic creature of her apparent power and self-sufficiency that lead to heightened feelings of persecution. If all goes well, these feelings are worked through when the child becomes aware that the mother is a whole object who contains love and hate. Feelings of remorse set in for having damaged the object's goodness.

One can see this psychological journey depicted in the film *The Piano*, both through the characters of Ada's daughter 'Flora' and her husband 'Stewart'. In Flora's case, we see the Oedipal jealousy of her stepfather transformed into a jealousy of her mother 'Ada' (Holly Hunter) and her lover 'Baines' (Harvey Keitel) when they embark on an affair. She betrays her mother by telling her stepfather of the affair and helps him to confine Ada, like a prisoner, in their house. Towards the end of the film, Flora is shown to feel remorse for her actions as she becomes close to her mother once more. Yet when she is asked by Ada to take a message to Baines, she betrays her mother again and this leads to Stewart's violent jealous revenge. Stewart's intense jealousy of Baines invokes Klein's description of the envious jealousy stirred up around the phantasy of an exclusive parental couple. Yet in the end, Stewart's capacity to acknowledge the difference and separateness of Ada and his desire to make peace with Baines, also resonate with Klein's description of mourning and its significance in working through the destructive, envious aspects of jealousy.

A good enough jealousy in this reparative context is associated with the 'depressive position' and is a sign that one has learned to mourn the lost object and that one is able to acknowledge its goodness and separateness (Klein, 1952: 79). However, Klein (1957) suggests there are nevertheless a number of possible outcomes for jealousy, depending upon the extent to which primary envy has been worked through and modulated. It may be that if the jealous subject is unable to relinquish his/her omnipotence and the primitive psychic defences associated with the paranoid schizoid position, then the jealousy may take on a manic and delusional quality or indeed may be denied altogether. Given the fragility of the jealous subject, relationships are impossible to sustain as he can only tolerate the other's existence by means of splitting, projection and delusional phantasy.[18]

Contemporary psychoanalytic research into jealousy

Shame and jealousy

Contemporary psychoanalytic research into jealousy also reflects current psychoanalytic and cultural concerns more generally. For example, contemporary work on the relationship between shame and jealousy mirrors the recent preoccupation with self-image and embarrassment in an image-conscious 'narcissistic' society (Mollon, 2002; Rose, 2003). Mollon's study of jealousy and shame exemplifies the shift from an emphasis on the Oedipal roots of jealousy, towards the relationship between jealousy and more borderline narcissistic disorders, where pre-Oedipal anxieties about the fragility of the self predominate (2002). Mollon draws on Object Relations theory to argue that 'shame is about the broken connection between one human being and others – a breach in the understanding, expectation, and acceptance that is necessary for a sense of being a valued member of the human family'

(2002: 142). Developmentally, this 'breach' creates a predisposition to feelings of inadequacy. Thus shame occurs psychologically through a 'failure' in the maternal figure's mirroring responses to her infant. It is this 'breach' that creates a predisposition to feelings of inadequacy and shame in social situations. The perceived rejection that leads to feelings of jealousy will be experienced as another such breach and so jealousy is also shameful. Mollon's view is that degrees of jealousy are inevitable. Yet the experience of shameful jealousy may be made much more severe by a societal response that pillories jealousy as a purely negative emotion and a sign of narcissistic weakness.

Sibling rivalry and hysteria

A second recent development in psychoanalytic understandings of jealousy is in the area of sibling rivalry (Houzel, 2001; Mitchell, 2000). As Mitchell argues, sibling rivalry has been a recurring theme of psychoanalytic discussions (2000: ix).[19] However, Mitchell says that a coherent theory of sibling rivalry has not been formulated within clinical or theoretical psychoanalysis. Instead, psychoanalysis has historically neglected and displaced the 'lateral axis' of sibling rivalry and its determining role in the psychic construction of subjectivities for the vertical axis of Oedipal parent/child relationships. Mitchell believes that the murderous feelings and desires associated with the Oedipus complex are not primary, but instead are only evoked after jealous fantasies of displacement brought about by the arrival of a new (real or imagined) sibling (2000: 20–2). Thus Mitchell argues that all jealousy has a sibling quality to it and she explores the role of primary sibling rivalry and its relationship to the death drive and feelings of early 'primitive' jealousy.

The regressive and violent quality of sibling jealousy and the struggle for survival within the hierarchy of family relations have been a recurrent theme of Hollywood cinema, especially in gangster and mafia films. In *The Godfather* trilogy (1972, 1974, 1990), for instance, the depiction of rivalry between the Corleone bothers and other gang members recalls the early murderous fantasies that may be stirred up when trying to come to terms with a new sibling. The film *The Road To Perdition* (2002) also provides an example in this cinematic tradition, in which one lazy brother and his more deserving sibling each compete for their father's affection and place as head of the family. In *The Road To Perdition*, 'Mike Sullivan' (Tom Hanks), the loyal employee of gangster boss 'John Rooney' (Paul Newman), competes and loses out to the boss's cowardly and disloyal son 'Connor' (Daniel Craig), and in the end, is hunted down and dies as a consequence. Interestingly, any vulnerability or wishful fantasies regarding the mother are largely displaced in such films where the underlying homoeroticism of the intense father–son relationships are defended through the authoritarian violence of the narrative.

The fear of the feminine, and the murderous rivalrous feelings that can emerge in relation to the mother were more explicitly represented in Cronenberg's infamous film *Dead Ringers* (1988). The film tells the story of identical twin brothers, the self-assured 'Elliot' and the weaker 'Beverly' (both played by Jeremy Irons), who are both gynaecologists and who operate on and sleep with the same women. The confident twin Elliot passes on his sexual conquests to his brother (without the women knowing), and this arrangement continues without a hitch until Beverly meets and falls for a famous actress (Clair Niveau) at his clinic and sleeps with her. From then on and within the new rivalrous dynamics of this triangular relationship, we see Elliot lose control over his brother as Beverly's identity also begins to fall apart. The precarious balance of the twin's relationship begins to unravel, as misogynist fantasies against the maternal body take hold in the form of death and mutilation.

Mitchell makes a link between the experience of displacement associated with sibling rivalry and male hysteria:

> It is the catastrophic awareness that one is not unique which triggers the onset of hysteria, in which the displaced child regresses to produce the Oedipal and pre-Oedipal stages and also the terrors of the traumatic helplessness of the neonatal infant.
>
> (2000: 20)

Mitchell argues that in the past, this trauma has been dealt with culturally by gendering it as 'feminine' and projecting it on to women as a mysterious and unstable condition (2000: 21). The psychiatric focus and cultural fascination with female jealousy would seem to back up this view (Moi, 1987). Clearly, in psychoanalytic terms, the Oedipal model of masculinity has more redeeming qualities than the chaotic, circular and confused psyche of the jealous male hysteric. Interestingly, the notion of hysterical masculinity resonates with contemporary accounts of masculinity in crisis and popular films such as *Memento*, (2000), *American Psycho* (2000) and *Fight Club* (1999).[20]

A crucial aspect of the subject's first experience of jealousy is the moving away from the omnipotence associated with two-ness and the exclusivity of the maternal relationship and the coming to terms with third-ness (Richards, 1997). A recurring theme in psychoanalytic accounts is that the pain of jealousy provides an early lesson in the acknowledgement of loss and the experience of separation. Whereas Freudian accounts emphasize the role of the father in this process, those in the Kleinian and Object Relations tradition emphasize the 'phantasies' associated with the mother when the child enters the depressive position. In order to specify further the relationship between masculinity and the different accounts of jealousy as outlined above, this chapter will now turn to psychoanalytic perspectives on the shaping of male subjectivities.

Two psychoanalytic models of defensive masculinity and jealousy

1 Masculinity as castration and jealousy

Following Freud (1923, 1925), it is often argued that in the case of boys, rivalry with the father over the mother is given up following the fantasy of castration and the threat of the father's retaliation against the child and mother (Maguire, 1995; Mitchell, 1975). To compensate for the loss of the incestuous love, and to avoid the wrath of the father, boys identify with this fearful paternal figure and the phallic power he represents. The prohibitive laws of the father and patriarchal culture are internalized by boys in the form of the super-ego, which regulates the expression of taboo desire (Freud. 1921, 1923, 1925).

As the feminist writer Judith Butler argues, the internalization of the super-ego sets up an ambivalence at the heart of the boy's emerging identity and in his relationship with the father who is simultaneously feared and idealized (1990: 60–2). The boy also has to repudiate his femininity and all the qualities associated with the mother. So in this reading, the desires and processes of identification that feed into the construction of masculine subjectivities are defensive, shaped reactively against the paternal threat and in opposition to the mother and what the boy later comes to understand as 'femininity'. This refusal of the feminine contributes to the duality of gendered identities in which masculine identities are shaped in opposition to femininity. As the unmourned object, 'Woman' comes to signify 'otherness', and is not to be trusted (Butler, 1990); something that has important implications for male jealousy. In cases of paranoid male jealousy, one can argue that the creation of the imaginary jealous triangle enables the male subject to recall and project the repressed unmourned objects on to the partner and the imaginary rival. The partner may unconsciously collude with this, because her unconscious wishes about lost Oedipal desires may be picked up by the jealous subject, who in turn is able to use the partner's ambivalence about those objects to torment and unsettle her further.

In his development of Freud's work, Lacan argues that 'Woman' is an enigma, whose 'surplus enjoyment' or *'jouissance'* remains a dangerous, elusive and unknowable force to others (Benvenuto and Kennedy, 1986: 190). Male jealousy takes on a particular resonance in this context, as the French psychoanalytic writer Morel points out, 'The eternal else-where, or Other nature of woman is the source of jealousy in the man' (2000: 158). For Lacan, male jealousy is about the impossibility of ever knowing or possessing the other. As discussed earlier, he argues that jealousy is related ontologically to the search for the lost object and the desire for something or someone that one can't possess. For Lacan, the sexual relations of possession rest upon a fictional arrangement whereby men have the phallus and women don't, but instead make do with being one (Mitchell and Rose, 1982). Thus, heterosexual relation-ships are founded upon a fictional arrangement in which possession of the other is impossible, as something always 'eludes' the desirous, and always potentially lacking jealous subject (Morel, 2000). The image of the untouchable screen goddess exemplifies this fantasy. The imagined possession of idealized female stars and celebrity images through con-sumption, provides a means through which the contradictions of pos-session and loss can perhaps be momentarily dispelled. The *femme fatale's* status as a precarious object of triangular desire has also been a recurring theme of Hollywood narratives. Rita Hayworth in *Gilda* (1946), Kim Basinger in *L.A. Confidential* (1997) and Nicole Kidman in *Moulin Rouge!* (2002) provide examples of where the desirability of the heroine is also matched, ultimately, by her inaccessibility. When the woman challenges her position as the phallic object of possession, she is often punished for it through death, as in the James Bond film *Casino Royale* (2006), where the independence of the female star Vesper Lynd (Eva Green), who is the object of Bond's love, is symbolically rewarded by drowning, trapped in a cage.

The jealous subject's desire to establish control over the other through the possessive gaze resonates with the more general Freudian narrative of masculinity and sexual difference. Butler argues that Freud and Lacan's theories emphasize the act of looking and present 'a scopic economy of desire' (1990: 56). As I discuss in Chapter 3, the voyeuristic aspects of the jealous gaze share much in common with cine-psychoanalytic theories of the possessive male gaze (Mulvey, 1975).[21] From the perspective of the castration complex, fantasies of possession play a crucial role in the male Oedipal journey. It arguably follows, as a number of empirical studies suggest, that later loss-provoking situations are experienced in a far more brutal and sudden way by men than by women (Baumgart, 1990: 187). In Freudian terms, women have less to lose in terms of their already castrated status, and so are more likely to experience depressive loss on a daily basis, in a more protracted way (Moi, 1987). Whereas the questions asked by a jealous woman are said to revolve around the theme of self-blame, the question asked by men in the same loss-provoking situation would seem to revolve around the loss of possession (Day Sclater and Yates, 1999). This view is borne out by those working therapeutically in the field of marital conflict, who describe 'the violent, burning, active rage' of their jealous male clients, where feelings of loss and separation are experienced in a form that is 'similar to the reaction of a sudden threat of a bleeding wound' (Baumgart, 1990: 187). The notion of a 'good enough jealousy' appears difficult to countenance in this model where male jealousy is over-determined by castration anxiety. As I now go on to discuss, the same can be said for the second model of defensive masculinity and its construction, where the power of the pre-Oedipal mother and the ambivalent phantasies about her are emphasized.

2 Envious masculinity and jealousy

Following the early psychoanalytic writings of Karen Horney (1926, 1932) and later feminists from the Object Relations School (Chodorow, 1978; Dinnerstein, 1987; Sayers, 1991), contemporary feminist writers such as Minsky (1996, 1998) argue that the origin of gendered subjectivities is not related to the father, but instead lies in the separation from the mother. In these accounts of masculinity, the separation is more problematic for boys because they have to carve out a male identity that is separate from the mother. The focus upon the pre-Oedipal roots of masculinity and the male struggle for individuation has been influential in highlighting both the potential 'fragility' and the defensive nature of the male psyche, and may also reflect current male anxieties about the perceived loss of patriarchal power and the more visible presence and influence of women in the public sphere (Maguire, 1995).[22] Here, it is argued that the defensive psychic mechanisms of splitting and projection are used regularly by men in their relations with women. More vulnerable aspects of the self are denied and projected on to women as a means of protecting the ego from persecutory elements associated with the mother (Minsky, 1996).

The Kleinian concepts of breast and womb envy have today again become popular with contemporary psychoanalytic feminists (Maguire, 1995; Minsky, 1998; Wieland, 2000). They re-work earlier theories (Horney, 1924; Klein, 1957; Riviere, 1932), to argue that male subjectivities are shaped by destructive, envious feelings, which have their roots in the first maternal relationship when the dependent boy resents the mother for her power and envies her plenitude. Again, this model implies that masculinity is shaped in a defensive way against femininity and so provides an explanation of the relationship between masculinity and misogyny, seen in films such as *American Psycho* for instance or *Dead Ringers* perhaps.

The kind of jealousies that are associated with this formation of masculinity are likely to be over-determined by paranoid and sadistic phantasies associated with the pre-Oedipal mother, including phantasies of greedy oral possession and envy of the combined parent (Klein, 1957; Riviere, 1932). The male jealousy of the woman who appears to be concealing a male lover provides a good example of male paranoid jealousy in this context. Here, the unconscious desire for the father, and his penis as phantasized as in the phallic mother's possession, works defensively in denying the phallic mother's power (Yates, 2000). Phantasies such as these take on a particular relevance in the current psychosocial context of uncertainty where many men feel socially 'betrayed' and insecure about the perceived loss of status in relation to women (Faludi, 1999).

As Minsky (1996) and others have argued, envious phantasies are regularly projected on to women who are then derided as objects of contempt or who loom large as castrating monsters in the cultural imagination. Creed argues that the recent 'crisis' of masculinity has provoked a regressive, envious response to change, in the form of paranoid anxieties about the 'phallic mother' (1993). The powerful castrating woman has, at different moments in history, been a popular cultural trope, and was particularly ubiquitous in film in the late 1980s and early 1990s as part of the backlash against feminism.

At the level of theory, the two psychoanalytic models of defensive masculinity that I have outlined so far provide a depressing picture of the possibilities for male subjectivies and fantasy and the potential for positive change in relations between men and women. One is also perhaps in danger of slipping into essentialist generalizations about the inherently problematic nature of masculinity as a reactive outcome of some inevitable pathological journey, whereby the male child is either caught up in rivalrous phantasies about the archaic phallic mother, or is in conflict with what Bollas has called the 'frightful' presence of a castrating Oedipal father (1992: 230). These two highly precarious and defensive models of masculine subjectivities imply an inability to cope with emotional ambivalence and a tendency to split the object in the face of uncertainty. The kinds of jealousy that are likely to accompany these modes of subjectivity are also therefore likely to be destructive and overly narcissistic. However, I now turn to a third psychoanalytic model of masculinity which, in contrast to the other two, provides the space to think about the possibilities of 'a good enough' male Oedipal journey. I theorize the implications of this more positive reading for male jealousy.

The complexity of gendered subjectivities and good enough jealousy

The term 'good enough' was first used by Winnicott (1971) to refer to the 'good enough mother', inferring that mothers should not be too good or too bad because either of those extremes may inhibit the development of the child. Being 'good enough', then, connotes both a stage of early child development and an attitude that acknowledges the contradictions and fallibilities of being human; it implies there is no perfection and that some difficulty is always present when relating to others and that such difficulty may indeed be a necessary aspect of object relations. One can apply this concept of being 'good enough' to other developmental stages and psychosocial phenomena. For instance, the psychoanalyst, Bollas (1992), uses the language of Winnicott to explore the notion of the 'good enough' Oedipus complex, which has less pathologizing implications for Oedipal masculinity. Developing the ideas of Bollas, the concept of a good enough masculinity acknowledges its failures, yet at the same time it escapes the pessimism implied by previous models of masculinity. Drawing on the theories of Winnicott and Bollas, this model of masculinity implies a capacity to accept the vulnerability of the self as well as the inevitable frustrations that emerge in jealousy scenarios where feelings of loss and anger may predominate.

In his narrative of the good enough Oedipus complex, Bollas (1992) describes the child's intoxicating journey from the relative safety of pre-Oedipal 'matrilineal' infantile love, to the triangular conflicts and dilemmas of the Oedipus complex. The Oedipal wish to erotically possess the mother is not pathologized in Bollas's account as a source of guilt and anxiety, but rather is affirmed as a necessary stage in the development of the child's ego, before moving on to wider psychic horizons. Having internalized the mother, he says there is 'no doubt' about the child's 'claim' upon her, as the child moves into the broader complexity of social relations and cultural life (Bollas, 1992: 231). Bollas implies that a boy's gendered identity is not acquired through a hateful negation of the feminine, nor is it based on some defensive idealization of the father. Rather, the child's physical and erotic desires propel him forward to a psychic space in which he wishes to identify with more than just his father or his mother. Bollas describes this process in terms of the embracing of complexity and finding one's place within a generational context, and acquiring a sense of perspective in relation to oneself and others.

Bollas's approach escapes the dualistic assumptions inherent in the models of Klein and Freud, which tend to concentrate either on the maternal influences of the envious pre-Oedipal sphere, or on the castrating father who causes the boy to identify with him out of fear (Bollas, 1992: 230). There is little space in such models for a more fluid conception of male subjectivity, in which masculine and feminine modes of identification and desire are both allowed to exist, and are not perceived as threatening or diluting 'real' masculinity. The extent to which the response to the dilemmas of difference, when played out around sexual desire, are negatively driven, plays a crucial role in the ways in which one's jealousy is experienced. If one defensively takes up a sexual position out of fear or because one is too angry to cope with the implications of loss, then the defences needed to maintain a coherent sense of self become harder to manage and are played out in jealousy scenarios. Such responses also have implications for the expression of jealous anxiety in the cultural sphere, when, as in a climate of masculine crisis, images of dangerous femininity and risk may predominate. The popularity of *noir* films in the 1940s and 1950s, which took place against a backdrop of male insecurity following World War II, provide a case in point (Bainbridge and Yates, 2005). However, combining the insights of Klein's concept of the depressive position with Freud's awareness of gender and the importance of erotic desire, Bollas's ideas can be extended to provide a model of a masculine subjectivity that is not split and overly defensive, but which is potentially able to cope with the complexities of sexual difference and cultural change. Such a model provides a way to think through the more positive aspects of men and masculinities today and a more nuanced response to the processes of feminization and cultural change discussed in Chapter 1.

It is possible to apply this model of a 'good enough Oedipus complex' to the case of male jealousy in a way that reinstates the tolerant and liberal tones of Freud regarding 'normal' jealousy, even though working through it may cause difficulty and unhappiness. Drawing on the work of Bollas (1992), one can argue that male jealousy need not be overly governed by narcissism and the wish to control the other. Rather, his ideas open up the space to think about the possible reparative qualities of jealousy. As discussed earlier, in psychoanalytic terms jealousy provides a test of how one copes with ambivalence, and tests one's capacity to cope with loss and the separateness of the object. A good enough jealousy implies the capacity to respect difference without being indifferent; the loss of an object to another is acknowledged, understood and not denied or acted out. The intention of this discussion is not to moralize about jealous behaviour, (even though some kinds of jealous behaviour are bad). Rather, one can suggest that certain kinds of jealousy are also symptomatic of certain kinds of masculinity and male fantasy, and so it should be the case that one can tell us more about the other. Some forms of good enough jealousy demonstrate the capacity to love and to mourn the loss of an object and cope with internal ambivalence without resorting to defences such as splitting or idealization, described in different terms by Klein and Lacan.

Two of the three psychoanalytic models of masculinity and jealousy discussed so far, can be defined as overly defensive, *reactive* models of masculinity, implying that men and masculinities are unable to live with uncertainties of object relations and respond fearfully to the risks and losses of contemporary cultural life. The third, *good enough* model envisages a mode of masculinity that is more able to cope with emotional paradox, gendered fluidity and ambivalence and connotes a less defensive response to the shifting cultural perimeters of hegemonic masculinity today. *Reactive* and *good enough* masculine types can be viewed as corresponding (respectively) to overly possessive narcissistic and paranoid jealousies on the one hand, and less destructive, good enough jealousies on the other. Clearly, these categories are ideal types and they may overlap in different instances. However, in developing such an approach, one can, against the backdrop of the changing conditions of contemporary culture, begin to imagine the possibility for less rigid and defensive modes of masculinity, in which the other is allowed to exist and which provides possibilities for something else to emerge.

These models of masculine jealousy can also assist in assessing whether some cinematic representations of jealous men challenge the reactive, narcissistic formations of hegemonic masculinity. A feature of 'good enough' representations is that they contain a degree of ambiguity In relation to issues of masculinity, jealous possession, the acceptance of sexual difference and the rivalrous other. Many of these themes come together in the film *The Quiet American* (2002) in which Michael Caine plays a cynical British *Times* correspondent 'Fowler' in Saigon, who has 'gone native' and is in love with a beautiful Vietnamese woman 'Phuong' (Do Thi Hai Yen). However, Fowler loses Phuong to the American 'Pyle' (Brendan Fraser), who wants to save her from what he believes to be Fowler's corrupting influence. There are different strands of jealousy at play in the narrative, which invite a range of complex and often contradictory readings from the spectator, including identifications with the poignant depiction of Fowler's jealous unhappiness at the loss of his mistress to Pyle. The film does not provide a consoling or heroic narrative of male loss and revenge, as Fowler's questionable behaviour as a white married colonial reporter is emphasized throughout. Yet the film manages to convey both a sense of his longing and jealousy and her desire for escape, thus allowing the spectator to hold in mind her difference within the complexity of this particular jealousy narrative. The film also draws an analogy between Pyle's questionable desire to rescue Phuong from Fowler, and the desirability of an American 'moral third force' to resolve the conflict in Vietnam, thus making a link between the fantasy of jealous 'rescue' and American foreign policy.[23]

Films such as *The Quiet American* allow space for less defensively driven modes of spectatorship that challenge the narcissistic structures of hegemonic masculinity and the reactive fantasies that have, until recently, often dominated the narratives of mainstream Hollywood cinema. These themes of masculinity and spectatorship are explored further in the following chapter.

3
Theories of Masculinity, Cinema, Spectatorship and the Jealous Gaze

Psychoanalytic studies of the cinema suggest that, once sitting still and quiet in the darkened auditorium, the spectator is lulled into a state close to dreaming. In this state, the boundaries between conscious and unconscious are no longer as secure as they remain in waking life. In dreams, and at the cinema, infantile ways of thinking and fantasising come to the fore once more.

(Radstone, 1996: 197)

Introduction

Hollywood has played a central role in creating the myths of masculinity in Western popular culture. Throughout the twentieth century, narrative cinema has been dominated by images of male heroes and stories structured from a male point of view (Cohan and Hark, 1993; Kirkham and Thumim, 1993, 1995; Mulvey, 1975). These images have also played a key role in the shaping of gendered subjectivities, where social discourses and unconscious fantasies intersect to produce subject positions for the spectator:

Not only is it [the cinema] an important supplier of paternal representations, but it orchestrates for the male subject the projections so necessary to his sense of personal potency. Its images, sounds and narrative structures are drawn from the ideological reserve of the dominant fiction.

(Silverman, 1990: 113)

The identifications, desires and pleasures stirred up by cinematic images have received a great deal of attention from psychoanalytic writers in film and cultural studies.

42

As Lebeau argues, there is a 'correspondence between the cinema, and the unconscious mind', both in terms of '*how* and *what* the mind thinks' (2001: 6). Watching a film is also a public and shared cultural activity and as Mulvey (1975) and others have argues in relation to notions of the patriarchal unconscious, films reflect and articulate the prevailing ideologies, myths and discourses of a given society:

> From this point of view, cinema is something like the royal road to the cultural unconscious; it takes up the place occupied by the dream in Freud's classic account of psychoanalytic interpretation.
>
> (Lebeau, 2001: 6)

From this perspective, the film works like a dream and the process of watching it is akin to 'dreaming in public' (Lebeau, 2001: 3).

Hollywood films invest in the relationship of the audience to the text and this is important in understanding the context of production and consumption. The role of the spectator is understood as a 'subject position' determined firstly at the level of the unconscious and secondly in terms of the lived social experience of the audience. Recent criticism foregrounds the importance of both dimensions in formulating an interpretation of a film (Kuhn, 1994: 22–3).

A recurring theme in psychoanalytic film criticism has been that in classical cinema, 'the spectator is always male' and that Hollywood narratives follow a male Oedipal journey in which the hero learns to accept the symbolic death of the father, separate from the mother and find love with another woman. Until the 1980s, when studies of masculinity began to emerge within film studies,[1] the depiction of heterosexual masculinities on screen was largely taken for granted and images of heterosexual men were perceived as the agents against which women and gay men were problematized as 'other' (Neale, 1983: 9). As Mulvey (1975, 1981) famously argues, in the classical Hollywood cinema, male heroes are usually positioned as bearers of agency and of the narrative – they act and look – whereas women tend to be acted upon and looked at. However, over the past two decades, film studies has increasingly focused on masculinities and the implications of those images for issues of spectatorship and male fantasy (Bainbridge and Yates, 2005; Cohan and Hark, 1993; Kirkham and Thumim, 1993, 1995). As I go on to discuss, Mulvey's model of masculinity and the omnipotent male gaze has since been developed to incorporate the differences and ambiguities of masculinity within contemporary culture.

This chapter reviews and traces the changing psychoanalytic theories of masculinity and cinema. The aim is to provide an overview of the relationship between masculinities and spectatorship in psychoanalytic film theory, from the all-powerful male gaze of 'apparatus theory', to more recent concepts of male trauma and the hysterical male gaze. The chapter discusses the implications of these theories for masculine jealousies and the notion of the possessive male gaze.

Mulvey's Lacanian inspired work on the mastery of the male gaze (1975, 1981) set the terms of the debate about gender and cinema within feminist film criticism and cine-psychoanalysis for years to come. Before Mulvey however, the field of 1970s cine-psychoanalysis was dominated by apparatus theory as applied by the male French theorists Jean Baudry (1970, 1975) and later, Christian Metz (1975) who took as given the male spectator and the male unconscious (Kaplan, 1998: 277). Their ideas are important because they provided the foundation for later developments in the psychoanalytic study of cinema and masculinity and I now turn to their work.

'*Screen* theory', cinema and the apparatus of the mind

Baudry (1975) and Metz (1975) use Lacanian psychoanalysis within what has come to be known as 'apparatus theory', to analyse the relationship between the 'machinery' of the cinematic apparatus, which includes every institutional aspect of its production and projection and the mental/psychic 'apparatus' of the spectator (Baudry, 1975: 763). They use Lacanian theory to argue that the cinematic apparatus simulates the unconscious construction of subjectivity, and liken the psychic state of the spectator to that of a dream. Baudry and Metz played a considerable role in the development of what has come to be known as 'Lacanian film theory', which was also part of the complex intellectual development in British film studies (and to a lesser extent in the US) referred to as '*Screen* theory'. The journal *Screen* introduced French ideas about film to an Anglo-American audience and set the intellectual agenda for film studies for a generation.

Screen theory uses theories of the French Marxist, Althusser, to critique the role of Hollywood cinema as reproducing the dominant ideology of the ruling classes and the capitalist economic system. The power of the cinematic apparatus to induce a psychological effect upon the spectator was the key theme of Baudry's and Metz's work. Baudry and Metz emphasize the unconscious and ideological power of the cinematic experience and how the specific cinematic conditions of watching a film determines one's enjoyment of it. Baudry's essays (1970; 1975) use the analogy of the 'prisoner' in 'Plato's cave' to describe both the 'womb'-like conditions of the cinema, and effects for audiences when the lights go down. He draws on Freud's (1900) *Interpretation of Dreams* to emphasize the regressive dream-like quality of the cinematic experience and its similarity to the 'hallucinatory' satisfactions associated with infantile narcissism and the mother's breast. Baudry (1970: 347) argues that the institutional and psychic apparatuses of the spectators become locked into each other and the flickering light or 'eye' of the projector captures the spellbound eye of the spectator. The subject experiences a totalizing sense of narcissistic unity and control in relation to the characters on the screen, which ideologically masks the real ontological fragmentation of the self and society (Baudry, 1970: 347).

Likening the experience of watching the film to Lacan's (1949) description of the mirror phase, Baudry argues that the spectator regresses into a dependent infantile state, in which the regressed infantile psyche of the spectator identifies with the characters (or ideal images) on the screen (1970: 353). This experience of narcissistic fusion is enhanced by the narrative form of classic Hollywood cinema, in which the story appears to unfold seamlessly in front of the audience, who sit passively, gripped by the unfolding story (Baudry, 1970: 352). In ideological terms, all contradictions are denied and resolved, when, for example, as at the end of the film, the hero kills the villain and rides off into the sunset with his narcissism intact. Thus for Baudry, issues of narrative, ideology and the unconscious processes of looking are interlinked: 'The cinema can thus appear as a sort of psychic apparatus of substitution, corresponding to the model defined by the dominant ideology' (Baudry, 1970: 354).

Whereas Baudry focuses on the pre-linguistic, and (in Lacanian terms) the *Imaginary* narcissistic modes of identification, to understand the power of the cinema, Metz (1975) discusses the Symbolic aspects of cinematic identification associated with the Oedipal crisis.[2] Metz suggests that when watching a film, the spectator suspends disbelief for the duration (1975: 802), and this process is similar to that described in classical psychoanalysis in terms of 'disavowal' (Freud, 1924, 1927). The latter concept is used in psychoanalysis to denote the refusal to acknowledge sexual difference, in the face of overwhelming castration anxiety. Metz (1975: 812–13) argues that when presented with these ideal images in the film, the spectator (who by implication is male) can use these ideal images to compensate for and deny his feelings of lack and inadequacy. Yet at the same time, these same images (for example, of beautiful women and powerful men) remind the subject of his own imagined inadequacies and wounded narcissism, and feelings of castration anxiety will once more come to the fore. To cope with this, the cinematic apparatus (in unison with his psychic apparatus) defends against such anxieties associated with difference through fetishizing the objects on the screen.

Drawing on a Lacanian reading of the Oedipal crisis, Metz highlights the feelings of loss that accompany the subject's entry into patriarchal culture and the acceptance of the incest taboo (1975: 808). For Lacan, the loss of the Oedipal mother becomes the imaginary other (*objet petit a*) that underpins desire and instigates an endless search for the lost object. From this perspective, the cinematic narratives work to restore an imaginary unification for the viewer, and help to mask Oedipal anxieties and compensate for the 'lost object' and frustrated desire. Thus, Metz argues that the Oedipal frustrations that underpin Lacan's account of subjectivity are resolved for the spectator when watching Hollywood films, as the classic realist narrative structures of the stories on the screen reflect the struggles of the (male) Oedipal journey (1975: 808).

Both Metz and Baudry have been criticized for their mechanical explanations of the relationship between the institutional apparatuses of the cinema and the spectator. A common criticism is that apparatus theory implies passivity on the part of the audience, and the relationship between the text and the spectator leaves little space for contradiction or resistance (Cook and Berinck, 1999: 349). A related criticism is the universalism and a-historicism of their psychoanalytic approach and the assumption of an undifferentiated mass audience (Kuhn, 1994: 55). As feminists have argued, the hypothetical spectator in apparatus theory is always assumed to be male (Kuhn, 1994; Penley, 1985). Metz's account is implicitly gendered because the experience of unity, which films promise to create for the spectator, is also bound up with the male search and Oedipal conquest for the lost female object. The (usually passive) positioning of the feminine object of (his) desire is more-or-less taken as given, without problematizing the political implications of that desire in terms of the cultural politics of gender.

Laura Mulvey and the pleasures of the male gaze

Laura Mulvey (1975, 1981) takes up these feminist issues, developing the Lacanian methodology of apparatus theory to argue that the narratives of mainstream cinema work ideologically to reinforce the psychic structures of patriarchal masculinity:

Psychoanalytic theory is thus appropriate here as a political weapon, demonstrating the way the unconscious of patriarchal society has structured film form.

(1975: 833)

Mulvey argues that the pleasures of watching Hollywood films (as in her later analysis of King Vidor's (1946) *Duel In the Sun*) are far from 'innocent', as their narratives are geared towards the male gaze and contribute to the reproduction of 'the patriarchal order'. Mulvey advocates 'the destruction of pleasure as a radical weapon' (1975: 834), which is necessary in order to 'conceive a new language of desire' (p. 835). Mulvey's theories emerged from a specific context of cultural and second-wave feminist politics, and she intended that her ideas should go hand in hand with a new practice of feminist cinema, which would disrupt the gender binary relations of looking and appearing in front of the camera.[3]

In her 1975 paper 'Visual Pleasure and Narrative Cinema', Mulvey uses Lacanian psychoanalysis to analyse the relationship between the screen and the spectator. She argues that the male gaze occupies a central place in that relationship. She spells out the gendered implications of Baudry and Metz's film criticism; that popular cinema is geared towards bolstering male narcissism, and that it is this narcissistic appeal which underpins the patriarchal construction of masculinity. Mulvey argues that popular cinema is based upon a division between narrative and spectacle. Men have ultimate control of the narrative action, whereas women are positioned passively as spectacles, as objects of male desire (Mulvey, 1975: 838). This positioning is achieved through a series of three 'looks': first, in terms of the way in which the camera looks at the women; second, the way that the male actors look at the women; and third, the way that the audience is positioned to look at the women in the same way as the camera and the male actors (Mulvey, 1975: 839). She argues that this sexual division of (male) looking and (female) being, reflects the gender imbalance in society more generally, and is underpinned by the psychic mechanisms associated with narcissism, and scopophilia, the sexual pleasure of looking.

In Freudian theory, scopophilia is associated with the controlling, sadistic gaze of the voyeuristic subject who looks unseen at his object from a safe distance (Freud, 1905: 70). The underlying motivation of the voyeur is the need to ward off castration anxiety by returning to the 'trauma' of the primal scene, to investigate from a distance and from a position of power, the original scene of trauma, to possess and punish the m/other for her Oedipal infidelity and difference. The voyeuristic pleasure in scrutinizing the object from a distance has much in common with the obsessive jealous stalker, who wants to possess and punish his chosen object of possession and desire. This variation of the jealous gaze is represented in films such *Taxi Driver* (1996), *One Hour Photo* (2002) and *Caché (Hidden)* (2005), where the voyeuristic look of the camera reproduces the jealous gaze of the stalker.[4] The relationship between the pleasures of fetishism and the male gaze is also discussed by Mulvey. Freud (1927) argues that fetishism is linked to a male fear of female castration and a desire to look away, and instead create an alternative, less threatening object or fetish of desire.[5] Close-ups of faces of female stars or fragmented shots of the body are cited by Mulvey as examples of such fetishism. Other examples are when the woman's entire body may be turned into a phallic symbol and be unconsciously used to deny the losses and conflicts associated with difference. The fearful fascination and desire to possess and control female sexuality is illustrated in the film *Basic Instinct* (1992), when the camera adopts strategies of voyeurism and fetishism, simultaneously searching out and focusing its gaze on the sexual allure of Sharon Stone's body, whilst also pulling away and fetishizing her body through shots of her mouth smoking a cigarette or crossing and uncrossing her legs.

Mulvey, like Metz, argues that Hollywood narratives are structured by male Oedipal conflicts associated with castration anxiety and loss, which, as we have seen, are dealt with through psychic mechanisms of voyeurism and fetishism. However, in contrast to Metz, who assumes, but does not problematize, the male gaze, Mulvey's aim is to spell out the costs of this 'scopophilic regime' and thereby change it (1975: 833). Mulvey's model of gender infers that patriarchal masculinities are fraught with unresolved Oedipal jealousies and possessiveness, and that the cinema with its narratives of Oedipal mastery, provides endless imaginary opportunities and solutions to ward off the rival and to punish and investigate women for their infidelities. However, Mulvey's (1975) analysis of the patriarchal cinema has been criticized for its over-arching claims and for a rather deterministic use of Lacanian theory, which positions women as passive and lacking (Buscome et al., 1992). Yet implicit in her application of psycho-analytic theory to the images of Hollywood films, is her determination to persuade us that these images are not timeless or natural, but can be challenged and contested on a critical and practical basis (Creed, 1998: 84).[6]

Mulvey's analysis has been enormously influential. The notion of 'the male gaze' has been central in setting the terms of the debate about gender and spectatorship ever since. One can argue that it still has relevance today, when applied to big-budget male action films such as the *James Bond* series, which continue to place the omnipotent male hero at the centre of the narrative. However, both Mulvey and Metz (1975) present an image of patriarchal masculinity as only powerful and possessive. There is little space for images of male vulnerability or the ambiguities that characterize many contemporary cinematic images of masculinity, such as Brad Pitt in *Se7en* (1995), Hugh Grant as the bored and lonely singleton in *About a Boy* (2002), Tim Robbins as the formerly abused and bullied school friend in *Mystic River* (2003), Guy Pearce as the confused amnesiac in *Memento* (2000) or Kevin Spacey as the husband having a midlife crisis in *American Beauty* (1999).

Mulvey's theoretical approach (along with apparatus theory more generally) has also been criticized for reproducing the binary division of gender, whereby femininity is positioned as 'other' (Copjec, 1982). This also has implications for masculinity and its theoretical depiction as a monolithic entity, which fails to reflect the cultural and historical differences *between* masculinities and the ambiguities of erotic desire (Mackinnon, 2003).[7] Indeed, there is also little space in Mulvey's theory for less phallocentric, bisexual modes of identification on the part of male spectators.

The anxieties and pleasures of masculinity as the object of the gaze

Since Mulvey, the study of masculinity and cinema has produced a number of readings that have explored the unconscious symbolism of masculinity, and its relationship to erotic desire, bisexuality and the sexual politics of the male gaze. These issues were put on the agenda by Neale (1982), who focused on the idealization of cinematic masculinity and its relationship to fantasies of the idealized father. Using the film *Chariots of Fire* (1981) as an example, he argues that the perceived crisis of masculinity at the cinema did not signify a threat to hegemonic masculinities. By contrast, Pam Cook (1982) points to the contradictions of narcissistic, idealized images of masculinity in films such as *Raging Bull* (1980), which undermines traditional representations of masculinity. Richard Dyer (1982) also explores images of masculinity, focusing on the homoerotic aspects of male imagery and the male gaze. In his paper about male pin-ups, Dyer (1982) argues that men are not always positioned as masters of the gaze, but instead, they may also be objectified and looked at by men and women as objects of desire.[8] Dyer says that although the macho poses of male pin-ups suggest a celebration of the phallus, such images are also inherently contradictory for the male viewer, as they signify the gap between the fantasy and reality of phallic power and what it means to be a man (1982: 274).

Neale's paper 'Masculinity as Spectacle: Reflections on Men and Mainstream Cinema' (1983), also focuses on the objectification of the male body and the strategies used to disavow castration anxiety and bisexual desire potentially aroused by such images. Neale explores the mechanisms and contradictions of heterosexual masculinities and their inscription in Hollywood cinema. He engages critically with Mulvey's ideas, both in terms of 'images of men on the one hand and the male spectator on the other' and he explores the mechanisms of identification and narcissism (1983: 10). Like Mulvey, Neale argues that the classic Hollywood film is structured by the male Oedipal journey, but he also argues that processes of masculine desire and identification are more fluid than Mulvey supposed. Neale suggests that although men identify narcissistically with the 'human figure' of the male hero on screen, they may also identify in a more disparate manner with a range of different characters on the screen, including women (1983: 10–11). In this sense, mechanisms of identification are always 'fractured and multiple' and, unconsciously, bisexual. Nevertheless, Neale emphasizes that films also work hard to maintain sexual divisions, and social discourses of gender work powerfully throughout to ensure that men continue to identify with their own sex (1983: 11). This is reinforced unconsciously through narcissistic modes of identification, because the latter also involve omnipotence and fantasies of mastery and control, and so complement and reinforce patriarchal images of heroic masculinity. Neale cites a number of classic Hollywood films and heroes to illustrate his argument, including the silent tough hero personified by, for example, Clint Eastwood, whose silence can be read as a narcissistic self-sufficiency (1983: 12).[9] However, Neale argues that whereas Mulvey only addresses the active 'look' of the male hero and its attraction for the male spectator, these narcissistic identifications always carry with them a subtext of doubt, conflict and absence (1983: 13). For the perfection of these cinematic ego ideals may also remind men of their own inadequacies and lack. Neale suggests that images of 'male authority and omnipotence' provoke a passive, masochistic relationship between the audience and the image, which is not only related to male identification, but also to erotic male desire (1983:16). But as Neale suggests, this homosexual voyeurism, which undermines the ideology of heterosexual masculinity, may provoke guilt and anxiety for the male spectator (1983: 14). However, Neale argues that such anxieties are offset by visual strategies that depict bodily mutilation and scarring, or through the violence of action scenes where the body is harmed in some way. The fetishistic use of guns and phallic weapons is an obvious example here and Neale also cites the fight scenes between friends in films such as *Spartacus*, (1960). More recently, one could include films such as *Gladiator* (2000) and *Troy* (2004) as examples of this kind of sadomasochism in action.

Neale identifies a number of contradictions related to male narcissism and mainstream Hollywood cinema, in which anxieties always accompany the pleasures of watching the hero on screen. For instance there may be a contradiction between the 'social authority of the law' and the 'narcissistic authority' of male fantasy, in which the film's hero resists the social demands for 'integration' into the social order, as symbolized by the intrusion of femininity and marriage. Instead of marrying the woman, the narcissistic hero (as in traditional Westerns) often rides off into the sunset alone. Nostalgic male narcissism is a constant trope of Westerns, which Neale argues are about 'doomed lost narcissism and the threat posed by women' (1983: 15). This contradiction is often partly resolved in Westerns by a socially responsible male figure, often played by John Wayne, as in *The Searchers* (1956) who also represents 'the anachronistic social outsider' (1983: 15).

Neale's problematization of heterosexual masculinities has inspired more recent books on the subject, of which there are still relatively few (see, for example, Cohan and Hark, 1993; Kirkham and Thumim, 1993, 1995; Lehman, 2001; Powrie, Davies and Babington, 2004). The significance of Neale's paper for this discussion lies in his insistence on the plurality of cinematic masculinities, which combine active and passive images, associated with masculinity and femininity. Neale's psychosocial approach provides insights into issues of spectatorship, as he emphasized the fluidity and bisexuality of the spectator's unconscious desires and identifications.[10]

Masochism and the male gaze

Since Neale's essay, there have been a number of other developments in the field of cine-psychoanalysis and cultural studies that have influenced the study of film and masculinity. These developments have continued to emphasize the fluidity of identification and the bisexual male gaze. For example, throughout the 1980s, new work emerged around the theme of passive, masochistic masculinities and male spectatorship (Modleski, 1988; Silverman, 1988; Studlar, 1985). Following Neale (1983), these theories challenge Mulvey's notion of the monolithic, possessive and sadistic male gaze, by returning to Freud's theory of the bisexuality of men and women:

> All human individuals, as a result of their bisexual disposition and of cross-inheritance, combine in themselves both masculine and feminine characteristics, so that pure masculinity and femininity remain theoretical constructs of uncertain content.
>
> (Freud, 1925: 342)

Studlar (1985) focuses on the relationship between the male spectator and the regressive fantasies associated with the pre-Oedipal child. She argues that the male spectator often regresses to this infantile position and identifies with the female images on screen from a passive, a-sexual masochistic position. Modleski however, critiques this 'benign' model of male spectatorship, as it fails to include the ambivalence and 'dread' that also accompanies male identification with the feminine (1988: 11). She argues that pre-Oedipal modes of identification are always influenced by, and viewed retrospectively through, the lens of the symbolic sphere of culture, when castration anxiety and the cultural devaluation of femininity come to the fore. Drawing on the work of Silverman (1980),[11] Modleski argues that although the symbolic is associated with the suppression of the feminine (as a reminder of the male subject's own bisexuality), the feminine other may nevertheless be a source of ambivalent fascination for the male subject, who experiences a sadomasochistic relationship to images of women on the screen (1988: 11–12).

Primal fantasies and the fluidity of the jealous gaze

The mobility of the gaze and the fluidity of desire are further explored in Elizabeth Cowie's paper 'Fantasia' (1984), which addresses pre-Oedipal fantasies related to the origins of sexuality and the primal scene. Drawing on Laplanche and Pontalis's essay 'Fantasy and the Origins of Sexuality' (1964), Cowie presents a fluid psychoanalytic model of the psyche and the cinema in which the spectator both occupies and moves between masculine and feminine positions. Citing Laplanche and Pontalis, Cowie (1984) argues that desire for men and women is influenced by three 'original fantasies' of the primal scene, to which the subject unconsciously returns, in order to work through and explain the origins of subjectivity: 'Like myths, they claim to provide a representation of, and a solution to, the major enigmas which confront the child' (Laplanche and Pontalis, 1964: 19). These primal fantasies work in a mobile fashion and enable the subject to occupy a number of roles at once, in which in fantasy terms, he or she acts as both subject and object, as participant and observer. Laplanche and Pontalis also make less of a distinction between conscious and unconscious fantasy and they point to the 'continuity between the various fantasy scenarios – the stage-setting of desire – ranging from the daydream to the fantasies recovered or reconstructed by the analytic investigation' (1964: 28). Laplanche and Pontalis define the originary fantasies thus:

the primal scene pictures the origin of the individual; fantasies of seduction, the origin and upsurge of sexuality; fantasies of castration, the origin of the difference between the sexes.

(1964: 19)

Cowie argues that these primal fantasies have a cinematic aspect to them, because they are analogous to, and provide the setting or *mise-en-scène* for the staging of, active and passive desires and subject positions represented on the screen (1984: 359). Cowie's concept of fantasy enables the spectator to view a film as a staging and working through of these fantasies of the origins of subjectivity and sexual difference. The three fantasy scenarios cited by Cowie could also be said to underpin representations of triangular jealous scenarios, where it is possible to identify with all three positions simultaneously as a means to work through and resolve a jealous fantasy. The fantasy scenario described by Seidenberg in his paper 'The Jealous Wish' (1952), provides a good example of this. In the case of the latter, the jealous subject feels compelled to create and thus re-enact jealous triangles in order to simultaneously identify with the role of the active rival and the passive jealous husband.

Masculinity and fantasies of the engulfing mother

The image of the all-powerful male gaze within feminist theory has been further challenged by Kleinian interpretations of masculinity in film (Creed, 1993; Horrocks, 1994; Taubin, 1992).[12] In contrast to the Freudian and Lacanian emphasis upon fantasies of the castrating father, the ideas of Melanie Klein (1988 a, b) and Karen Horney (1932) address the unconscious 'phantasies' associated with the all powerful, castrating pre-Oedipal mother.[13] The male fear of the monstrous woman was first addressed by Freud in his paper 'Fetishism' (1927). There, Freud argues that the male terror 'at the sight of the female genital', is related to the fear of her castration. However, Karen Horney emphasizes the fear of Woman as the castrator and also the unconscious wish on the part of some men to be castrated and take up the position formerly associated with femininity (1932). As discussed in Chapter 2, psychological formations of masculinity are influenced by infantile phantasies of envy, something that is given added force when the child separates from the mother during the Oedipal phase (which begins earlier in the Kleinian account). Horney argues that boys find this Oedipal process especially difficult (1932). Phantasies associated with the experience of maternal loss and thwarted Oedipal desire may induce feelings of intense envy, fear and narcissistic rage, from which they may never fully recover. This envy of woman finds expression in patriarchal culture, where femininity is routinely derided and is subject to projections of male lack (Creed, 1993; Minsky, 1998).

As with Neale's (1983) ideas about male spectatorship and the pleasures and anxieties of male objectification, a Kleinian approach can be used to explore more masochistic images of masculinity in relation to the 'monstrous feminine' and the different anxieties they are likely to evoke for men and women.[14] Creed argues that images of 'the monstrous feminine' come in many guises, but they tend to find most clear expression in film at moments in history when male identity is under threat (1993: 1). For example, such images (in films such as *Gilda*) were clearly evident in the *film noir* genre in the 1940s and 1950s, following the upheavals of World War II in the guise of powerful man-eating *femme fatales* (Kaplan, 1978). In the 1980s and early 1990s, anxieties about the castrating mother could also be found in a number of anti-feminist 'backlash' films such as *Disclosure* (1994) and *Basic Instinct* (1992).

Cultural studies and its influences

As discussed above, throughout the 1980s and 1990s, apparatus theory was challenged and developed within cine-psychoanalysis. However, another influential source of criticism came from the growth of cultural studies, which critiqued *Screen* theory. Highlighting its ahistorical tendencies and its monolithic notion of spectatorship, cultural studies foregrounds the lack of attention to differences of social subjectivity in this work. An influential strand of this critique focuses on audience research and cultural reception and was first pioneered by Stuart Hall (1977) and later David Morley (1980, 1986). These studies emphasize the polysemy of texts, and challenge the notion that audiences are passive, 'cultural dupes' (Hall, 1977). This strand of cultural studies draws attention to the historical and cultural context of textual meaning and to the significance of both institutions and social audiences in the production and consumption of meaning (Ang, 1985; Staiger, 1992; Turner, 2002). Dyer's (1998b) work on stars provides a good example of this kind of cultural studies approach, where text and context are analysed for the production of meaning. The political significance of popular culture for purposes of reading against the grain has now replaced the image of the 'shackled' spectator seen in Baudry's rendition of Plato's Cave (1970). Instead, it is now regularly argued in cultural and film studies readers, that popular culture and popular Hollywood films provide a potential site for symbolic transgression and for political struggle, where hegemonic meanings are contested and transformed on a daily basis (for instance, Storey, 1996, 1999; Turner, 2002).

Today, the focus is on hegemonic struggles in popular cultural texts. These are not just related to categories of class, but instead are more complex and layered and include cultural groupings related to ethnicities, gender and sexuality (Dyer, 1997; Eleftheriotis, 1995). As Connell argues, the negotiation of images also extends to the struggles around hegemonic masculinity and what it means to be a man (1995). Mainstream cinema provides an important site where patriarchal masculinities are regularly tested and transformed and this notion also underpins the approach taken in this book regarding discussion of masculinity and cinema.[15]

Contemporary psychoanalytic understandings of masculinity and cinema

Both cultural studies and film studies now share a greater critical understanding of diversity and an acknowledgment of the plurality and differences between masculinities (Cohan and Hark, 1993; Eleftheriotis, 1995). Cine-psychoanalysis has also become increasingly interdisciplinary. It now routinely interweaves psychoanalytic ideas with a range of theories and perspectives that historicize and take account of the psychic *and* social complexities of masculinities and issues of gendered spectatorship (for instance, see Bainbridge and Yates, 2005; Kirkham and Thumim, 1993, 1995).[16] Cook and Bernink note that contemporary film studies of masculinity focus less on issues of fetishism and voyeurism, and more on issues of hysteria, trauma and masochism (1999: 362).[17] This in turn reflects the social and cultural changes associated with the alleged crisis of masculinity and the feminization of contemporary culture, as discussed in Chapter 1.

The film case studies in this book combine cultural studies theories of popular culture and hegemonic struggle with those of psychoanalysis. They also address debates about the crisis of masculinity in cinema, and suggest that new ambiguous images of masculinity may be emerging that have a potential for something new and different – as in the model of 'good enough' masculinities outlined in earlier chapters. These images of masculinity are decentred further by narrative codes, plots and stylistic codes that subvert the more traditional representations associated with the classical realism of the Hollywood cinema, and the male Oedipal journey that underpins the plot and story-line resolution. One can define such representations as 'feminine', because of their textual openness and the lack of closure around meanings of the text (Kuhn, 1994: 17). Kuhn argues that defining a feminist film goes beyond trying to establish some criteria for a feminist text based around the notion of content and form (1994: 13–14). Kuhn also argues that to look at a text in cultural isolation makes no sense, as one also has to address the historical cultural context of its production and reception and the potential meanings that are opened up in that relationship between text and spectator. For Kuhn, a film which is textually polysemic and which thus provides a number of possible readings and identifications for an audience, holds the most potential as a 'feminine text' (1994: 13). She contrasts this with more 'closed' texts of the dominant Hollywood cinema, where meanings are more fixed and where potential spaces for a wider range of readings are closed down.

Yet as we have seen, new images have emerged over the past decade that have allowed a new psychological and critical space to emerge for male audiences. Radstone (1995b: 36) links this new imagery of masculinity with its potential for new, less narcissistic modes of spectatorship to psychic states of mind associated with mourning and the capacity to come to terms with loss and the fallibility of the self.[18] The implication is that this capacity to mourn is reflected at individual and cultural levels of fantasy. One can argue that it is the ability to cope with loss and emotional ambivalence that largely determines the formation of jealous fantasy and the experience of jealous triangles. The images of men described by Radstone not only suggest a qualitative shift in the textual representations themselves, but they also point to a change in the way male audiences engage and relate to the narrative themes and characters in the films. However, these so-called feminized representations of men may also be at the cost of representations of women. Their presence may be marginalized in relation to the portrayal of the 'new man', who may enviously colonize the cultural and psychic space formerly occupied by women. This may occur through more traditional narrative strategies, related to plot, themes and characterization, which deny them more complex representations of feminine subjectivities. 'The other' in this context does not only refer to Woman. Otherness can also refer to differences between men and the difficulties of tolerating these differences without slipping into destructive, rivalrous subject positions as a defence.

The themes of masculinity, jealousy and spectatorship are explored further in Chapter 4, where I discuss the methodologies employed in the case studies in Chapters 5 to 9.

4
Analysing Jealousy Texts from a Psycho-Cultural Perspective

Introduction

The shifting imagery and emotional narratives of popular cinema provide a rich and varied field for research into gender, emotion and contemporary culture. As a product of mass entertainment and plea-sure, films continue to be enormously popular and their narratives have an important role in the shaping of popular fantasy and the con-struction of gendered identities. As cultural products, films 'have a special tie to the life of the mind' (Lebeau, 2001: 3) and, as we saw in Chapter 3, there is already a useful body of work in film studies that has addressed the psychological intensity of the cinematic experience for audiences. The triangular Oedipal structures associated with jeal-ousy narratives have historically played a key role in the history of Hollywood cinema. The jealous subject's desire to establish control over the other and the voyeuristic aspects of the jealous gaze, share much in common with cine-psychoanalytic theories of the possessive male gaze (Mulvey, 1975).

This chapter examines the different elements of the psycho-cultural method used in the film case studies in Part II and the traditions from which they draw. In order to provide some context for that discussion, it begins by considering questions of interdisciplinarity within film and cultural studies today.

Film studies methodologies: questions of interdisciplinarity, text and reception

The psycho-cultural method used in this book follows a growing trend of eclecticism in film studies methods more generally (Hill and Gibson,

1998; Kirkham and Thumim, 1993, 1995). Such an approach takes account of aesthetic concerns related to the film text (for example, issues of *mise-en-scène*) and also questions of narrative, which are associated with traditional film studies methods of textual analysis (Bordwell and Thompson, 1997). However, it also includes perpsectives on the historical and cultural context in which the film is produced and received. Thus, such an approach combines issues related to the text and its mode of address,[1] with those related to spectatorship and the 'social audience' (Kuhn, 2002). In short, it takes account of the readers' socio-cultural and psychic relationship to the text and its meanings.

Staiger emphasizes the significance of the cultural and 'reception context' in the production of meaning (1993). Films can be used to tell us something about the historical context of their production and consumption. Yet Staiger also reminds us that the relationship between the film text and the cultural context of its reception can never be a straightforward mirroring process as certain social histories might imply. There can be no unified reading of a film and its stars because the discursive formation of any society is always 'uneven' and 'contradictory' (Staiger, 1993: 78). Gledhill also questions the relationship between the text and society by reminding us of the complexity of the (unconscious) relationship between the text and the reader (1995):

> [reading a text] is a diffuse and multiple experience which includes looking, emotional and visceral response, fantasizing as well as reflection and reminiscence.
>
> (Gledhill, 1995: 78)

Staiger argues that there is inevitably a tension between the 'ideal reader' associated with the film's mode of address and the 'real' viewer, whose response may be more contradictory and who may read against the grain (1993).[2] Staiger's (post)structural mode of textual analysis focuses less on the text in isolation and more on the 'discursive formation' of the film's cultural and historical context as providing the key to the meanings of a film. Conceptually, however, the links or *continuities* between a film text and its reception still play a key role in her model and this also applies to the film case studies in this book. This continuity is increasingly being emphasized by those such as Gledhill (1995), whose work sets out to make a bridge between the two methodological camps in film studies; between those who focus mainly on the film text and use psychoanalysis to analyse its mode of address, and those who use ethnographic or other methods to analyse the responses of audiences. The psycho-cultural approach taken here brings together many of the concerns of the different disciplines which have tended to focus on different aspects of films and their appeal. There is a particular focus on how interpretations of masculinity and its emotional significance can be brought under scrutiny through cinema, as the next section sets out.

Men and women reading men

In Kirkham and Thumim's first volume on masculinity (1993), it is perhaps significant that whereas the male writers choose action films to analyse masculinity, the women writers select melodramas as the focus of their analyses. Taking into account the potential problems of essentializing the gender of the reader/researcher, it is, nevertheless, possible to recognize the differences that may influence the focus of interrogation. This difference is acknowledged more generally in the film case studies in this book in relation to issues of spectatorship. As Neale argues, a film may facilitate fluid and 'mobile' identifications on the part of the spectator. However, the pull of culture and the gendered discourse which circulate though culture also work to reinforce the gender differences of the audience:

> A series of identifications are involved, then, each shifting and mobile. Equally, though, there is constant work to channel and regulate identification in relation to sexual division, in relation to the orders of gender, sexuality and social identity and authority marking patriarchal society. Every film tends both to assume and actively to work to renew those orders, that division. Every film thus tends to specify identification in accordance with the socially defined and constructed categories of male and female.
>
> (Neale, 1983: 11)

Whilst the focus of the films in this book is masculinity, representations of femininity and the positioning of those images (in relation to masculinity) are also addressed. Masculinity is constructed in relation to femininity and any discussion of one has implications for the other. A significant question is whether the feminization of masculinity as represented in images of jealous men, are portrayed at the expense of the women in the film who are marginalized or punished as a result.

New Hollywood and the cross-over film

There has been a renewed interest in the economic and socio-political role of the cinema industry and its institutions (Neale and Smith, 1998; Schatz, 1993). Such work can be seen as a move away from the perceived reductionism of just focusing on the text and its relationship to the psyche of the spectator.[3] Research into contemporary Hollywood cinema takes as its focus the loss of the traditional Hollywood studio system, which 'helped trigger the series of changes in structure, in practice and in style which marked the end of a distinct phase in Hollywood history and the beginning of something new' (Neale and Smith, 1998: xiv). This period is also associated with 'post-classicism'. The concepts of post-classical and postmodern cinema are sometimes used interchangeably and there is a growing body of work on the meaning of these terms and their relationship, together with the historical periodization associated with them (Neale and Smith, 1998). As part of this post-classical shift, Kramer emphasizes the changes in Hollywood images of masculinity which can be traced back to the 1950s, and which reflected 'a generation shift' in post-war America (1998).

The emergence of the 'New Hollywood' cinema is associated with a new commercial and industrial phase of cinema production funded, first and mainly, by the rise of large blockbuster films aimed largely at a youth market (Schatz, 1993). Secondly, the new Hollywood industry has kept itself running by using major stars to promote films made on a fairly moderate budget (Schatz, 1993: 202). However, alongside the dominance of blockbusters and films with big expensive stars, there also emerged in the 1980s a new 'small-is-beautiful, market-niche approach' (Schatz, 1993: 203). As Wyatt argues (1998), since the late 1980s, Hollywood film producers and distributors have also had to adapt to a more diverse market, and have done so by financing 'artistic' films such as Neil Jordan's *The Crying Game* (1992) and Steven Soderbergh's *Sex, Lies and Videotape* (1989). Such films are often referred to as 'cross-over films', because they incorporate many of the experimental techniques and aesthetic devices associated with art-house films, but are still accessible enough for a sizeable segment of a mass-entertainment audience (Polan, 2001: 18). One can argue that given their positioning on the cusp of mainstream and alternative entertainment, cross-over films potentially provide a site where new definitions of masculinity are negotiated and redefined. One can argue that most of the films discussed in the case studies relate in some way to this segment of the market.[4]

The mixed status of the cross-over film has a number of implications for film studies methodologies that often reinforce a dichotomy between the textual approach taken when analysing art-house films, and the methodology used when analysing the reception of mainstream films. As Crofts argues, in the case of the former, the 'aesthetic structures' of the film and the artistic intentions of the director tend to be examined, whereas in the latter, the reviews, box office receipts and audience are analysed (2000: 137). The cross-over film provides a useful model to disrupt the duality of such approaches and the links 'between text, circulation and reception' (Crofts, 2000: 152). Alongside an analysis of the text and its mode of address, it is also useful to discuss extra-textual factors associated with publicity about the film and its promotion in the UK press and their cultural significance. I draw on (mainly UK) press reviews to provide a broader cultural context for my analysis of the film and its star.

Film reviews and their uses

Film reviews and other publicity about the films and the stars occupy a number of roles in relation to the promotion and consumption of films and the relationship that exists between the film's textual mode of address and its reception at social and unconscious levels of spectatorship. On the one hand, they are related to the production and the promotion of the film, and contribute to the 'informal publicity' machine of the film industry (Kolker, 1998: 13). The publicity around a film helps to build up an 'aura' and a particular set of expectations for an audience (Benjamin, 1992). It is often said that whereas reviews of art-house films are spread by word of mouth, the reputation of mass-entertainment films is more usually related to the promotion and publicity of the film industry itself (Crofts, 2000).

One can argue that the reviews, along with accompanying publicity around the stars and the film more generally, are an extension of the Hollywood machine itself, and in ideological terms, provide another outlet for the reproduction of Hollywood values Cook and Bernink (1999: 39).[5] However, as audience studies have shown, this 'tight-fit' perspective does not account for the inconsistencies of audience response, and no amount of publicity can make consumers buy tickets for a film that has acquired a negative reputation through word of mouth or through the press (Basuroy, Chatterjee and Ravid, 2003). And just as audiences do not always respond positively to films in the ways hoped for by the film-makers and critics, mainstream critics are not an extension of the film industry and may respond negatively to films that have had vast amounts of promotional money spent on them, as with *Captain Corelli's Mandolin* (2001) and *Pearl Harbor* (2001). However, as Walker argues, if the reviewers do praise a film, as for example with *Bridget Jones' Diary* (2001), film companies will use the favourable comments of the reviewer to promote the film (2001: 13).

Thus there is no neat relationship between film reviews and the industry as a 'manipulationist' model of consumption might suggest (Dyer, 1998b: 12–14). The relationship between film reviews and the public is instead a complex mediation between the film text, the spectator and audience response and society. The significance of this relationship can be explored at two levels. Firstly, in terms of their influence upon spectators, one can argue that film reviews create a certain set of expectations around a film, which in turn influences the relationship between the spectator and the film text. Secondly, press reviews also represent an audience of sorts, and may provide a cultural barometer or a 'gauge' of how a given film was received at the historical moment of its release.[6] Thus, analysing the recurrence of certain textual themes within a collection of film reviews can tell us something about the cultural values and fantasies that circulate within a culture at any one time.[7]

One needs to be aware of the specificities of different media texts and audiences, for instance of UK tabloid and broadsheet national newspapers such as *The Sun* and *The Guardian* and more local newspapers. However, the anxieties that are conveyed in relation to the themes of gender and jealousy are often very similar, if written up in a different style. Sometimes, one can use reviews from different media environments (for example, magazines as well as newspapers) in order to explore a recurring theme that has emerged in relation to masculinity and jealousy. There is a distinction between the functions of film reviews and of other media texts on film such as article features about a film or about a star in a particular film. Dyer (1998b: 60–1) divides media texts about film into two groups; 'promotional texts' are material that is generated by the industry to put the star or film in a good light, and second, more general 'publicity' is not controlled by the star or the industry. Film reviews tend to fall into the latter camp.[8] The boundaries between these different textual categories may become blurred and the two kinds of texts may interact. This process of intertextuality, whereby different media texts may interact and inform each other, also contributes to the meaning of films for spectators (Storey, 1996: 71).

The inter-textuality of star and film text

The concept of inter-textuality (the way in which 'one text is marked by the sign of another' (Storey, 1996:71)) is also relevant when discussing the construction of jealous masculinity as mediated through the image of a particular film star. Stars are central to the pleasures of cinema going and the inter-textuality of the film text, the body of the star on the screen and the star's public persona all feed into the construction of meaning for the spectator. The construction of stars has received increasing attention over the years, reflecting perhaps the increasing fascination with celebrity culture more generally.[9] Male stars provide a useful focus to explore particular relationships between masculinity and jealousy and Dyer's approach to the study of stars is useful in this respect. He uses methods from cultural studies, semiotics and sociology to analyse the appeal of stars and their value as polysemic sign systems. For Dyer, stars should be read as complex texts which are constructed through promotional material as produced by the film industry and more broadly by the general publicity surrounding the star (1998b: 61). Dyer's approach does not seek to uncover the biographical truth of the star, but rather to describe the narrative that has been constructed for public consumption. As Phillips argues: 'a star is an image [and] a cultural signifier', and also (usually) 'an object of desire' (1999b: 181). The star comes to embody all that a particular culture projects on to him and her, and s/he also comes to 'em-body a set of values which are fashionable and which capture the *Zeitgeist* – the spirit of the time' (p. 181).

However, stars, like films, cannot be used simply as sociological mirrors; they do not reflect society in a straightforward way. Dyer argues stars have an ideological function insofar as they reinforce the prevailing ideologies of the day (1998b). Yet the star masks or reconciles competing ideologies, in complex and contradictory ways. Dyer also suggests that stars may embody 'values that are under threat' (1998b: 28). This can be seen in the image of a star such as Ralph Fiennes, who frequently depicts a nostaligic portrayal of a lost English masculinity. It is also seen in images of Michael Douglas as an 'angry' man and in the very un-PC version of white American middle-class masculinity that this conjures up. The nostalgic appeal for some reviewers of De Niro's portrayal of Travis's reactionary chivalry is another pertinent example of the variable, ideological pleasures of identifying with stars. Thus for Dyer and others, the star is a condensed sign of different aspects of society. When the social order is fragmentary and unstable, the star may appear especially 'charismatic', working as a kind of narcissistic foil for cultural anxieties.

Phillips suggests that just as a star can be viewed ideologically as a cultural image, the star's 'persona' also needs analysing (1999b: 181). Here, he is referring to the 'merging of the real person and the roles they play'. In my analysis of the different male stars, space is given to the discussion of their biographies as shaped in the press and to the fantasies that are evoked for the consumer/spectator as a consequence. Whilst this is done with an awareness of the constructed nature of the biographical narratives, those narratives are nevertheless significant because they mediate the affective reading of the star in question and reinforce a sense of narcissistic identification with those stars and their film roles. For example, the life of De Niro is constructed in terms of his status as a 'real' method actor, who is edgy, introverted and difficult to know. This public image of De Niro's masculinity complements the roles he played at the height of his career as tough and awkward heroes living on the margins of society. As I discuss in the following chapter, the viewers' identification with the loneliness of Travis in *Taxi Driver*, complemented the public persona of De Niro as an outsider. Dyer (1998b) argues that the fantasies and identifications that may be invested in stars can be extremely powerful and charged with emotion. The psychoanalytic implications of these identifications and their narcissistic underpinnings have been discussed by Mulvey (1975) and others, reminding us of the affective pleasures involved when reading about stars.[10] Yet, the emotional aspects of the film text have often been neglected in film studies and I now turn to that.

Emotional texts and affective spectatorship

It may be that the cultural studies emphasis on the role of 'negotiation 'and 'resistance' has lost some of the insights of earlier psychoanalytic film studies, as it ignores the emotional aspects of cinema and the pleasures of unconscious fantasy. As Pearce argues: 'Emotion – how can we name it, talk about it, evaluate its significance – may be seen as one of the few remaining wilderness areas of textual analysis and reception theory' (1996: 374).

As Pearce goes on to say, if the role of emotion is addressed, it is often done in rather broad terms, as for example, 'an expression of liking or not liking the character concerned'. Pearce argues that we need to discuss the rich variety of emotions that are engaged by the cinema, including 'fear, jealousy, hope, devotion, tenderness, frustration joy, agony, fulfilment' (1996: 416). The case studies in Part II arguably contribute to such a project through an exploration of masculine jealousies as depicted in those films. The different aspects of these 'jealousy texts' are now outlined below.

Jealousy may be conveyed textually in a number of ways. Emotions are represented and communicated through the aesthetic and formalistic properties of the film text, including the film's *mise-en-scène* and the structure of the film's narrative (Bordwell and Thompson, 1997: 72). I address each of these elements below, and then I go on to discuss the representation of jealous bodies on the screen and the feelings they are likely to engender in the spectator.

The jealous *mise-en-scène*

I have used the term 'jealous *mise-en-scène*' to connote the different fantasy environments for the jealous dramas in each story. The term *mise-en-scène* literally means 'to put on stage' and in film studies refers to the setting in which the drama takes place.[11] Gibbs provides an expanded definition:

> So in talking about *mise-en-scène*, one is also talking about framing, camera movement, the particular lens employed and other photographic decisions. *Mise-en-scène* therefore encompasses both what the audience can see, and the way in which we are invited to see it. It refers to many of the major elements of communication in the cinema, and the combinations through which they operate expressively.
>
> (2002: 5)

This notion of the film's setting and its potential for 'expressive' communication can be extended to incorporate the notion of 'fantasy' to refer to the film's setting for the enactment of desires and their frustration. From this perspective, fantasy is not located as the object of desire, but rather as in the *setting*, the *mise-en-scène* of desire (Cowie, 1984: 368). As Neale argues (1986), a film cannot tell us what to desire, but it can provide the fantasy settings for the staging of those desires.[12] As I discuss in later chapters, the jealous *mise-en-scène* in *Taxi Driver* can be described as a paranoid setting for the persecutory jealousy that takes place. In *A Perfect Murder*, the jealous *mise-en-scène* is largely characterized by the pleasurably opulent, materialistic setting of the husband's environment, which sets the scene for his acquisitive and territorial jealousy. However, the ethereal, fluid strains of the music provide a more feminine pre-Oedipal counter-narrative to the husband's envious jealousy and possessiveness. The jealous *mise-en-scène* in *The End Of The Affair* is often ambiguous. At times, the muted lighting together with Nyman's musical score is poignant and wistful and connotes the pathos of lost love (Neale, 1986). At other moments, the film recalls the paranoid settings of *noir* films. *The Piano* also conveys aesthetically the textual ambiguities associated with an art-house *mise-en-scène*. In fantasy terms, the visual strangeness and beauty of the film suggests the pre-symbolic realm of the feminine and sets the stage for the ensuing jealous drama which evokes the struggles of coming to terms with the Other, and living with sexual difference.

Jealousy narratives

It is useful to explore the structure of narrative in relation to jealousy, as the question of 'what happens next?' may, for example, arouse emotions related to jealous anxiety, fear and jealous suspicion. The narratives may have a psychodynamic quality, if emotionally the depiction of jealousy helps to move the narrative along. Such a narrative, for the spectator, may unconsciously evoke a particular psychological journey between different psychic states. This method is most often associated with the use of films made by psychotherapists (Berman, 1997; Gabbard, 2001). However, writers in film and cultural studies have also used films to track developmentally a particular psychosocial journey.[13]

The jealous narrative has implications for issues of spectatorship and the emotional work involved when watching a film. It can help us to understand the ways in which the spectator may be drawn into and captivated by the triangular dramas enacted on the screen and may provide insights into the trajectory of jealous affect and jealous subjectivities. It may be easier for the audience to witness action in the form of jealous retribution, than, as in the film *The Piano*, to identify with a more complicated form of jealousy that does not have a clear resolution in the form (for example) of 'a shoot out' between two rivals. Jealousy is uncomfortable for others to witness; as, amongst other things, it may remind them of their vulnerabilities and powerlessness in the face of loss and betrayal (Clanton and Smith, 1986: 90; Lasch, 1979: 192–3). The depiction of jealousy on screen may create a similar effect on spectators, who may physically cringe or experience adulterous pleasure as the point-of-view-shots conspire to exclude the jealous character.

Homoeroticism and jealous endings

Freud argued (1922) that there is a close relationship between the repression of homosexuality and morbid jealousy and rivalry. This relationship arguably has implications for representations of jealousy and the toleration of sexual difference. For example, two of the film case studies (*The Piano* and *The End Of The Affair*) depict the possibility of an alternative outcome between the jealous men. In contrast to more traditional stereotypical images of aggressive rivalry, Bendrix the jealous lover in *The End Of the Affair*, ceases to hate his rival, the husband, and adopts a close affectionate relationship with him instead. From a Freudian perspective, the affection between the two men is less defended in its depiction of masculinity, and by implication, the repression of homosexuality appears lessened, resulting in a withdrawal of negative projections between the rivalrous parties concerned. This ending would suggest a shift from what Leslie Fielder has described as the 'violent repression of homoeroticism in the history of Hollywood films' (1970: 348). Fielder defines the repression of homoeroticism as an 'authoritarian defence' and argues that female characters have carried the projections associated with this denial in the form of the masterful gaze (as discussed by Mulvey, 1975; and Neale, 1983). Fielder also argues that homoeroticism underpins the depiction of strong male friendships in the American novel and in Hollywood 'buddy' movies (1970: 348). Radstone takes up this theme:

> Typically, the repression of homosexuality has been associated with violence between male characters, as well as with its pejorative denial. Certain films, particularly male buddy movies, blur the boundary, however, between pejoration and titillation.
>
> (1995a: 163)

Representations of destructive male rivalry in jealousy films can also be seen in this light as 'an authoritarian defence' against homosexuality and the differences implied by femininity. Yet today, the jealous endings in these films are often ambiguous. They promise a different settlement between the parties concerned, which in turn has implications for the ways in which masculinity is depicted and imagined. Nevertheless, the positive aspects of these jealous endings are compromised and come at a cost. As in *The End of The Affair*, the woman still dies as men embrace over her dead body. The death of the adulterous woman is generically a common outcome in film melodramas and it is a sign of postmodern cinema that the jealous outcomes of such melodramas are no longer so certain.[14]

Jealous bodies

Jealousy is a painful and visceral emotion, which in everyday life is often experienced and talked about in physical terms (Baumgart, 1990).[15] Within the context of film studies research, this has implications both for issues of representation and spectatorship and the way representations of jealousy on the screen can make us feel. Witnessing jealousy may induce the same physical feelings of disgust, embarrassment and shame in film spectators as in real life. In psychoanalytic terms, jealousy threatens the loss of possession, and may evoke early shameful anxieties associated with narcissistic losses of infancy (Mollon, 2002). This is particularly the case with depictions of male sexual jealousy, with all its cultural associations of cuckoldry and masculine humiliation. In cinematic terms, the Hollywood fantasy solution is often a violent one, in which the jealous subject gets to kill the rival in a cruel and bloody manner. The spectator can derive pleasure from such violent solutions as the illusion of narcissistic integrity is thus restored.

But the jealous narratives of today are often not as straightforward as that. In each of the case studies, the rivalrous boundaries between the hero and the 'baddies' are not so clearly defined, and the suffering of the jealous man is often expressed through the body in ways that leaves the man looking weak and fragile. The spectator is thus confronted with the uncomfortable physical excesses of the jealous body and the connotations of loss associated with it.[16] One example of this is Michael Douglas's portrayal of the jealous and possessive husband in *A Perfect Murder*. The ruthlessness of his actions are often contradicted by his body language, which at times conveys a certain masochism in the way he seems to give into and become overwhelmed by his feelings. The flush pallor and fleshiness of Douglas communicates a vulnerability, which can make one recoil, and contrasts with the excessively pale and stiff Britishness of the husband Henry (played by Stephen Rae) in *The End of The Affair*, and the furious jealous lover Bendrix (played by Ralph Fiennes) whose jealous paranoia recalls generically earlier depictions of masculine insecurity in 1950s *film noir*.

Masculinity is culturally associated with hardness and rigidity (Lupton, 1998). One can see this expressed in the body language of De Niro in *Taxi Driver* whose physical rigidity parodies the machismo of the reactionary chivalrous hero.[17] However, the wounded vulnerability of Travis is also apparent and is symbolized physically by the scars on his body. Three of the male characters discussed in the case studies are physically marked by wounds or tattoos. Alongside Travis, who has scars on his body, in *The End Of The Affair*, Bendrix has a wound on his leg, and in *The Piano*, Baines's body has Maori tattoos. These marks convey to us the potential vulnerability of these men, and their difference and their flaws in relation to hegemonic masculinity. They also recall the potential ambivalence of the son's relationship to the father, who in the myth of *Oedipus Rex*, jealously spiked the foot of his son (the baby Oedipus) before abandoning him in the desert (Benjamin, 1990). At a mythical level, the scars on the bodies of the jealous protagonists serve as a poignant reminder of patriarchal authority and the wounds it can inflict on its sons. Another reading might be that these scars and markings are eroticized in such a way as to fetishize the male body, thus masking and displacing any possible identification with jealous loss.

Towards a psycho-cultural case study approach to film analysis

This chapter has set out the psycho-cultural approach used in Part II of this book, where the aim is to explore the shifting cultural and psychic patterns that occur in relation to emotional masculinities as encoded in representations of male jealousy. Nichols has defined the goal of film study research as reaching a greater 'comprehension effect' of the field or area under investigation (1985). With this in mind, the case studies draw on a range of primary and secondary sources to analyse films where jealousy is central to the narrative. The films in question also deploy images of male stars who can be seen to represent distinctive and culturally salient types of masculinity. Part II explores the emergence of cultural spaces where 'good enough' images of masculinity and male jealousy are at play.[18] Each study discusses the psychic, emotional and cultural meanings of the film concerned, and uses a range of media sources to historicize the meaning and appeal of the film within a broader (Western) cultural context. Each chapter takes into consideration issues of race, ethnicity, sexuality and gender, critically placing such themes in their historical contexts.

Although one needs to be wary of making generalizations from such a small sample, the case studies have certain features in common. For example, all five films were released (and in one case re-released) in the 1990s and early 2000s, so they share features related to the socio-cultural context of their production and reception. To say that these five films have characteristics in common, is also to suggest the possibility of some broader underlying cultural pattern related to the shaping of masculinity and sexual difference during that period as encoded through the films' images of male jealousy. It is hoped that the analysis of the five films will contribute to a greater understanding of the relationship between jealousy and masculinity within these broader cultural and cinematic contexts.

Part II
Masculine Jealousy in the Movies

5
Taxi Driver: The Psychopathic Hero and the Rescue Romance: How Jealousy Drives the Narrative Along (*M. Scorsese, USA, 1976*)

> Taxi Driver ... has been re-released to mark its 20th century anniversary. But it hasn't aged so much as triumphantly metastasized. Since the mid-70s, the movie has become presciently emblematic of our emotionally diseased, violence-prone culture.
>
> (Howe, 1996)

Taxi Driver remains one of the most acclaimed films in the history of cinema. One can point to the iconic status of Travis Bickle, played by Robert De Niro, whose masculinity, both then and now, captures for his audiences the narcissistic instabilities of the tough Hollywood hero (Bainbridge and Yates, 2005). The complexity of De Niro's performance as the troubled anti-hero Travis anticipates more contemporary images of ambiguous masculinities, which are a feature of the other films discussed in this book. The film works as a critique of chivalric noble jealousy, exposing its violent underpinnings through the depiction of Travis's paranoid desire to save the woman from the evil third party. *Taxi Driver* was first released in 1976, and reissued in 1996 (for the cinema and on DVD). It remains significant for contemporary discussions about changing debates about masculinity in cinema because it was made at a moment when more traditional images of heroic masculinity were being overtly challenged. As the 1976 press reviews suggest, the success of the film was connected to the specificities of that historical moment in the West, when white patriarchal authority was being undermined by a number of forces associated with feminism, black civil rights and the Vietnam War.

However, *Taxi Driver* still has relevance for male audiences today and its themes resonate with contemporary popular debates about the crisis of masculinity. The more recent positive press reviews that accompanied its re-release at the cinema and on DVD testify to its continued popularity. For example, in a DVD review, John Larsen (1999) argues that *Taxi Driver* 'has become so ingrained in the pop psyche that it is hard to avoid it. I know people who still use the "talking to me" bit in their everyday lives'.[1] *Taxi Driver* is now viewed as a 'classic' film, and reviews and personal retrospective accounts of first viewings can be found on a number of internet 'classic' movie sites.[2] *Taxi Driver* can provide insights into contemporary discourses and fantasies of masculinity, and the press reviews in 1976 and 1996 also contribute towards a discussion of psychosocial changes that have taken place since the moment of its release.

Male sexual jealousy provides a driving force behind the narrative and occurs at key dramatic points in the film to alert us to Travis's psychosis. A central element of the film's narrative of jealousy is the 'Rescue motif', a term used by Freud (1910) to refer to the male fantasy of rescuing distressed women from a third party. Although the depiction of Travis's heroism reproduces the narrative pleasures of the traditional male gaze, it also works critically to alert us to the violent underpinnings of chivalric masculinity, which may mask a more violent wish for revenge. The portrayal of Travis's jealousy is related to the representation of his misogyny and racism as the film re-enacts a number of social, political and psychological conflicts that existed in the 1970s and the threat presented by the 'other' to the white male cuckolded psyche.

Masculinity under siege: the psychopathic jealous hero

Taxi Driver was released during a period of enormous social and political change in the Western world. It was made in 1976, a year after the United States pulled out of the Vietnam War. Political corruption associated with Watergate was also a strong factor for the American audience and the film is imbued with the failure and guilt of that experience for Americans (Taubin, 2000).[3] Against that socio-political backdrop, *Taxi Driver* can be grouped alongside those films influenced by the counter-culture of the 1960s and early 1970s, which drew on radical political discourses and images to critique the old myths and stereotypes of the traditional Hollywood cinema and society. The film's director Martin Scorsese was part of a group of young directors of the time, who wanted to produce a new kind of cinematic experience that challenged the old Hollywood tropes and methods of film making. The most cited examples here of what some have called the 'New Hollywood' cinema were films such as *Bonnie and Clyde* (1967), *Easy Rider* (1969) and *The Graduate* (1967), that challenged the status quo, were characterized by 'taboo subject-matter', experimental cinematic conventions, techniques and narratives, and aimed to unsettle the viewer in new ways (Kramer, 1998: 297). Such films also feature alienated and vulnerable male characters, who contrast with more traditional heroes exemplified by actors of the Classic Hollywood period, such as John Wayne in the 1940s and 1950s, where heroic representations of masculinity dominate the narrative.

Historically, *Taxi Driver*, with its themes of male suffering and alienation, contributed to a more radical and politically progressive Hollywood cinema. Yet despite its 'art-house' credentials, some feminist critics have argued that *Taxi Driver* is part of a masculinist rightwing backlash against the cultural uncertainty of the period and the more liberal forces that were pushing for change (Mellen, 1977; Taubin, 2000). One can cite a number of cultural, social and political anxieties in the 1970s that dented the confidence of white masculinity; something which is represented at overt and covert levels in the film. The perceived threat posed by the increasing demands for equality and independence from women and also from black civil rights groups, also underpin the film's depiction of male anxiety and aggression (Taubin, 2000). Thus one could argue that *Taxi Driver* falls into the category of a 'backlash' movie, defending the rights and position of hegemonic masculinity under siege. Yet *Taxi Driver* also goes against that rightwing anti-feminist backlash. In contrast to other representations of masculinity in films of the 1970s, such as *Dirty Harry* (1971) or *Death Wish* (1974), *Taxi Driver* challenges the kind of traditional macho images of men, where narcissistic masculinity is naturalized and represented unproblematically.

Throughout the film, we are alerted to the instability of Travis's masculinity, by ironic references to macho screen heroes such as John Wayne and Clint Eastwood (Taubin, 2000: 24).[4] Travis increasingly acts out in an exaggerated manner the persona of 'the tough guy', which heightens the sense of his paranoid anxiety and psychological fragility. The 'are you talking to me?' scene is a good example of the film working reflexively to throw the wishful identification back to the spectator. Viewers are presented with the spectacle of Travis confronting himself in the mirror, and we in turn are left begging the question of just who or what it is that Travis is addressing at this moment. This scene appears to encapsulate Travis's rivalrous relationship to the other, and both men and women can enjoy the mock-heroic aggression of this scene, which provides a memorable spectacle of performative masculinity.

Taxi Driver anticipates postmodern approaches to film making insofar as it draws on genres past and present across the Hollywood spectrum; as, for example, in the Western, with its self-conscious references to John Wayne and *The Searchers* (1956), or the existential angst of French New Wave cinema. *Taxi Driver* also evokes aspects of *film noir* of the 1940s and 1950s, a genre, which is associated with masculinity in crisis (Kaplan, 1978). This is no coincidence, as the dilemmas of masculinity depicted in *Taxi Driver*, which refer to the wounded soldier returning home in the 1970s, have parallels with the post-war situation in the late 1940s, when the *film noir* genre also picked up and expressed the crises of identity many men experienced when returning home after the war (Westerbeck, 1976).

De Niro's portrayal of Travis Bickle was a central factor in the film's success and as Taubin (2000) argues, it was he that made Bickle a figure 'worthy of identification'. To explore his allure as a star, I now turn to De Niro's performance and the construction of his star persona.

Robert De Niro as Taxi Driver

> De Niro's performance ... forces you to question the rigid and sentimental codes of masculinity which he clings to even as they destroy him.
>
> (Williamson, in Jeffries, 1993: 6)

De Niro first emerged as a star at a time when new images of masculinity began to be available in mainstream Hollywood films. In contrast to the heroic images of leading men in the classical Hollywood era,[5] new Hollywood stars emerged that represented an urban, East-coast life sensibility, associated with Europeanness and an edginess that reflected the uncertainties and neuroses of the modern city. De Niro can be placed in this context, alongside actors such as Al Pacino and Dustin Hoffman, who looked very different to WASP blondes like Robert Redford, for instance.

In 1976, the film critic Pauline Kael (1976) described De Niro as 'the greatest living American actor' and more recently, the film and cultural critic David Thomson has reminded us that De Niro has been hailed as 'The American Olivier' and 'the greatest actor of his generation' (1998b: 12). In contrast to Pacino and Hoffman, De Niro is more classically handsome, and his status back in 1976 as 'the new' but "shy" Brando' affirmed his sexual desirability and status as a screen idol for men and women (Davis 1976; Kael, 1976).

When *Taxi Driver* was first released, De Niro was already a star from *Mean Streets* (1973) and *The Godfather Part 2* (1974). Fantasies of Italianness, as represented by De Niro in the Mafia film *The Godfather, Part 2*, are inextricably bound up with popular images of male rivalry and jealousy. By the time of *Taxi Driver,* De Niro's image was already associated with a particular kind of tough masculinity, able to defend what was his, through violence if necessary. However, the old-fashioned theme of vengeance and redemption is conveyed as motivating Travis's actions and provides a point of identification for the audience. The film critic Pauline Kael (1976) points out that the main difference between his role in *The Godfather, Part 2* and *Taxi Driver* is that in the case of the former, his violence is 'more controlled'.[6]

Tales of De Niro's acting technique of transformation and his ability to inhabit the bodies of his characters have reached mythical proportions.[7] In *Taxi Driver,* his capacity for bodily transformation is both mirrored and demonstrated in Travis's physical transformation into an urban psychopathic warrior with a mission. Travis's obsessive exercise regime, his hard, white body combined with his adoption of a mohican haircut, has all the connotations of narcissism pushed to its pathological extremes. But alongside the toughness, De Niro simultaneously exudes a vulnerability that promises hidden depths, which in *Taxi Driver* is also marked on the body by a scar (appropriately) on his back. Stoddart argues that such scars suggest a 'sadomasochistic suffering' and establishes a history of 'machismo-driven heroism' (1995: 195). The scarred body may also carry a certain homoerotic frisson and invite a sadomasochistic gaze from the audience (Neale, 1983).[8] Robert De Niro fits these varied and multi-layered criteria as an object of identification and desire for men and women. This is reflected in the reviews of De Niro when *Taxi Driver* was first released. For example, in 1976, journalists such as Pauline Kael (1976) combined descriptions of De Niro's famed 'deep intensity' in his portrayal of Travis, with praise for his more erotic qualities: '[he has] an erotic aura ...' and is able to 'reach into himself'.

Contemporary nostalgia for De Niro as Taxi Driver

Dyer argues that stars embody values that are felt to be under threat (1998b: 28). Much of the praise from critics in the 1990s is steeped in nostalgia for the 'early' De Niro, particularly in his role of Travis Bickle. His early roles now appear to embody a lost era of the 'true' and really great male Hollywood method actor. In her discussion of De Niro's performance as La Motta in *Raging Bull,* Cook (1982) suggests that De Niro/La Motta represents a nostalgic 'ideal' of lost masculinity and yet at the same time, fails to live up to that fantasy. One can argue that something similar is happening in the contemporary press reviews of De Niro and *Taxi Driver* when they speak of the young De Niro and his credentials as a 'real' working actor. The disappointment of respected critics about his later roles, which also touches on the more squalid descriptions of De Niro the man/star, and his involvement with 'call-girls', appears to confirm his fall from grace (Thomson, 1998a: 5; Thomson, 1998b: 12). The desire for the return for the original 'authentic' De Niro of the past was summed up in an article in the following way:

> Have you seen this man? And if not, how did you miss him? ... De Niro should learn to just say no ... It has been about five years since critics and audiences started sounding the alarm bells over De Niro who as he rounded the curve toward 60, began taking more comedy and light character roles.
>
> (Zacharek, 2005: 7)

Critics demonstrate a nostalgia for his early roles in *Taxi Driver, Mean Streets* (1973), *The Godfather* (1974) and *The Deer Hunter* (1978), and the 1990s reviews of *Taxi Driver,* which universally praise De Niro's portrayal of Travis, can be seen in the light of a nostalgic looking back. Broadly, then, in these reviews the nostalgic appeal and *fantasy* of De Niro as an actor (as exemplified in *Taxi Driver*) is that he allegedly embodies a particular kind of (lost) masculinity that contrasts with what is perceived to be the more lightweight and unprofessional stars of today, such as Leonardo Di Caprio, whose hedonistic lifestyle has, according to press reports, evoked the fury of De Niro's erstwhile director Martin Scorsese:

> Di Caprio arrived on set last week to a public roasting in front of cast and extras. The director of *Raging Bull, Taxi Driver* and *Goodfellas* let loose a 10-minute tirade that left his leading man speechless.
>
> (Carroll, 2000: 26)

The theme of loss is a strong theme in the film reviews of *Taxi Driver* from both time periods. This is often expressed in terms of the loss of the real and the depiction of Travis's struggle to survive in a sordid environment and his search 'for something human along the rubbish-strewn, neon lit street with their listless loungers' evokes sympathy (Shorter, 1976: 11). Some relate this loss to the falseness and changing values of consumerism in an increasingly materialist Western world, and in particular 'the great façade' of consumer culture (Coleman, 1976).[9] As one journalist puts it: 'He's been (like most of us) deceived by false advertising, phony movie and tv dramaturgy, vote hungry politicians' (Murf, 1976).

The loss of the real is echoed in the film's depiction of Travis's paranoid relationship to his environment, and provides a powerful backdrop or *mise-en-scène* for the film's jealousy narrative to unfold.

The jealous *mise-en-scène*

Throughout *Taxi Driver*, white masculinity appears to be under threat from a number of forces in the environment. The story is narrated by Travis, whose minimal voice-over commentary jars with the lurid imagery on the screen and the paranoid world-view that underpins the film's hellish *mise-en-scène*. The emotional disconnectedness of the relationship between Travis and his environment is heightened by the way the cab almost appears to have a life of its own. One can liken this depiction to postmodern descriptions of the loss of the 'real', in which it is argued that the categories of difference that have hitherto played a central role in defining subjectivity and cultural meaning are now falling apart (Baudrillard, 1985; Jameson, 1985).

The loss of the real in the film and in the reviews is equated with an increasingly menacing and shallow society, where beautiful women have become ruthless and ambitious and are not to be trusted. It appears that for Travis, the slippage between subject and object, between categories of difference, are experienced in increasingly paranoid terms: 'women, they're all the same, they're just like a union' (Schrader, 1990: 35). For Travis, the environment is overrun by bad objects:

> They're all animals anyway. All the animals come out at night: whores, skunk pussies, buggers, queens, fairies, dopers, junkies, sick, venal. (*A pause.*) Someday a *real* rain will come and wash all this scum off the streets.
>
> (Schrader, 1990: 7)

Throughout the film, the representation of male rivalry, jealousy and misogyny are closely entangled with representations of racism and fear and loathing of the 'other'. The depiction of Travis's split and racist psyche is further conveyed by the colours of the *mise-en-scène* and the lighting. De Niro's body is very white, and Betsy is also white, blue-eyed and blonde, and her white clothes ironically convey Travis's idealization of her. This whiteness contrasts with the reds of the night, the dark *mise-en-scène*, and the images of black pimps and gangsters who, in racist fantasy, make cuckolds of white men. Interestingly, Travis's racism was not discussed by press reviewers in 1976, as the film's script writer Schrader pointed out:

> The movie is riddled with suggestions of racism. It runs all the way through. But so far the only person to be disturbed by it was someone at the Amsterdam news.
>
> (Arnold, 1976)

The music is also important in cueing us to Travis's state of mind. Bernard Herrmann's score moves between ominous military drumbeats providing an ironic military flavour to Travis's 'mission', and the sleazy, tender strains of the saxophone to connote the poignancy of desire and lost romance.[10] Sometimes the music complements Travis' s point of view and invites us to collude with Travis' s fantasy of love and the idealized Betsy, whereas at other moments the lush excesses of the saxophone create a sense of distance, pointing to the ludicrous or comic aspects of Travis's perverse relation to the world. Elsewhere, the drumbeats build up into a crescendo whilst he is driving around in his cab like a military policeman, and at other moments, the full-blownness of the music works ironically, to alert us to the unreliability of Travis's point of view.

The jealous 'rescue motif'

As we have seen, white masculinity appears to be under threat from a number of forces in the environment. Throughout the film, the representation of male rivalry, jealousy and misogyny are closely entangled with representations of racism and fear and loathing of the 'other'. The narrative is structured by the representation of Travis's jealousy, in which the loss of the woman (Betsy) and male rivalry spur him on to violence. For Travis, it is as if the creation of rivals provides a temporary solution for the inability to acknowledge or cope with the loss. Although Travis's jealousy plays a key role in driving the narrative, the audience may not be consciously aware of this. This may be because

Travis's jealousy is not represented in ways that we associate with jealousy, as Travis does not whine or overtly express jealous loss. Instead, the jealousy is displaced and discharged in a more destructive fashion, through guns and violence. The hiddenness of the jealousy enables him to be a hero to the public (in the film) and for spectators who are shielded from the more helpless castrating aspects of jealousy.

One definition of jealousy is to protect and (jealously) guard, and in the Romantic tradition this has certain noble and idealistic connotations (Baumgart, 1990; Van Sommers, 1988). The trope of the man who jealously protects and rescues the defenceless woman in distress is a good example of this. Throughout the film, Travis draws on the old chivalrous discourse of the wronged helpless female to justify his wish for revenge. There is an element (however bizarre) of Travis acting out and taking to extremes the parody of the male hero who looks after his lover and seeks to protect her from a male villain/trespasser. Although one can argue that the discourse of male chivalry has lost much of its social legitimacy, the rescue fantasy of the knight in shining armour still remains a seductive one in the Western cultural imagination (Berman, 1997). The portrayal of Travis's reactionary chivalric heroism illustrates the rescue fantasy taken to its destructive extreme where chivalric discourse may mask a more violent wish for revenge. The so-called heroic wish to rescue a third party echoes the American foreign policy rhetoric of the Vietnam War, which is evoked throughout the film.[11]

In Kleinian terms, the rescue fantasy underpins a particular mode of object relation, which necessitates a third party from whom the woman must be saved. As we have seen, it was Freud (1910) who originally named this mode of relating 'the rescue motif'. His argument is that for many men, jealous triangles become the pre-condition for their 'object choice'. As discussed in Chapter 2, Seidenberg (1952) names this 'the jealous wish' because the subject takes a certain perverse pleasure in becoming jealous.

Cowie (1984) argues that film narratives provide an opportunity for spectators to identify fluidly with protagonists from the perspective of different fantasized scenarios that relate to primitive sexual fantasies associated with the primal scene. In *Taxi Driver*, one can argue that something similar may be happening for the audience in relation to the pleasures of the jealous gaze and the triangular wishful fantasies of sexual transgression and chivalrous rescue enacted by Travis. For example, one could identify passively with the wish to be rescued and incite jealousy in the other, or with the rival who is doing the adultery, or the one whose possession is threatened and feels compelled to protect and jealously guard what is his. *Taxi Driver* illustrates this jealous reaction formation and the guilty desires associated with the primal scene. From this Freudian perspective, it is as if Travis's desire for Betsy and Iris is denied and, in a perverse swerving away, finds representation through gun fetishism, voyeurism and rivalry with the politician and the pimp. Travis acts out the fantasy of the jealous hero who feels compelled to rescue the helpless young woman from the villainous third party, who is in fact himself.

The female objects of rescue and desire

The rescue fantasy is most evident with Iris, but is also a recurring theme of the early scenes between Travis and Betsy. For example, when Travis first meets Betsy and asks her out, he looks deep into her eyes and in effect offers to rescue her:

> Well Betsy Ma'am, I drive by this place here in my taxi many times a day. And I watch you sitting there at this big long desk with these telephones, and I say to myself, that's a lonely girl. She needs a friend. And I'm gonna be her friend.
>
> (Schrader, 1990: 21)

The joke is that she looks twice as resilient as he, and the image of her as someone in need of rescue is shown to be a projection on his part. And yet in this scene, De Niro is at his most seductive and we want his character to succeed in this courtship ritual. Betsy's colleague Tom is set up as a rival as he resents Betsy's attraction to Travis. This rivalrous encounter between the two men is potentially more enjoyable because such is the intensity of Travis's conversation, he seems to be oblivious of Tom's jealous presence. Thus Travis, the loser, has a moment of mastery, and gains supremacy in this brief triangular moment.

For Travis, Betsy is an 'angel' and she becomes the object of his idealization. Betsy's name has all the connotations of American apple pie and her blonde WASP identity is presented as an important ingredient of Travis's adoration. Her whiteness (along with her name) places Betsy, in the paranoid and racist imagination, on 'his' side, rather than on the side of difference and the black men and women who are presented as the bad objects in Travis's persecutory world. Not all the prostitutes, pimps and thieves in Travis's paranoid vision are black, but most are and there are no virtuous or respectable black characters in the film.

In psychoanalytic terms, the representation of Travis's paranoid world-view conveys a split mode of relating, and the binary construction of woman as whore or Madonna is symptomatic of this (Hollway, 1987).[12] The breakdown of this structure is alluded to in the scene when Travis takes Betsy to see a porn movie. Travis's sexually repressed world appears to contain a fascination with, and a puritanical disgust of, bodily excess, which is equated with the otherness of femininity and black skin. It is as if he is unable to sustain the splitting of femininity into the good and the bad, the fair and the dark respectively. In the breakdown of the structure, the sadistic punishing wishes against feminine excess overtake fantasies of idealization. When Betsy rejects him, Travis appears to try to compensate for that loss by creating a bad rivalrous father object in the guise of the politician Pallantine, for whom Betsy has been working. From the perspective of this paranoid jealous narrative, the saintly Betsy now becomes the whore who cannot be trusted. This theme is also echoed in many of the reviews, which describe her character in negative terms as a cold *femme-fatale*, as the 'class-conscious', 'cool socialite' (Coleman, 1976; Mackie, 1976), who in effect makes mincemeat of Travis, and reviewers show sympathy for 'Travis's rejection at the hands of middle-class Cybil Shepherd' (Schnickle, 1976).

Taubin argues that in taking Betsy to a porn film, Travis's behaviour is akin to a real violation, such as 'date rape' (2000: 21). In 1976, a number of reviewers show sympathy for Travis, whose inappropriate choice of film is seen merely as a careless social gaffe (as one reviewers puts it: 'He [Travis] makes all the wrong moves and is rejected' (Hutchinson, 1976). More recent reviewers are keener to distance themselves from him at this stage (Sutcliffe, 2000). As Schrader's script notes indicate, not only does this scene signify Travis's 'out of touchness with "the real world"', it also demonstrates Travis's cruelty and a wish to humiliate the healthy and wholesome Betsy:

> There's something that Travis could not even acknowledge, much less admit: that he really wants to get this pure white girl into that dark porno theatre.
>
> (Schrader, 1990: 30)

When Betsy has become the rejecting bad object who is not to be trusted, she joins 'the others' in the camp led by Pallantine, who then becomes a rivalrous object. Travis next meets Iris, the 12-year-old prostitute who replaces Betsy as the angel who needs saving. Another imaginary triangle is created between Travis, Iris's pimp Sport (Harvey

Keitel) and Iris (Jodie Foster) and the rescue fantasy becomes dominant once more. Iris provides the perfect object for Travis's rescue fantasies because of her status as an under-age prostitute. However, Iris is not so sure she wants to be saved, and she does not position herself in relation to the rescue fantasy without ambiguity. Thus Iris represents more than a powerless under-age victimized prostitute. Rather, her character points to other possibilities beyond those inscribed by older patriarchal discourses of femininity. As she says to Travis, who wants her to go home, 'God! Haven't you ever heard of women's lib?'[13]

In the scene where they meet for breakfast, Travis appears bemused at Iris's independence and her assertion that she is in charge of her life. In some ways the scene is a comic one because Travis, with his fixed and reactionary codes of morality, appears to be speaking from a completely different place to Iris; indeed, it is as if they are talking at cross purposes. Like Sport in an earlier scene, she looks in disbelief at Travis, who seems so 'square' and out of touch with the times. Travis struggles to understand Iris's libertarian narrative of communes where, by implication, the rules of jealous possession are a thing of the past. However, in refusing to be put off by what he perceives to be the more wholesome scent of 'home', Travis keeps on with his mission to save Iris and return her to her proper place.

Throughout this scene, Travis jealously attacks Iris's pimp Sport whom he accuses of being a 'killer' and of holding her against her will. Because she is so young, some viewers might identify sympathetically with Travis in this respect. What is arguably repressed, in this and other scenes, are the sexual aspects of Travis's jealousy and his desire for Iris. Indeed, the heroic reading of Travis's behaviour depends upon this repression. For example, when he first visits Iris in her room, Schrader's script indicates that when Iris begins to seduce him, Travis has to struggle to resist her, to the point where he is 'falling apart' (1990: 68). However, in the film itself, Travis's desire is more disguised and his sexuality is played down. Travis pushes Iris away as if to save her from both herself and the role her pimp forces her to perform. Yet, he is also saving her from himself. In this instance, the differentiation between himself and (the rival) Sport shows its weakness, as he projects his illicit desires for Iris on to Sport who becomes the bad rivalrous and envied object. Thus, the depiction of Travis's heroic rescue fantasies is underscored by sexual guilt and anxiety, which are exacerbated by the connotations of his desire for the girl-woman prostitute.

This tension is also present in the *Taxi Driver* reviews from both time periods. On the one hand, they signal Travis's chivalry in rescuing the 'under-age prostitute' from the pimp and punters. On the other, they write suggestively of Foster's sexually provocative appearance. Like Travis, they point to her corruption by Sport and the New York streets. In 1976, Jodie Foster/Iris's sexual desirability is strongly implied, especially in the tabloids who carry images of her standing suggestively in her infamous hot pants: 'Baby Doll Hooker in Hot Pants' (Cashin, 1976), 'Foster says "Taxi Driver didn't teach me anything I didn't know already"' (Blake, 1976). No mention is made of Travis's possible desire for Iris because this would complicate his potential status as a hero – and 'our' possible identification with him – as a vengeful crusader. Thus the public may collude with the character's defences. In the case of 12-year-old girls, feelings of jealous possession retain their social legitimacy only if they are devoid of sexual desire. If it were otherwise, Travis would be seen as bad as the pimp whom he (and society) reviles. It would also detract from the identification with the romantic image of the celibate knight, who pursues justice for a higher purpose than the reward of physical pleasure. Sexual jealousy depletes this image and makes Travis less worthy of identification, implying a closer relation to the pimp than perhaps he or we would like.

Morbid jealousy and male rivalry

The creation of rivals is a significant part of the rescue motif which, as we have seen, compels Travis to act jealously throughout. *Taxi Driver* is steeped in aggressive male rivalry and fear of the other. In psychoanalytic terms, Travis's rivalry provides the temporary solution for a refusal to acknowledge loss and the separateness of others. From the psychoanalytic perspective of Melanie Klein, this unacceptable loss and separation reaches back developmentally to infantile defences against the depressive position, which causes a breakdown into extreme paranoid splitting as a consequence. Arguably, the film's mode of address evokes for the spectator, feelings and defences such as these. I have also discussed the implication of the rescue motif with respect to a more classically Freudian perspective. Here, the pathological defences are activated against intolerable guilt and anxiety engendered by the Oedipus complex. The villainous Oedipal father (or brother) must be killed off, or alternatively the Oedipal child self is projected on to the rival and, again, destroyed so that a guilt free purity can remain.

Freud (1922) argues that morbid jealousy and the loathing of the rival, is also linked to the repression of homoerotic desire. The refusal of this desire is expressed through the intensity of the hatred of the other man as a jealous rival. Travis's jealous rivalry with Sport provides an example of this scenario. In traditional phallic terms, and in contrast to Travis, Sport appears to have everything – good looks, women, money, and a phallic power which is combined with a femininity that Travis fears and desires. The homoerotic component of Travis's jealousy is expressed in the phallic symbolism of his murder of Sport, with the words 'suck on this' as he does so. The film critic Kael (1976) argues that 'Keitel's pimp is slimy all right', but his playful manner is also 'oddly winning'. Taubin (2000) suggests that Keitel's sympathetic portrayal of Sport decentres the 'moral balance' of the film, thus challenging the traditional patriarchal binary distinction between the noble moral crusader and the villain.

Gender and jealous paranoia in reviews of *Taxi Driver*

Despite Travis's psychopathic qualities, many critics past and present, appear to have strongly identified with his character and the depiction of his jealous paranoia and this identification appears to be divided along gender lines. One can argue that the film may hold a different set of pleasures and identifications for the female reader, as female reviewers past and present, appear to identify less with the character of Travis and his point of view and resent 'the camera rubbing our noses into the congealing blood' (Kingsley, 1976). There were far fewer contemporary female press reviews of *Taxi Driver*, which in itself may reflect the popularity of the film and its 'classic status' for male audiences. For example, in 1976, Margaret Hinxman (1976) argued that while she found De Niro's performance 'brilliant', she nevertheless thought that his character was 'deranged' and that his relationship to Betsy was that of 'voyeur'. More recently, the cultural critic Amy Taubin (2000) suggests that the themes of sexual repression, misogyny and jealousy are central to the film's narrative. Taubin argues that at a recent screening, male reviewers were 'communing' with Travis in a way that she, as a female spectator, could not, and she was aware of her 'non-empathy' for the character (1993: 57). Taubin refers in particular to the male identification with Travis's 'malevolent gaze, in the armed 'n' ready musculature rigid with rage'.

Many of the 1990s reviewers speak of the film's power to evoke memories of its first screening, and remain haunted by the violence and blood of Travis's 'cathartic' shoot-out (Taubin, 1993: 57).[14] In psychoanalytic terms, 'catharsis' implies that some kind of positive insight has accompanied the repressed energy that has been released

(Laplanche and Pontalis, 1988: 60–1). In the press reviews from both periods, the Freudian sexual symbolism that underpins the notion of cathartic release combines with the discourse of 'innate male sexual drive' (Hollway, 1989), to imply the inevitable desirability of Travis's murderously jealous outburst at the end.[15] Alexander Walker is one of the few reviewers from 1976, to point to the interaction of hatred and revenge underpinning Travis's jealous rescue fantasy. Walker does not find the massacre at the end an emotional cathartic release, but sees it more in terms of rape fantasy and writes of 'his impotence armoured by a multitude of weapons' (1976).

In addition to identifying with the depiction of Travis's 'cathartic' violence, many male critics from both eras also appear to identify with the depiction of Travis's emotional vulnerability, as if he was just an over-sensitive, 'socially inept' man pushed 'over the edge' (Cannon, 1997). In both eras, his misogyny and racism is mostly ignored. Instead, they focus on Travis's social alienation and political exclusion as being the cause of his descent into madness and violence: 'We have all felt as alone as Travis. Most of us are better at dealing with it' (Ebert, 2000).[16] Interestingly, this theme of social exclusion speaks of being left out, the very thing which provides the basis of jealous feelings.

In both eras, the themes that frame the response of male reviewers are shot through with the language of paranoid jealousy, in which the themes of betrayal and loss predominate. For example, the environment, which is seen as the cause of Travis's problems, is summed up by them as 'deceitful' (Murf, 1976) and untrustworthy, and in particular, they point to the betrayal of corrupt and 'sleazy politicians', and the 'stuck-up' women who are greedy and manipulating (Cameron, 1976; Howe, 1996). Travis's misogyny is more often reproduced in the 1976 reviews, where the language of jealousy and class converge, suggesting that Travis's emotions are more authentic and 'sincere' then those of the 'superficial' Betsy, the untrustworthy, 'class-conscious' careerist who lets him down (Cameron, 1976; Mackie, 1976).

Conclusion

The strong sympathy of male reviewers for the psychopathic qualities of Travis and his emotional vulnerability resonates with the feminist debate about cinematic depictions of emotional masculinities and the significance of these images for less narcissistic modes of spectatorship and for good enough masculinities. As we have seen, in cinematic terms, *Taxi Driver* was distinctive in its break from traditional

Hollywood modes of representation of masculinity, and anticipated contemporary postmodern representations of masculinity (Butler, 2000).[17] *Taxi Driver* is structured and narrated from the point of view of the male protagonist Travis, who is represented as the paranoid and vulnerable victim of forces beyond his control. In many ways, he is romanticized as a lonely hero, who searches for an identity and justice in a world that shows him no kindness. The popularity of the film and the reviews suggest that alongside his loneliness, the film also evokes identification with Travis's paranoid anxieties and envious fantasies about women and their power to betray men. In contrast to the complexity of more reparative modes of working through emotions, the narrative trajectory of Travis's jealousy illustrates – albeit in an extreme form – a mode of jealous masculinity characterized by narcissistic illusion. The refusal to acknowledge loss and the temptation to resort to omnipotence and idealization accompany more destructive forms of jealousy in *Taxi Driver*. Similar imaginary solutions seem to have been sought by many who have written about the film and perhaps also many others who have seen it, in their understandings of it.

It is too simple to relate the film's mode of address to more negative critiques of hegemonic masculinity, which position the film in relation to a rightwing backlash against feminism and the uncertainties of contemporary culture, and which argue that we now slip more easily into paranoid schizoid ways of symbolizing the world. Aesthetic devices in the film, such as the musical score and the jealous *mise-en-scène*, also create a critical distance that invites the audience to refuse conventional positions associated with the narcissistic male gaze. *Taxi Driver* retains a radical edge, unsettling the audience, alerting it to the political and sociological conditions of contemporary culture and the legacy of the Vietnam War for men. This critical awareness also plays a part in reviewers' and audience's identification with Travis's subject position.

The 1976 reviews suggest that the audience may have been more shocked and moved by the social environment, and use the sociological language of social exclusion to describe Travis's plight. However, by 1996, the language used to describe Travis's story is more psychological, more focused on loneliness, emotional vulnerability and male loss. What both sets of reviews have in common is the assumption that Travis's violence at the end is inevitable, whether caused by inner psychological forces or outer sociological ones. In none of these reviews is there the suggestion that Travis could have taken a different path and changed his life. Indeed, there is sympathy for Travis's narrative of chivalry, which I have argued is underpinned by the fantasy of jealous rescue, sadomasochism and the projection of sexual desire. Despite the ambiguity of Travis as a character who is both macho and vulnerable, De Niro's portrayal of Travis the psychopathic hero remains seductive for those for whom the rescue fantasy retains its power. The contemporary appeal of *Taxi Driver* is, I have argued, largely related to De Niro's depiction of Travis, and to the nostalgia for the lost masculinity within this representation.

Travis's psychopathic behaviour may be perceived as the perverse and outdated revenge of the male hero who no longer has a place. However, from the point of view of a sympathetic audience, his jealous 'rescue' does enable Iris to go to college, Betsy to admire him and himself to erase the pimps who seem to have all he both despises and desires. However outdated in social and political terms, the seductive power of Travis's fantasy remains strong. Travis invites sympathetic identification, partly because of De Niro's portrayal, and also because of the seductive power of the rescue motif, which however misguided and violent, works as a displaced solution for cultural and psychological anxieties about male loss, sociologically indexed in the 1970s, more psychologically inflected today. The underlying and continuing instability in the movie hinges upon who it is that actually needs rescuing.

6
Michael Douglas: Envy, Greed and Jealous Desire in *A Perfect Murder* (*A. Davis, USA, 1998*)

A Perfect Murder (1998) provides an overt portrayal of sexual jealousy in a triangle between a husband, wife and lover, emphasizing material greed and sexual betrayal. The film stars Michael Douglas, and his performance as the jealous husband is mediated by his charismatic star persona and the highly charged brand of emotional masculinity with which he is often associated. When the film was released, Douglas had become a symbol of embattled American middle-class masculinity, a theme which is evoked throughout the film through its representation of the cuckolded white male psyche.[1]

A Perfect Murder is a Hollywood re-working of the Hitchcock suspense thriller *Dial M for Murder* (1954). In contrast to *Dial M For Murder*, however, where the money goal was presented as the motive for murder, male sexual jealousy and the struggle for supremacy within the jealous triangle are central to the contemporary film's narrative. Michael Douglas's character 'Steven' appears to embody a mode of jealous masculinity in which the envious desire for possession is central. *A Perfect Murder's* screenwriter, Patrick Smith Kelly, has said that 'the basic thrust of the film is about possession' (BFI, 1998). The film's narrative pleasure is mainly driven by an invitation to identify narcissistically with Steven's omnipotence and his need to maintain possession and power over his wife (the object) and her wealth.[2]

A Perfect Murder, with its themes of jealousy, rivalry and possession, also illustrates a cultural struggle between values and qualities associated with femininity and masculinity, and sheds light on contemporary attitudes and fantasies about gender and sexual difference. This gendered struggle, which is played out in the narrative of the film and in the reviews, mainly takes place in relation to 'Steven'. On the one hand, Douglas's depiction of emotional vulnerability illustrates the potential feminization of masculinity in popular culture. Yet on the other, his character embodies a sense of continuity with an earlier mode of narcissistic patriarchal masculinity, and as we shall see, for many in the press, that was largely part of his appeal.

Michael Douglas: an icon of wounded, cuckolded white masculinity

> There is always the added pressure when someone in your family is in the same business. I mean look at me, I'm 53 and people still want to talk to me about my dad.
>
> (Douglas, in Muir, 1997: 15)

Many of the reviews for *A Perfect Murder* show a distinct nostalgia for the kind of confident unapologetic masculinity represented by Douglas, both on and off screen. Douglas's brand of middle-class white masculinity taps into a narcissistic fantasy of male continuity, something that is also reinforced by his 'second-generation status' as Kirk Douglas's son. Every press cutting I surveyed of Michael Douglas since 1969, positions him in relation to his 'famous father', as the son of 'legendary' and 'immortal' Kirk Douglas (BFI, 1998). It has become somewhat of a joke that, in the past, Michael Douglas had to keep reminding interviewers 'I am *not* Spartacus' (Pickering, 1988: 18–19). His positioning as 'Kirk's son', together with the fantasy of his so-called biological 'genetic destiny' (Anon, 1995: 16), extends to the use of biological language to describe his apparent capacity to express 'instinctual' aggressive emotions, something that has informed reviews of him ever since.[3]

Douglas's films and the characters he plays, often appear to mirror his own life, or at least the one that is publicized for our consumption in the media. A good example here is how his much-publicized 'real life' addiction to women dovetails with his screen performance of the adulterous husband in the enormously successful *Fatal Attraction* (1987).[4] *A Perfect Murder* follows in this tradition of his movies paralleling Douglas's real-life dramas. For example, there was criticism of the credibility of the age gap between Douglas and Paltrow in the film:

> 'I've got to be careful what I do', said the 25-year-old actress, who found starring opposite Douglas unsettling. 'It was impossible to regard him as a peer. I always regarded him as my father's friend'.
>
> (McDonald, 1998: 2)

The reported 'jealousy' of Paltrow's father and grandfather in relation to this was dismissed by Douglas with the same aggression and confidence as Steven in the film: 'So, she is a young woman playing a "trophy wife"? So what! – That's always happened!' (LWT, 1999).[5] At around this time, Douglas left his wife for a much younger famous actress, Catherine Zeta Jones, which again blurred the lines between the fantasy and reality of Douglas's performance on and off screen. This slippage reflects, perhaps, the willingness of the critics to blur the boundaries of their reviews, in which the identification with Douglas's brand of potent masculinity may work as a defence against the wounding and potentially feminizing connotations of Steven's character of the cuckolded husband.

Douglas has gained a reputation for starring in controversial 'erotic' thrillers: *Fatal Attraction* (1987), *Basic Instinct* (1992) and *Disclosure* (1994). In each case, he plays the part of the embattled male, falling for and fighting off powerful and glamorous female sexual predators (Ambrose, 1988: 9). The latter seems to confirm his role as the leading man in a popular cultural backlash against feminism and establishes his status as the *bête-noir* of many Western feminists (Coward, 1999a; Faludi, 1991, 1999). At the same time, following his role as the beleaguered and embattled white American middle-class male in *Falling Down* (1992), his star persona has come to represent 'the lascivious middle-aged white guy who has something to prove', turning 'male angst into big bucks' (Anthony, 1995: 12). The rapturous response from many of the male critics to Douglas's portrayal of Steven in *A Perfect Murder*, points to the powerful and continued appeal of Douglas's 'intelligent' and emotionally wounded image of masculinity, certainly for many white middle-class male cinemagoers today.

At the end of the twentieth century, Douglas won more respect for his work as an actor and as a producer, and even some feminist critics revised their views, showing a new appreciation of Douglas as a masculine icon.[6] For instance, the feminist cultural critic Camille Paglia has spoken in rapturous terms about Douglas as 'a model of intelligent masculinity' and second-wave feminist Ruby Rich has cited with admiration his capacity to express a certain kind of 'defensive', 'wounded masculinity' (LWT, 1999).[7] While reflecting contemporary feminist concerns about the fragility of masculinity and the feminization of men, Douglas's apparent capacity to convey a certain woundedness, also presents a more complicated picture of the *range* of identifications he is able to evoke. As I now go on to discus, this range extends to a more visceral, homoerotic response, which allows the contemporary viewer to pleasurably engage with the more taboo aspects of masculinity.

Jealousy, greed and the fantasies of the instinctive, jealous body

The publicity surrounding Douglas's addictive personality with all its connotations of innate bodily urges complements the physicality of his acting style. This style exudes a form of masochism and an emotional vulnerability that makes him an ideal actor to portray the more difficult and even humiliating aspects of emotional subjectivity. As the film critic Thomson argues, 'Douglas's acting is remarkably free from vanity ... he (has) displayed an unusual appetite for his own sexual humiliation. He easily presents a strong image. But he is also drawn to strains of weakness and neurosis in the protagonist' (1995: 22). Thus, the heroic narrative of his struggle to control his emotions has been central to his appeal as an actor.

In *A Perfect Murder*, Douglas does not entirely allow his emotions to let rip, but rather he conveys a taut sense of 'self-restraint' and control over what he invites the audience to imagine are the innate, testosterone-fuelled emotions that drive him and which bubble under the surface (Queenan, 1998: 16–17). In this way, his performance taps into a romantic fantasy about the struggle to curb innate emotions such as jealousy, in the face of a world that no longer deems them acceptable. The fact that he seems to give into them at the end of the film is a big disappointment for the reviewers: 'It only hurts more that his [Douglas's] character is saddled with such a pathetic excuse for an ending' (Prigge, 1998).

The Warner Brothers' publicity places Steven's jealousy as central to the film.[8] Although the publicity poses the question of whether Steven was motivated by 'jealousy' or 'greed', the implication is that the two are very much bound up together and the critics pick this up in their reviews:

> You're never quite sure why Douglas wants Paltrow out of the way. Is it for the trust fund she owns? Is it for his own self-esteem? Is it because like the art on the walls, she's lowered her market price by sleeping around? Douglas keeps us guessing and therefore intrigued.
> (Walker, 1998: 26)

The guilty pleasures of identifying with his portrayal of greedy masculinity is a dominant theme of the reviews, which often adopt an ironic tone when referring to their enjoyment of Douglas's aggressive performance of bourgeois villainy. The journalist Matthew Sweet provides a good example of this in action:

> This week I learnt to love Michael Douglas. And what did it for me? That gelled hair that curls over the back of his neck. His Alan Partridge leather gloves. That sinister fold of middle-aged fat that brims over his too tight collars. That snarling, desiccated voice, like Marge Simpson's psycho brother. His glacial nastiness. His horrid Bob Monkhouse tan. I could probably go on all day, but that's how it is when you're in love.
>
> (1998: 5)

As in the above quotation, descriptions of Douglas's portrayal of Steven are often very visceral, and the language of oral greed and aggression is a strong element when describing the physicality of the performance.[9] For example, reviewers speak of Steven as 'the inheritance hungry husband' (Andrews, 1998: 22), and of his 'fleshy malevolence' (Steyn, 1998: 14). As Steyn goes on to say: 'Douglas is a sleek conqueror, tall, tanned, luxuriant hair swept back to expose a forehead as big as a football pitch.' The same journalist makes the perceptive point that 'Hitch was supposedly in love with Grace Kelly, but it's nothing to how Davis dotes on Douglas' (Steyn, 1998: 14). Often, as in Matthew Sweet's love letter above, there is a slippage between identification and desire by critics, who speak ironically of their 'unhealthy admiration for Michael Douglas' (Queenan, 1998: 16), and of 'the joy' of 'seeing Douglas sink his teeth and sex appeal into the role of another rich, middle-aged American bastard' (Christopher, 1998: 44). This homoeroticism connects with the film's depiction of rivalry and the restructuring of the jealous triangle through the renegotiation of male desire.

Rivalry, homoeroticism and the imaginary father

> And he has begun to pick up the clenched vocal mannerisms of his father Kirk.
>
> (Matthews, 1998: 49)

Steven's rivalrous, possessive persona is evident from the moment the rivals make a pact to murder the wife, they become entwined as reverse images of one another. The lover, to quote Stephen, is the 'potent and trashy' artist who is the opposite of the worldly and successful cuckold husband. As Alexander Walker points out in his review, they are portrayed as 'two sides of the same avaricious coin: one poor, one rich and like brothers, or father and son, they even share the same dimpled chin' (1998: 26). The rival represents the husband's alter-ego, or a split-off part of his character, which he gets to kill his wife. The lack of differentiation between the two men signifies something psychotic, sometimes in the manner of a sadomasochistic father and son relationship. At other moments, a repressed undercurrent of homoerotics desire appears to exist between the two.

Douglas's character is positioned as the older powerful male patriarch, who bullies and sneers at the younger man. Even if audiences do not associate him with his father Kirk, there might, as we have seen, be a certain amount of nostalgia in watching his performance of an un-PC man in expensive suits, unapologetically patriarchal and omnipotent. Douglas draws on a traditional discourse of the wronged, cuckolded husband to explain Steven's jealous rage:

> Steven is a real mixture: a successful, charming man and a conniving potentially lethal mate ... he makes a murderous decision when he learns his wife has been unfaithful, a choice that makes him easy to hate, but I wanted the audience to care what happens to him anyway – to understand he loved his wife, how many pressures he was carrying inside himself, and what a blow to his ego it was for him to come face to face with the man who had cuckolded him.
>
> (BFI, 1998: 6)

Douglas (as Steven) almost parodies himself when he delivers speeches that sound oddly out of place, even 'hammy', and in certain scenes he evokes discourses of jealousy and patriarchal possession, more usually associated with his father's generation. For example, when Steven first confronts his rival, he struts about aggressively, dressed in a dark suit and coat and black gloves, and he draws explicitly on an old-fashioned clichéd discourse of the wronged husband that recalls an earlier generation, when the rules of sexual possession were more certain. His melodramatic speech about the 'envy' of his rival seems completely over the top, especially given the almost sulky ineffectual presence of the actual rival in question:

> Steven: That's it? You steal the crown jewels of a man's soul and your only excuse is some candy-arsed Hallmark card sentiment ... even if that was true, that's not good enough!

One can draw on a Freudian explanation of male jealousy to argue that Steven's masculinity suggests a powerful rivalry and identification with an imaginary patriarchal presence. A fantasy of phallic masculinity must be evoked to bolster a fragile narcissistic ego, which needs to be constantly guarded in the face of castration anxiety and life's uncertainties. The concept of the imaginary father can be used to explore the fantasies of masculinity that continue to dominate Hollywood film. Radstone (1995a) applies Freud's (1913) analysis of the myth of the Primal Horde to argue that the fantasy of the primal father and his idealization underpin the shaping of patriarchal masculinities and the yearning for an idealized father.[10] Drawing on such work, one can argue that Douglas's portrayal of Steven's rivalrous battle evokes the ongoing struggle that men are facing through the loss of the old patriarchal order, together with the continued rivalry with the imaginary father and the old order. It may be that for some (as in the reviews cited earlier), this imagined rivalry is given added impetus because of Douglas's similarity to, and publicized rivalry with, the absent father figure of Kirk.

Freud (1922) argues that all jealousies contain an element of bisexuality. *A Perfect Murder* also contains elements of repressed homoeroticism and the words used by the husband in the murder of the rival are telling, if clichéd, in their Freudian symbolism. In *A Perfect Murder*, Steven stabs his rival with the words 'how's that for wet work?' The characters of Steven and David are also put into a sexual relation with each other through their desire for the same woman. The pleasure for audiences who identify with Steven's power and mastery in the triangle may relate to Steven's ability to intervene in his wife's relation to her lover, to then challenge her possession of him by controlling the actions of her lover and turning him against her. As Steven puts it, after his meeting with her lover, 'I made him an offer', and this sexual innuendo is a strong theme throughout the film. Thus there is the implication of erotic rivalry not only between the two men *for* Emily, but also *with* Emily for David, the lover.

Voyeurism, jealousy and new technology

Neale argues that 'Voyeurism is marked by the extent to which there is a gulf between the seer and the seen' (1983: 16). As discussed in earlier chapters, this 'look' is central to the pleasures of cinema viewing, and has elements of sadism in it that are related to castration anxiety and guilt. The pleasure lies in projecting that guilt on to the object or figure of desire, in finding out and ascertaining guilt. Voyeurism is often a component in extreme, destructive jealousies, where the desire to control the other dominates. The painful, if compulsive, fascination of watching one's beloved in the arms of another is a familiar trope of the obsessively jealous, and has been documented by psychoanalysts (Freud, 1910; Seidenberg, 1952) and in novels such as Greene's *The End of the Affair* (1951), Proust's 'Swann's Way' (1913) and Tolstoy's *The Kreutzser Sonata* (1890). The masochistic pleasures of voyeuristic jealousy may be used to act out forbidden incestuous or homoerotic desires, or may be related to destructive, envious impulses (Klein, 1957). Both of these aspects are represented in this film, where from the opening scene, the searching voyeuristic gaze of the camera finds the adulterous couple making love.

Mulvey argues that an important feature of the voyeuristic look is that 'sadism demands a story' and needs to 'make ... something happen' (1975: 14). In *A Perfect Murder*, there is a perverse pleasure to be found in watching Steven's voyeuristic cruelty when he attempts to orchestrate and listen to Emily's death from his mobile phone. The phone enables him 'to make something happen'. We watch intercut scenes of Steven and Emily, as he listens to her struggle with the intruder. At this stage of the film, everyone believes the intruder to be the lover. This scenario is indicative of how the film portrays the gendered relationship between new technology, jealousy and power. In contrast to Steven, Emily is represented as having a more benign relationship to the phone and new technology more generally. Whenever the phone rings, Emily is lying down. For example, when Steven first phones his rival David, Emily is in bed with him. In the scene of her attack, when the phone rings, she is again lying down in the bath. Surprisingly perhaps, for a millionairess with a mock waterfall for a bath, she has no telephone near to hand, as instead, for the plot to work, she has to get up and go down to the kitchen to answer it. When she does, she is attacked, whilst her husband listens. Thus, while the husband is updated in the modern film, she is still, in this important respect – and like Grace Kelly almost 50 years previously – positioned passively in relation to the phone and (initially) the attack. Femininity in this instance is defensively anchored in historical mores, a view which is reinforced further by the critics, who deride Paltrow's Emily as passive and weak.

The jealous *mise-en-scène*: globalization, consumer culture and jealous desire

The relationship between masculinity, jealous possession and the feminine other are evoked through the film's jealous *mise-en-scène*. The pleasurably opulent, materialistic setting of the husband's environment sets the scene for his acquisitive and territorial jealousy. This visual emphasis on the pleasures of wealth also complements the film's jealousy narrative in which Emily, the 'trophy wife', is reduced to an object that has possibly lost her value by sleeping with another man (Walker, 1998: 26). The rivalrous struggle between the husband and the rival is as much about the possession of money as it is about love. The film's *mise-en-scène* has a fetishistic quality to it, something that may reinforce the identification with Steven's possessive gaze. Steven and his affluent metropolitan setting visually reflect the commodification of lifestyle and relationships associated with global capitalism and late consumer culture (Featherstone, 1991).

However, although the global nature of multinational capitalism is emphasized, the imagery of ruthless, colonizing acquisitiveness is also implicitly challenged throughout by the wife Emily, and different aspects of the *mise-en-scène* that allude to a more inclusive feminized culture where real and imagined boundaries are less jealously guarded. In contrast to her ruthless jealous husband, whose relationship to the world is shown to be mediated by computers and financial deals, Emily signifies a more relational and less colonizing relationship to the environment. Her work as a US translator appears to symbolize very different possibilities for the new global social relations. Thus, throughout, Emily becomes associated with a less rigid and more positive reading of ethnicity and difference, which can be encoded as 'feminine', challenging the film's more pessimistic definitions of consumer culture and subjectivity, where colonization and the impulse for mastery predominate. Emily's place in the new global order also signifies a link with the future. This is made more concrete when she communicates with the Arab detective in his own language, and asks him about his child. The reference to the child takes the film's point of reference away from narcissistic concerns of the present to those of the future, and confirms Emily's link to other generations and also to other cultures that symbolize different possibilities for the new global order.

The detective Mohamed Karaman, played by David Suchet, was universally praised by critics both for the subtlety and moral gravity that he brought to the part.[11] For example, journalist John Wrathall argues that Suchet 'deserves an award for the first ever sympathetic Arab-American (character) in a Hollywood movie' (1998: 11). Perhaps part of his appeal is his lack of difference in terms of a fantasy of his *non*-ethnicity, or rather, what Suchet himself calls his 'ethnically neutral' interpretation of the role (BFI, 1998). His 'ethnically neutral' interpretation may also appeal, partly because it adds to a more universalized image of paternal gravitas, and it provides an image of the benign 'world' cop that can appeal to a globalized audience. This global theme is also reflected in the background music of female voices, which is present from the very beginning of the film, working partly as a counter-narrative to the more traditionally masculine themes of the film and related to the jealousy narrative. Kristeva's work on the semiotic 'chora' is apt here (1974: 93). She applies this term to certain forms of artistic expression to connote the feminine qualities of pre-Oedipal and pre-verbal experience associated with the child's first relationship to maternal body.

Jealous megalomania

In psychoanalytic terms, the representation of Steven's jealousy does not evoke for the spectator 'good enough' feelings of jealous loss based on attachment for his wife; in fact, quite the reverse is the case. Steven is portrayed as an omnipotent megalomaniac, without a shred of emotional vulnerability. It is this that makes him such an appealing and escapist character for those who are reminded daily of the contemporary frailties of masculinity. It is not as though we are being asked to identify with feelings of jealous loss, even when faced with the representation of his wife's adultery. Jealousy is represented in the character of Steven as being dealt with defensively, through a form of jealous displacement, where the jealous hurt gets transformed into a compulsion to maintain possession at all costs. His jealous emotionality is transformed into making money and he turns the desperate situation of having an unfaithful wife into a financial transaction.

The cuckolded Steven has plenty to be jealous of, given that his young wife is having an affair with a much younger man than himself. If this were a jealousy based on attachment and a fear of losing the beloved, then one might think that the killing 'should' be between the two male rivals. But in this instance, we are given a scenario in which the two men mutually agree to kill Emily, the so-called object of desire. Steven may have dreamt up this perverse plan, but David readily goes along with it for the money, thus reducing Emily, and the money that her dead body represents, to the status of an object of exchange between the rivalrous men. Moi cites a number of psychiatric studies that show that in murderous cases of male jealousy, it is usually the female partner that tends to be killed and not the rival (1987: 147–8).

She applies Lagache's concept of *amour captatif* to the problem of murderous male jealousy, suggesting that jealous men are characterized by a 'sadistic desire for mastery' and are unable to cope with the separateness of the love object.[12]

The powerful narcissistic underpinnings of such jealousy imply that the jealous subject would rather destroy what he loves than share the desired object with another person. One can draw on the psychoanalytic language of Klein to argue that Steven's jealous megalomania is depicted as 'paranoid-schizoid' in character: feelings of loss are defended against, destroying whatever presents a threat (Klein, 1957). Money is an important signifier in this scenario. Alongside the more obvious power dynamics of class, money is also bound up with the representation of Steven's lack of 'generational consciousness' (Bollas, 1992). In contrast to his wife who represents 'old money' and who has a family she is close to (and, in particular, it is the maternal connection that we see as a powerful source of Emily's strength), Steven's 'new money' signifies further his lack of history and a lack of connection to the past. Steven appears to have no family, past or present, and compensates for this through his relentless struggle for money. In contrast to the portrayal of other powerful business anti-heroes on the screen such as *Citizen Kane* (1941), whose motivation to make money was depicted as being related to a search for the lost object ('Rosebud'), Douglas (as with his role 'Gordon Gekko' in *Wall Street,* 1987) here invites a more a-historical and narcissistic interpretation of male subjectivity.

The defensive hegemonic struggles about gender that take place in the film narrative also take place in the press reviews. Douglas's performance elicits a similar response from the critics, indicating the sociohistorical construction of masculinity in both the film text and the press and the unconscious fantasies which may accompany those constructions. The contrasting depictions of the husband and the wife in *Dial M For Murder* (1954) and *A Perfect Murder* (1998) arguably reflect the shifting nature of these textual constructions, and at a meta-textual level, may work defensively to maintain the patriarchal hierarchies of gender.

Dial M For Murder (1954) and the re-make of a jealous hero

Douglas's acting style contrasts with the more cool and detached performance of Ray Milland in the 1954 version *Dial M For Murder,* who received a mixed response from reviewers of the time. Although his alleged portrayal of 'smug duplicity' was praised by some (Lejeune, 1954; Whitefait, 1954), others said his performance was not 'physical' enough (Houston, 1954). Hinting at the character's lack of heterosexual credentials, the implication of those press reports appeared to be that he was not a manly enough villain. Instead, for these critics, he seemed 'too troubled by psychological insight', and had 'a touch too much of Hamlet' to be a really convincing villain (Anon, 1954).

The flawed hero is a recurring theme of Hitchcock films, signalling the instability of masculinity more generally and the extent to which the crisis of masculinity is not restricted to the late twentieth century. The greater space given to the drama of Steven's jealousy in the later film, however, is suggestive of the greater 'emotionalization' of masculinity in the 1990s (Lupton, 1998). Nevertheless, as we have seen, the positive implications of such imagery for less defensive, and more fluid, good enough masculinities can be questioned. For example, one can argue that the representation of Steven's jealous emotionality is dealt with in a hysterical manner, through Douglas's melodramatic acting and also by the ultra fast pace of the dramatic action and the excesses of the *mise-en-scène*. In *Dial M For Murder*, the wife's love affair is not central to the plot, whereas in *A Perfect Murder*, Emily's affair is very much alive and central to the story of Steven's jealous revenge. The greater emphasis on Emily's sexuality, together with her independent work status, reflects the changes in cultural and sexual politics that have occurred since the 1950s when *Dial M for Murder* was made.[13]

In contrast to the sympathy shown for Grace Kelly as the wife in 1954, the 1998 reviews are far more complimentary about Michael Douglas's performance as the non-PC, ruthless and controlling husband than about Paltrow's performance as the adulterous wife. Paltrow is almost universally criticized by critics for her portrayal of Emily, who is seen as irritating and passive, failing to live up to the performance of Kelly in the earlier version; as one journalist comments:

> for Paltrow, the film is a disaster. The part is dependent on a star quality that she hasn't really got, and the film's flat lighting somehow succeeds in making her look zitty and washed out.
>
> (Sweet, 1998: 5)

The Warner Brothers' publicity states that Steven's motivations are ambiguous because he appears to be as much motivated by money as by sexual jealousy (BFI, 1998). The husband's envy of his wife's wealth and status is perhaps more understandable to modern audiences than those of 1954, partly because the envy of others and the desire for instant gratification may have become more socially acceptable in the late twentieth century culture than jealousy, with all its connotations of weakness, loss and dependency (Craib, 1994; Lasch, 1979). In the contemporary version, it is as if Emily/Paltrow, who is a privileged woman with a good job, a lover and a rich husband, invites a more sadistic response in the media.

Steven's envious gaze was frequently reproduced in the negative, even misogynist reports in the press where there is often a slippage between Emily, the fictional character, and Paltrow, the actor. This slippage is reflected in the hostility of the comments reportedly from Douglas about Paltrow: 'Much of her media success came out of who she's dated' (Lawrence, 1998: 7). This envious hostility is interesting at a meta-textual level, as it suggests that the crisis of masculinity is played out beyond the film text, in the context of its reception. For example, Paltrow is described in terms of her being 'at her droopiest', which 'only enhances one's pleasure as Douglas sets about bumping her off' (Billson, 1998: 8). As the reviews indicate, it may be that as an intelligent, educated, 'guilt-free adulterous woman', she doesn't appear to need or invite our sympathy, as she can look after herself (French, 1998: 6). The modern audience may identify with Steven's jealousy, but it is a jealousy that is shot through with envy of the woman.

Emily as the active curious subject, or the passive object of jealousy?

The film's portrayal of Emily's challenge to her objectified position in the jealous triangle is contradictory. On the one hand, she is certainly pictured as having more independence than Grace Kelly's version of the wife, insofar that she has a job and a lover, kills the intruder, eventually solves the murder mystery and finally kills her husband. Yet on the other, as the press reviews emphasize, it is primarily the qualities of passivity and lifelessness that come across.[14] As we have seen, this is illustrated in the scenes with the telephones. However, what Emily lacks in new technology savvy, she eventually makes up for with traditional feminine intuition (as symbolized by the key). In *Dial M for Murder*, the English detective plays the investigative role, but in *The Perfect Murder*, Emily plays a more important role in unmasking and finally killing her husband. The way this is most clearly represented is when she gradually unravels the mystery of the missing key. More generally, the symbolism of the key that opens locked forbidden doors and secrets has an almost archetypal significance in relation to femininity and the transgressive curiosity of women in patriarchal cultures (Atwood, 1998). For example, one can recall Angela Carter's interpretation of 'Blue Beard' in *The Bloody Chamber* (1995), where the young heroine is punished (and in this feminist interpretation is rescued by her mother) for opening the door to the forbidden chamber. The symbolism of the key in the film is presented both as a practical dilemma and (as in *The Bloody Chamber*), as a puzzle that she must solve in order to find out the truth about her murderous husband. As in 'paranoid woman's films' such as *Rebecca* (1940) and *Gaslight* (1940), where a psychotic husband projects his madness onto the woman, the underlying question is not so much about the mystery of femininity, but rather it asks 'what do men want?' (Gallafent, 1988). The task of the woman in films such as these is to find out the truth and expose the husband as a murderer.

In a more classical Freudian vein, the key also has phallic connotations, symbolizing penetration. Thus, the key symbolizes at least two relevant themes for jealousy; namely curiosity or the desire for knowledge, and sexuality. Emily, with whom the key is associated, is a condensed sign for these different aspects of the jealous psyche. However, as we have seen, she finally reverses its more objectifying connotations by taking possession of it and returning to the scene of the crime to challenge its totemic significance. Emily's curiosity can unlock doors and challenge the limits of her husband's omnipotent fantasies that limit her world.

Conclusion

This chapter has used *A Perfect Murder* to think through the dilemmas and possibilities of contemporary masculinities and their ambiguities in contemporary culture. A key theme of recent discussions about emotional masculinities has been that the alleged 'feminization' of culture has facilitated the emergence of new, more feelingful modes of cultural masculinities (Bainbridge and Yates, 2005). However, a recurring feminist argument is that despite the increase in more nuanced, feminized images of men on the screen, these are often achieved at the expense of women (Butler, 2000; Rowe, 1995). The appeal for popular critics of Douglas as the jealous husband Steven appears to be his *non*-PC capacity to be tough and *non*-feeling in the 'traditional' feminine sense. As Steven's character illustrates, it would be a mistake to conflate

all definitions of emotionality with the kind of nurturing images traditionally associated with femininity and, among men, with the 'new
man'. The character of Steven in this film is intensely emotional, but
his emotionality is associated with a mode of masculinity which is
going out of fashion. The ruthless, possessive, angry emotions displayed by the unreconstructed character of Steven are certainly there at
the expense of the female protagonist, but perhaps only in a more up-
front way than with his more 'feminized' contemporaries, and for
critics this is part of his appeal.

It is the more villainous and aggressive aspects of Douglas's character
that are conveyed most. There are, however, qualities of masochism
and vulnerability that come through in his acting, which provides
space for a more complicated reading of his portrayal of jealous masculinity and the identifications it evokes. The potential for a critical
gaze also extends to the portrayal of the relationship between the patriarchal jealousy of the husband and the cultural environment in which
he is seen to operate. At its roots, morbid jealousy is about objectifying
the other and the refusal to acknowledge difference. *A Perfect Murder*
makes an analogy between the cuckolded psyche of its protagonist and
the possessive colonizing practices of late twentieth-century global capitalism. For most of this film, the audience are invited to identify with
Steven and his struggles for possession within the jealous triangle. It is
his omnipotence that is tested, his capacity to carry out 'a perfect
murder' and then to cover it up afterwards. The term 'perfect' is
significant here, given that everything else in the film appears to be
about the perfection of image and appearance and the perfection that
money can buy. In the end, Steven's inability to control events and the
objects around him undermines his masculinity, and also works as a
broader critique of an overly materialist, image-based society, where
the selfish and superficial values of narcissism predominate. To an
extent, the blurring of boundaries in the press reviews between
Michael Douglas and his character, and their identification with
Douglas's celebrity status more generally, lend credence to this view,
reinforcing the narcissistic world-view represented by Steven.

At the beginning of this chapter, I argued that a hegemonic struggle
takes place in the text between the values associated with Douglas's
depiction of overly possessive, narcissistic masculinity and its associated values of rivalry and territorial aggression, versus those of the
independent wife who refuses to be his possession. Her character represents a different set of cultural values and is depicted as having a less
narcissistic, more relational stance to others – both in terms of *time*

(she has a family and a history) and *place* (it is implied that she has a more open and respectful relationship to other cultures). From a French feminist perspective, one could argue that Emily rejects the 'masculine' controls of the symbolic order, and registers that refusal in the intuitive spaces beyond speech, through music and the intuitive strategies which challenge the boundaries of her husband's control (Irigaray, 1985). Nevertheless, the significance of this challenge to Steven's patriarchal masculinity can be qualified somewhat. Despite the depiction of Emily's independence, for example in her job as a translator, her representation is still undermined by aesthetic strategies which reinforce her marginal status within the narrative and set her up as a passive object of identification.

Moreover, the balanced portrayal of emotional subjectivity is provided ultimately not by her, but by the detective whose depiction of the benign cop incorporates what is best about masculinity and femininity, to produce a non-threatening, paternalistic view of the law. On the one hand, his rhetorical question at the end, 'what else could you do?', implies a sanctioning of her adulterous affair and the murder of her husband, affirming that the law is no longer on the side of the jealous husband, but rather with the person who is the object of the jealousy. Nevertheless, one can argue that hegemonic masculinity is restored, as the reassuring detective also re-establishes male authority and a sense of continuity with the fantasy of the good father.

7
Englishness, Nation and Masculine Jealousy in *The End Of The Affair* (*N. Jordan, USA/UK, 1999*)[1]

Introduction

The End Of The Affair (1999) is a historical drama about an adulterous love affair in London during World War II. The film is based on the 1951 novel by Graham Greene, and was directed and adapted by Neil Jordan. It stars Ralph Fiennes as the jealous lover 'Maurice Bendrix', Stephen Rea as the husband 'Henry', and Julianne Moore as the wife and lover 'Sarah'. In many ways *The End Of the Affair* offers a more radical cinematic treatment of jealousy than other mass-entertainment films such as *A Perfect Murder* (1998) and provides an opportunity to explore a less rigid and predictable portrayal of jealousy and male rivalry. In *The End of The Affair*, the depiction of masculine jealousy is linked to questions of faith and its betrayal, together with the impossibility of love and desire.

The film's story chiefly belongs to the jealous lover Bendrix, but his narrative is constantly undermined by other voices and by the events that take place. Throughout the film, Bendrix struggles to know everything and to possess all the facts, but he can't. The film does not offer the spectator any comfortable identificatory positions within the jealous triangle. For example, identifying with the lover rather than the husband does not necessarily invite the pleasures of possession and resolution that one might otherwise expect of a Hollywood treatment of jealousy; but neither is Bendrix, as the fiercely possessive lover, demonized. In this chapter, I explore the extent to which the alternative portrayal of male rivalry in this film opens up the possibility for a less narcissistic and potentially more emotionally complex response from the spectator.

The analysis of masculinity and the troubling of jealous boundaries are also evoked through the film's depiction of nation, Englishness and cultural heritage. Ralph Fiennes as Bendrix is redolent of a particular type of English masculinity, in the tradition of classically trained actors such as Jeremy Irons and Lawrence Olivier. His star persona brings to the fore romantic fantasies about English masculinity as an intense, tortured, emotional sensibility, an image which is also mediated by fantasies of nation and otherness. Alongside an analysis of the jealousy film text and its star, I shall explore the discourses about the film in the UK reviews, where fantasies of nation, Englishness and jealous possession predominate.

The jealous *mise-en-scène*: a postmodern take on heritage and jealousy in *The End Of The Affair*

The End of The Affair contains, but in a critical, re-worked form, stylistic features associated with heritage films.[2] The visual period details, in terms of the props, costumes and settings, all work to create an authentic sense of damp and gloomy 1940s London. The lighting creates an effective setting for the jealousy, including a muted yellow (traditionally the symbolic colour of cowardly jealousy and nicotine-stained old station waiting rooms), and also green (the most common association with jealousy today), which, as one critic commented, was the 'colour of pea soup' (Andrews, 2000: 18). Thus, the symbolic connotations of wartime packet soups, illicit meetings in fogs and station cafés come together to evoke a particular sense of wartime Englishness, connoting as they do the most famous English World War II adultery film *Brief Encounter* (1945).[3]

However, the authentic period details are undermined by the flashbacks, the dark, shadowy lighting, and the jealous gaze of the camera that looks for what can't be seen or found. Michael Nyman's modern, repetitive and circular film score works as a counter-narrative to the 1940s period details, and it also helps to convey a sense of the tortuous circularity of jealousy and the difficulties of resolving it. At times its repetitiveness gives the film a heightened sense of male melodrama and a vulnerability, which contrasts with the hard bitterness of Bendrix's voice-over that narrates his jealousy. The ambiguities of the film's *mise-en-scène* are tantalizing and seductive, and often work in a critical manner to disconcert rather than reassure the spectator. Jordan subverts the conceits of English heritage films that idealize history, and instead he evokes the atmosphere of the 1940s in such a way as to unsettle the audience and its response to the dramas of male jealousy as enacted on the screen. This is clearly illustrated in the scene of

Sarah's depression during VE day, where her feelings of alienation are equated with the emptiness of British propaganda and the victory parade.

The critical portrayal of the past in terms of 1940s England also extends to the depiction of Bendrix's own critical relationship with his own past and an understanding of the events and fantasies that sparked his jealousy. The film not only reveals the constructed nature of Englishness and patriotism, but also the constructed nature of male subjectivities, which helps the film to create a less self-deluding relationship with the past. The spatial and temporal shifts of the non-linear narrative disrupt Bendrix's point of view, and his memory of events. This aspect of the film's form also calls into question the legitimacy of the jealous subject; while undermining Bendrix's *claim* to be jealous, in terms of Sarah's adultery as its cause, it undermines his entitlement to be jealous in the first place.

The film's expressive lighting is often reminiscent of paranoid *film noir* detective films of the 1940s and 1950s, a genre which, as we have seen, is associated with masculinity in crisis. The narrative works partly in the manner of a *noir* detective story and Bendrix's voice-over sometimes brings to mind Raymond Chandler's stories. Throughout the film, the theme of the detective is reinforced by the self-conscious voyeuristic camera shots that play with the spectator's perhaps shameful wish to know more, to sniff out the trail of Bendrix's jealousy. For example, we vicariously watch Sarah through the eyes of the detective and in particular the son, who Bendrix calls the 'vicarious lover'. At other moments, the camera focuses accusingly upon Bendrix himself; as, for example, when he goes to visit the detective agency. Here, we follow him walking through a darkly lit passageway and then, when he arrives, the camera closes in on his uncomfortable-looking body, biting his lip and sitting awkwardly in his chair, his white face perspiring, and his eyes almost blinking in the light. Thus the camera's shifting focus upon the subjects and objects of jealousy also invites the audience to take up numerous identificatory positions in relation to the jealous triangle on the screen.

Ralph Fiennes as an English hero

Ralph Fiennes's portrayal of Bendrix received almost unanimous praise in the UK press. The boundaries between the imaginary, constructed public persona of Fiennes and that of Bendrix are often blurred in these reviews. The main themes that have emerged in the publicity

around Fiennes, his films and the construction of his life history, contribute to the reading of Fiennes as Bendrix the jealous lover. As a cultural sign, Ralph Fiennes attracts a particular set of fantasies about a
lost, romantic, white English masculinity, which combines more traditional elements of a wild, romantic Byronic sensibility with Freudian
discourses about his instinctual emotional subjectivity and his status as
the troubled son of the Oedipal mother.

Fiennes's star persona can be grouped alongside other romantic classically trained English actors in the tradition of Lawrence Olivier, Alec
Guinness, and more recently, Jeremy Irons and Daniel Day Lewis.[4]
Throughout his career, Fiennes's interviews have been awash with
signifiers that point to his 'Englishness'. For example, journalists recall
'sipping Earl Grey tea' with Fiennes (Jones, 1992: 29–31), his 'perfect'
manners and his identity as the 'perfect Englishman' (Gritten, 1992:
34–9).[5] Alongside his Englishness, the terms most often used to
describe him tend to converge around the image of his emotional
'intensity' and his 'dark' hidden depths (Johnston, 1999: 7). This deep
and tortured aspect of Fiennes is said to coexist alongside his 'integrity'
and 'intelligence' as an actor (Berens, 1995: 116–19; Martin, 2000: 13).
These different facets of Fiennes's star persona are also present in the
reviews of *The End of the Affair*. For example, the ecstatic review given
by Bradshaw in *The Guardian* newspaper is fairly typical in this respect:

> Fiennes himself is simply remarkable. There is no other actor who
> could have played this role and, as with his Onegin last year, there
> is an unmatched maturity and complexity to his screen presence: a
> jaggedness, a simmering *amour propre*, a neurotic obsessiveness, an
> importunate yearning.
>
> (2000: 4)

The narrative of the romantic Englishman with hidden and dangerous depths has a long tradition in English literature, but within the
cinema, one can locate it in relation to the idea of 'the British romantic
lead'. This figure dates back to Ronald Colman in the 1920s (Amidon,
1996: 4). According to the film critic David Thomson, it was Colman
who established the tradition of the slim and well-mannered British
hero with 'the seductively restrained voice', with all its associations of
decency, silk cravats and flannel trousers, but who is also 'capable of
deep romantic obsession' (Amidon, 1996: 4).[6] The continued appeal of
the English romantic lead is arguably related to a nostalgia for a lost
masculinity, represented by Fiennes, who lends an aura of authenticity

to the role of the wartime jealous anti-hero Bendrix. However, the fantasy of Fiennes as the 1940s Englishman is not just related to the old-fashioned quality of his voice and appearance; it also rests with the 'real' way in which he is able to convey his emotions on screen.

Ralph Fiennes as a modern Freudian hero

Since the early 1990s when he first became a star, Fiennes's emotional subjectivity has been a central theme of his reviews.[7] One can argue that the 'authenticity' Fiennes is able to bring to the portrayal of emotions such as jealousy, resonates with audiences steeped in the culture of therapeutic values and Freudian pop psychology. The qualities associated with an old fashioned 'antique' Englishness described above (Sutcliff, 2000: 5), are given fresh meaning for audiences in the light of contemporary therapeutic concerns. Fiennes has reportedly said that

> acting has therapeutic dimensions ... maybe acting is a way to know yourself, because even when you're acting, you're always yourself in some way – it's a very primitive impulse to inhabit who you are.
>
> (Sandler, 2000: 9)

Fiennes's publicity draws on a discourse of Freudian instincts to explain his emotional sensibility. We are told that, for Fiennes, emotions are like a 'primitive', 'instinctual force', and that he is often 'consumed' by them, rather, he says, like the desire to act itself (Smurthwaite, 1992: 9).

Related to stories of his instinctual behaviour is the representation of Fiennes's powerful and innate heterosexual 'sexual charisma' (Fisher, 2000: 37). We are told that he has a very keen sense of his own sexuality, as his defence of the love scenes in *The End Of the Affair* illustrates: 'I don't think the sexuality in the film is sadistic, abusive or based on violence or control. It's mutually consenting adults making love' (Martin, 2000: 13). However, Fiennes's heterosexual masculinity does not only work to reassure and flatter his audiences. For example, the censors of *The End Of The Affair* were more concerned and disturbed by his nudity than the naked feminine form of Julianne Moore, who played his lover. One can argue that the censorship derived less from the portrayal of an aggressive sexual virility, but rather from a physical vulnerability, which is unusual in cinematic representations of heterosexual masculinity. It is fascinating that his heterosexual status is asserted, given so many signifiers of castrated masculinity within the film, and the homoerotic dynamics of the film's closure. Fiennes is not a big muscular actor and his body is able to convey a sense of woundedness, which contributes to the portrayal of Bendrix's neurotic and jealous sensibility. From the beginning, Bendrix's vulnerability is signified visually by his nervous and awkward bodily disposition, his limp and the scar on his leg (which he tells Sarah came from the Spanish civil war). Thus, from the beginning of the film, Bendrix is wounded and his jealousy also symbolizes that woundedness.

In *The End Of the Affair* there is also something of the childish Oedipal boy about Fiennes's portrayal as Sarah's lover. In one scene, after making love, we see Bendrix in his dressing gown, dressing Sarah, telling her that he's jealous of 'this button', and that he is jealous of her 'stockings' and so on. The jealousy in this scene shows Bendrix's jealousy in a romantic benign light, and reinforced by his boyishness, as if illicitly dressing a flirtatiously protesting mother. This maternal Oedipal theme complements the much publicized aspect of his life history, where the inspirational role of his 'adored deceased' mother, has reportedly played a central role in his 'vocation' to be an actor:

> Mr Fiennes told *Hello* magazine last month that his mother had taught him to appreciate 'art and love and poetry – what a gift to leave a son'.
>
> (Anon, 1995: 31)

At his mother's funeral, Fiennes reportedly 'brushed her hair and later described her as more a friend than a mother' (Covenay, 1997: 20).[8] One can contrast the construction of Fiennes's maternal Oedipal subplot to that of Michael Douglas, whose father is always central to the public construction of his life history. For the less overtly macho Fiennes, his mother occupies centre stage and contributes to a more 'feminized', sensitive, public construction of his emotional identity as a star (Gerrard, 1999: 30).

Bendrix: the reflexive jealous hero or drama queen?

Fiennes's emotional identity as a star arguably contributes to the reading of him as the emotionally tortured Bendrix. Bendrix's preoccupation with his own jealousy is a major theme throughout the film and provides a central narrative focus for his memories of jealous loss and desire. And yet his relationship to his jealousy is paradoxical because while he seems to be utterly taken up with his jealous feelings, he is nevertheless able to observe them, to use his skills as a writer to record and analyse them. Bendrix's ambiguous jealous sensibility embodies a mixture of character traits associated with modernity and late modernity. For example, as a writer, he is in many ways portrayed as the postmodern subject *par excellence* who can deconstruct himself as he tells the story, highlighting the reflexive and performative nature of masculinity.[9] This, in turn, provides the space for a more critical relationship to the jealous protagonist, where one is invited to identify and question him at the same time.

As the film's director, Neil Jordan, has argued, Bendrix's angry insecurity and quarrelsome manner may make him an 'unlikely hero' (Case, 2000: 22). But he nevertheless offers the audience an example of reflexive, feelingful masculinity as throughout the film, he constantly articulates his jealousy in the mode of a Freudian confessional and shares with us even his most nasty feelings of jealous possession. In this way, he is at once all surface and depth, and (to quote numerous press reports) his star persona helps to convey a 'brooding intensity' that also adds to an aura of hidden depth and emotional suffering (Johnston, 1999: 7).

In contrast, say, to the characters of Steven in *The Perfect Murder* and Travis in *Taxi Driver*, Bendrix's jealousy can be symbolized, he can name it and he wrestles with it because he knows it is his demon and treats it as such. Paradoxically, what he can't do is allow the separateness of Sarah, the love object. Sarah tells him there are different ways of loving, but not according to him; he is very much the empiricist, who must touch and observe what he is feeling. In this respect, his attitude is on the side of the modernist subject, and his jealous subjectivity could be read as a parody of masculinity in the scientific age of the Enlightenment. For example, Malcolm Bowie has written about the 'comedy of misapplied intellect' of the obsessively jealous subject, and how jealousy may (as in the case of Proust's narrator in *La Prisonniere*), be acted out and experienced in the mode of the empirical scientist who is embarked on an endless search for mastery of the facts and empirical truth, and who 'relives in the solitude of his own body, the general human quest for knowledge' (1987: 50). Jordan observes the underlying frustration experienced by the jealous subject and he argues that jealousy is potentially 'as endless as love', particularly if one is a writer:

> If you act on jealousy you have to act on those areas of somebody's life that you haven't actually got access to. It's like a form of fiction

in a way. It made absolute sense to me that being a novelist, he could be infinitely jealous.

(Case, 2000: 22)

Although Bendrix can deconstruct his jealousy, this understanding does not necessarily enable him to transform or change his jealousy and his capacity to imagine and symbolize it may even perpetuate it. Lacan names this circular and tortuous jealousy *jalouissance*, where the jealous person tortures himself by endlessly imagining possible scenarios between the rival and the lover (Morel, 2000: 158). The rival works as a narcissistic mirror for the jealous man, who becomes subject and object of his own jealous gaze.

To return to Jordan's analogy of jealousy as fiction, one can argue that one way of controlling the story is for the jealous subject to experience the perverse pleasures of masquerading as the rival, so that one's own voyeurism and sexual jealousy is aimed at one's own image. This is the case in *The End Of The Affair* with Bendrix, who uses the private detective and his son to spy on himself as Sarah's lover and he clearly enjoys hearing Parkis recall the details of the meeting while he shaves in front of the mirror and smugly recalls his role as 'the lover'. In this way, it is not only Parkis who becomes the 'vicarious lover', watching, recording and 'sniffing out love' on his behalf; but Bendrix also becomes implicated as the subject and object of his own jealousy. These different elements, which feed into the portrayal of Bendrix's jealousy, partly confirm but also disrupt the narcissistic gaze of the male subject, and help to produce more varied and critical spaces for audience identifications.

The sanctification of Sarah as a jealous object of desire

In the main, however, the more complex and nuanced portrayal of Bendrix's jealousy is achieved at the expense of the female protagonist, whose subjectivity is given less narrative depth and instead is idealized in a fairly traditional manner. Moore does not bring to her performance of Sarah the same neurotic edge seen in Deborah Kerr's portrayal of her in the 1955 version of the film. Kerr's performance remained true to the novel, appearing more flawed and worldly wise and seeming to possess a troubled psychological edge that Moore's Sarah lacks. In the earlier version of the film, the complexity of Sarah's character is given greater recognition throughout, as we watch her wrestle with a number of philosophical and theological dilemmas about the value of rationalism and nature of Christian belief. This aspect of her struggle is ignored in this film and so, like Bendrix, the audience are also saved that particular struggle with the complexity of her psyche.

God may have been played down in Jordan's treatment of the story, but at times Sarah appears to have been sanctified instead. The 'miracle' of removing the boy's strawberry birthmark by kissing him on the cheek is perhaps the defining moment of this, when her 'maternal softness' and spiritual goodness come together to signify Sarah's otherness in relation to the material world represented by men such as Bendrix and his detective. Images of the mysterious female other come to mind here.[10] For Lacan, women are able to access a state beyond that of knowing and rational thought, but rather, as in his example of Bernini's statue of Saint Teresa in Rome, are raised to mystical levels of experience and states of religious ecstasy (Lacan, 1991: 115). Lacan's account of male jealousy is apt when applied to the story of Bendrix and Sarah, whose enigmatic presence evokes Lacan's description of the unknowable mystical woman, and Bendrix, of the endless desiring jealous subject, in search of the *objet petit a* that is forever out of reach. Sarah is thus a more romantic and removed figure in this film than in the earlier 1955 version where, despite the lack of physical nudity and sex, she seemed to be more flawed and embodied.

A section of the narrative is told from Sarah's point of view and is narrated by her in the form of a voice-over. However, what we *see* is *his* vision of what she is saying and so her story is mediated by his inter-pretation of events. In giving his interpretation of her story, Bendrix also steals her narrative, something that reinforces his theft of the diary within the story itself. This scenario illustrates feminist debates in film studies about whether recent representations of a 'new', more feel-ingful masculinity in popular culture signify a meaningful cultural shift, or whether these popular images of emotional masculinities rep-resent something more superficial (Bainbridge and Yates, 2005). One could argue that in the case of Bendrix in *The End Of The Affair*, it is *his* story of emotional unhappiness that remains dominant throughout. Like an emotional transvestite, he steals her clothes and, vicariously, she is given space to become a player in Bendrix's psychodrama of jeal-ousy and lost romance. In the meantime, she remains largely enig-matic, silent and unknowable and finally dies a tragic death.[11]

Homoeroticism, and male rivalry: the tensions of sameness and difference

There are two portrayals of male jealousy in *The End Of The Affair*: Henry, the cuckolded husband, and Bendrix, the lover. Bendrix's jealousy resonates at a number of levels; the search for the lost object, a quest for knowledge and truth and the lacking jealous subject who projects everything on to the idealized other. Henry is portrayed as emotionally repressed and lacking in sexual passion, which from the standpoint of the Western modern secular audience makes Sarah's adultery appear understandable. Henry confesses his jealousy early on, but it is only at the end of the film, when he generously asks Bendrix to move into their house and, in effect, suggests they 'share' Sarah, that the depth of his love for Sarah is conveyed. Until the final act, the film's narrative mainly belongs to Bendrix, and the impression is given that Henry is unaware of Sarah's affair, as the film's narrative depth is not extended to him. Thus, Henry is made to appear all the more vulnerable and Rea's portrayal of the depressed cuckolded husband does not readily invite identification. It is not until the last act that Henry's other more sympathetic qualities are conveyed and made more apparent.

The film challenges more traditional patriarchal narratives of jealousy, which usually involve two men jealously hating and killing each other over a woman. The rivalry between the husband and lover is portrayed less rigidly than is normally the case, and the boundaries between the two men are more fluid, as they end up living together and finding friendship with one another. Henry's generosity to Bendrix at the end is poignant, when for the first time he tells Bendrix (and us) that in fact he always knew that Sarah was having an affair, but that he never thought it was him: 'but the thing is Bendrix, I'm glad it was you'. Henry's generosity in this scene disrupts the traditional oppositional model of male rivalry within jealousy triangles, and provides another, if at times ambivalent, way of relating between men. Thus, as the film draws to a close, audiences are able to appreciate that Henry's jealousy stems more from love than hate or mindless male rivalry.

In psychoanalytic terms, the homoerotic charge between the two men in this scene is rather interesting because it upsets the Freudian assumption that heterosexual men defend against homosexual love through the deployment of jealous projections and rivalrous relations. In *The End Of The Affair*, the ambiguity of the jealous ending promises a different settlement between the parties concerned, which then in turn has implications for the ways in which masculinity is depicted and imagined. The lessening of the projections between the two men at the end of the film implies an acceptance of *sameness* between them. One can point to the contrast between this and other models of rivalry, where the masculinity of the jealous subject and rival is more usually constructed in terms of *difference*, as a defence against any possible desire between them.

The embrace of the rivals implies a coming to terms with lack and loss, and in contrast to the earlier version of the film, it also connotes a refusal to accept the law of the father. At one level, God represents the father, who takes Sarah from Bendrix, and Bendrix hates him for it. God represents a challenge to Bendrix's materialist, empirical sensibilities and the narcissistic need for mastery and control. God keeps wrong-footing Bendrix, and as the one with more power, God represents factors that cannot be controlled. Corny though the symbolism may be, one can, in a Freudian vein, argue that the bombs represent the rumblings of the Oedipal father/God. Throughout their affair, they are in constant danger, and in the end it splits them up. So God is a castrating figure who curbs his omnipotence and Bendrix never forgives him for that.

Neil Jordan's interpretation of jealousy: a view from the outside

The more complex portrayal of male jealousy in *The End of the Affair* is related to the subtlety of Greene's original book, but also to Jordan's screenplay and his interpretation of the novel. As mentioned, there was an earlier film adaptation of the book made in 1955. In that version, the religious aspects of Greene's novel are emphasized, together with the moral dilemmas of Sarah's infidelity, which appeared more sensational to audiences of the day.[12] Jordan's version of *The End of The Affair* plays down the religious aspect of the story, but in contrast to the 1950s film, he returns to the non-linear structure of the book; a mode of narrative which also resonates with postmodern approaches to film making. Jordan is renowned for making controversial films that include disturbing themes, ambiguous narratives and characters that refuse easy points of identification and subject positions for audiences (Radstone, 2007).[13] In interviews, he positions himself somewhat romantically as 'the outsider' to the British establishment and he draws on the discourses of authenticity and nation, but in an oppositional way, to discuss jealousy both as a marker of 'real' male passion, and also as a marker of national difference between the repressed English and the more liberated Irish:

> It was very interesting making this film as an Irish person, because our relationship to emotion in language is far more combative. We have extreme explosions of emotion. For me to be dealing with this degree of understatement was fascinating ... The image means much

more. It's a very un-Irish thing ... The Standard English accent is
part of a culture which is designed to conceal emotion.

(Case, 2000: 20–2)

Jordan argues that Greene did not conform to the model of the emotionally repressed Englishman, and in this respect Jordan identifies
with, and says he feels empathy for, the man and his work. As some of
The End Of The Affair publicity documents indicate, the original novel
by Greene was based on his affair with his mistress Catherine Walston,
with whom he shared a cottage in Ireland for many years while they
had an adulterous affair (Kennedy, 2000: 4). This connection between
Greene's affair with Walston and Ireland has (alongside his conversion
to Roman Catholicism) endeared him to Irish writers such as Jordan,
who claim an affiliation with him and his work (Case, 2000: 20–2). The
inference is that, for Jordan, Greene is (like him) the 'outsider' in terms
of British masculinity, and he points to the unconventional eroticism
of his relationship with the 'decadent' Walston as evidence of this
(Case, 2000: 20–2). As Jordan goes on to say:

This is a 42-year-old novelist who was writing about a very un-
British exposure of sensuality, but writing with all the understate-
ment that would be natural to those characters.

As if setting out to expose the 'unspoken' and repressed aspects of
British emotional culture himself, Jordan also extends this interpretation of Greene's subversive attitude to the sensuality in his cinematic version of the story. The fairly explicit erotic portrayal of Bendrix
and Sarah's sexual affair caused a great deal of controversy within the
press and much to the publicized fury of Jordan and the cast, it
resulted in the film being given an 18-rated certificate.[14] As far as
Jordan was concerned, this was further evidence of the continued
'hypocrisy' of the British establishment and the difficult feelings
evoked by the film's frank portrayal of English male sexuality (Case,
2000: 20–2).

The theme of Englishness and the question of its authentic representation in the film is a recurring theme in the UK press reviews,
where reviewers are unsettled by the film's textual ambiguities.
One can read this as a defensive response to the images of masculinity made available through the film's exploration of jealousy. To
explore that response further, I shall now turn to that critical press
response.

Englishness, nation and the struggle in the UK press

Jordan's critical interpretation and treatment of Englishness in the film and his unconventional adaptation of Greene's work caused a certain amount of consternation in the UK press. Just as Jordan positions himself and appears to identify with the predicament of the lover and the romantic outsider, the UK journalists respond like angry cuckolds. They put up a more spirited jealous defence of the object, the object being Graham Greene and, in particular, Greene as a signifier of Englishness. The desire to recoup and control the potential un-pleasures of the text and its losses is thus dealt with in the UK press by focusing possessively on Graham Greene as a part of English heritage.

In the reviews, discourses of jealousy and nation converge about the fidelity of the film to Greene's novel and the national authenticity of the book's adaptation to the screen. The English reviewers also position Jordan negatively as an outsider and as a 'foreigner' (Andrews, 2000: 18), trespassing on the hallowed ground of Graham Greene, who they claim for their own. It is as if Jordan the Irish 'outsider' has trespassed on and taken liberties with Greene's novel and the British literary tradition, which Greene is deemed to represent (Patterson, 1999: 27).

There is criticism from reviewers about the liberties Jordan takes with the plot, especially in terms of the needless 'vulgar sexual reunion' of Bendrix and Sarah's trip to Brighton (Bradshaw, 2000: 4). It is as if this excessive representation of 'infidelity' itself constitutes an infidelity on the part of Jordan to Greene's novel and appears to have offended the sentiments of certain overly possessive English critics, who feel that Jordan has betrayed the authentic English literary heritage of Graham Greene (Patterson, 1999: 27).

The inferred jealous battle for literary possession of Greene's English literary heritage is, of course, absurd, given that he was a very interna-tional writer, and reportedly wrote the novel while staying with his mistress on the very sunny un-English isle of Capri (Kennedy, 2000: 4). However, issues of truth and authenticity, which are meant to be a defining feature of the heritage film genre, are a constant theme in the reviews. For example, English critics believe that despite all the authen-tic period details of the props, scenes and costumes and so on, the film nevertheless presents an inaccurate historical picture of Englishness during World War II. For instance, there is criticism that the clipped English voices of the American Julianne Moore and the Irish Stephen Rea were a trifle over done (Quirke, 2000: 3).

Critics comment on the choice of an American to play Sarah and an Irishman to play the cuckolded husband, but the choice of Fiennes for the part of Bendrix (whom Greene originally based on himself) receives widespread praise from British and American critics.[15] Fiennes's interpretation is universally praised amongst other things, because he *is* and *appears* to be so English, and his interpretation of Bendrix/Greene is said to be all the more authentic for that (Bradshaw, 2000: 4). Some also remark on his resemblance to Graham Greene, upon whom the character of Bendrix was originally based, thus adding new layers of authenticity and 'reality' to his performance. However, again the discourses of jealousy and nation converge in the criticisms of Moore's portrayal of Englishness, as critics question Jordan's choice of her rather than one of 'our own fine British actresses?' (Patterson, 1999: 27).

Conclusion: questions of faith and the jealous struggle for possession

This chapter has argued that *The End of The Affair* presents a more radical treatment of gender and sexual difference that potentially unsettles and blurs the boundaries that denote more traditional representations of gendered subjectivities. The ambiguity of these boundaries presents a challenge to more traditional narratives of jealousy which involve a story of two men jealously hating and killing each other. Instead, the film provides critical spaces for imagining a different kind of settlement between the rivalrous parties concerned and the different psychosocial forces that shape masculine jealousies. The jealousy that is portrayed in this film provides a good example of a *non-psychotic* jealousy and a more nuanced depiction of masculinity that allows for an emotionally complex response from the audience. The representation of rivalry is also less rigid than is normally the case in Hollywood films, and the jealous boundaries between them are less rigidly portrayed. However, the portrayal of male bonding is arguably at the expense of the female protagonist Sarah, whose subjectivity is given less space and has less narrative depth than the lover and the husband, who in the end embrace (almost literally) over her dead body. Thus, while the film does provide critical spaces for imaginative work around masculinity and jealousy, it also reproduces more traditional narratives of male suffering at the hands of an idealized and enigmatic feminine object of desire.

A central theme of this film is the question of fidelity and faith. Sarah has faith in Bendrix's love and in God, and Bendrix lacks faith in either. At the end of the film, he ceases to hate Sarah for her betrayal, but continues to hate and mistrust God. This gendered relationship to faith in the other, may well resonate more broadly for audiences within contemporary culture, where Western myths of masculinity and what it means to be a man are shifting. Although from a modernist 'enlightened' point of view, Sarah's belief in God and miracles places her on the side of superstition, her belief and hope in the future gives her a psychological dimension that he lacks. Bendrix's intelligence appears to get him nowhere and his inability to trust, together with his literal empiricism, is symptomatic of his lack of faith in the present and perhaps echoes the insecurities of some men in contemporary audiences. The film emphasizes the circular nature of love and jealousy, the futility of it, but also its inevitability. Bendrix is only released from the torment of his *jalouissance* by her death. The problematization of masculinity and its boundaries are evoked through the film's depiction of nation, Englishness and cultural heritage. The desire for visual authenticity, which is assumed to be a feature of heritage films, is also a feature of contemporary culture, where the search for the 'real' may be related to the loss of faith in the narratives that once defined and codified the myths and patriarchal certainties in the West (Bainbridge and Yates, 2005). In *The End Of The Affair*, this loss of faith, together with the disorientation and the emotional responses it evokes, is something that is echoed in the narrative and which is brought to our attention in a number of ways. One can cite the theme of Sarah's faith and Bendrix's lack of it, of his jealousy and his refusal to believe in her fidelity. These ontological uncertainties are also expressed aesthetically, through the ambiguities of the film's *mise-en-scène*.

In terms of the film's mode of address and its implications for spectatorship, a significant question to address is whether the depiction of Bendrix's jealousy is able to convey something meaningful to the audience or whether at a psycho-political level, it merely serves to reproduce more empty narcissistic representations of masculinity that deny and in effect work against change. It is sometimes argued negatively that a 'cult of authenticity' exists in heritage films that works to legitimate and reproduce a particular idealized and reactionary view of nation and of that nation's historical past (Hill, 1999).[16] In Neil Jordan's *The End of the Affair*, this desire for authenticity and historical truth is closely related to the loss of faith signalled above (Bainbridge and Yates, 2005) and can be read as an example of how Hill's position does not always hold true in relation to heritage cinema. In this particular film, the loss of faith and its associated sense of emotional disorientation are foregrounded extensively. Such disorientation and loss touch on anxieties about the strangeness of a settlement where the certainties of the borders, once constituted by the struggle for mastery and rivalrous possession, are left open and unguarded. However, as we have seen, the UK press responded defensively to the loss of mastery and the tensions of difference implied by these new spaces. This cultural resistance, together with the unconscious anxieties underpinning it, was articulated and channelled through the discourses of jealousy, Englishness and nation.

Such tensions and fears have a number of implications for the cultural shaping of masculinities, and the potentiality of new spaces in popular cinematic texts. In psychoanalytic terms, these resistances also point to the potential psychic anxieties about the strangers 'within' and without, and the imaginary others, which threaten the overly narcissistic borders of the Western patriarchal imagination (Kristeva, 1991; Yates, 2006). Films such as *The End Of The Affair* arguably provide critical spaces for imaginative work around masculinity and jealousy, while also reproducing more traditional narratives of male suffering at the hands of an idealized and enigmatic feminine object of desire.

8
The Piano: A Feminine Narrative of Masculine Jealousies (*J. Campion, Australia/New Zealand, 1993*)

Introduction

The Piano has almost become a cult film for feminists, who have written at length about the significance of its enigmatic heroine Ada. However, little has been said about the male characters in the film and the depiction of their different jealousies has not been addressed. *The Piano* provides an example of an alternative, feminist strategy for representing the plurality of male jealousies, including the possibility of a 'good enough' jealousy, and a different kind of resolution between the parties concerned. The themes of sexual jealousy and jealous possession, together with the psychological tensions and pleasures of living with otherness, are central to the film's narrative. These themes are played out in relation to gender and through the portrayal of male sexual jealousy and its relationship to colonial possession.

The Piano is widely cited as a key – though controversial – example of feminist film making because of its nuanced exploration of femininity and the otherness of female desire (Gillett, 1995; Margolis, 2000; Polan, 2001).[1] However, the film *also* unsettles the spectator in its subtle interpretation of the plurality of masculinities and the different forms of masculine jealousy that may exist. This plurality challenges the cultural binary divisions of gender and sexual difference associated with hegemonic masculinity, and illustrates the concept of masculinity as *difference* rather than as sameness.

The chapter begins however, by addressing Jane Campion's role as director and her contribution to the film's production of meaning and its feminist appeal.

Jane Campion and *The Piano* as a feminist text

It's hard to say if the film is made from a specifically female point of view ... It's not a political feminist thing; it's just me as a person making a film. I guess that includes the fact I'm a woman talking about love.

(Campion, in Andrews, 1993a: 26)

The Piano is an independent production, made in New Zealand, written and directed by the director Jane Campion, whose distinctive artistic style as a famous director also gives her the status of *auteur* (Polan, 2001: 12–13). As the above quotation suggests, Campion's relationship as a film-maker to feminism is sometimes ambiguous, although, as a director, she is frequently acclaimed for work that 'solicits a feminist spectatorship' (Gordon, 1996: 194). Campion's films are renowned for exploring the social and psychological intricacies of gender and sexual difference, and her films address the themes and issues consistent with those of feminism.[2] However, in *The Piano*, Campion also foregrounds issues about the complexity of heterosexual masculinity and the film usefully questions assumptions about patriarchal formations of masculinity that are grounded in sameness. The film shows how masculinity is also inflected by difference and this is important for understanding the triangular structures of jealousy that dominate the narrative.

It is often argued that the film challenges the male gaze of patriarchal narrative cinema discussed by Mulvey (1975), as, instead, it is narrated from the point of view of the female protagonist Ada (Gillett, 1995). She is unable to speak, but her desires are nevertheless forcefully communicated non-verbally throughout the film, mainly through her piano playing and her sign language. The film does not just provide a role reversal where the man becomes a feminized object of the gaze and the woman becomes the active subject who looks and initiates action in a traditional 'masculine' way. As Atwood (1998: 91) points out: in such a scenario, the roles may have changed, but the dominant/passive 'structure of looking remains the same'. Instead, she argues that the different relationships in *The Piano* provide a more complex portrayal of (non-verbal) communication and a desire to listen, where the 'specular logic' of the male gaze is challenged and offset.

The desire to challenge the active/passive binary divisions of gender, and to portray a different kind of masculinity, appears to have informed Campion's choice of actors. Reports tell us that she wanted to convey both the strengths and vulnerabilities of her male characters, as this chapter will go on to discuss below. The unlikely and even 'bizarre' casting of Hollywood stars was commented on by journalists and played a role in promoting the film (Johnston, 1993: 56). To understand that process more fully, I shall now turn to the construction of the film's male stars, Sam Neill and Harvey Keitel.

Sam Neill as Stewart

When *The Piano* was released in 1993, Sam Neill was known as 'New Zealand's most famous actor', and was already well known to British audiences from his roles on British television (Walker, 1993: 4). Throughout his career as an actor, Neill has consistently been described as 'an intelligent heart throb', and his star persona has an 'Englishness' about it which has been likened to the 'sardonic' and 'brooding' qualities of James Mason (Mann, 1984: 15). Neill's British colonial roots are a constant theme of articles about him. Neill's reticent, courteous and shy manner was, until the 1990s, often associated with a particular tradition of old-fashioned upper middle-class English masculinity.[3] His major career break came when he starred in the feminist film *My Brilliant Career* (1979), where his identity as an intelligent, egalitarian and sensitive actor emerged and was promoted at that time in press reports: 'I don't mind being used to further feminist causes if that is how the film is seen' (Neill, in Bamigboye, 1980: 15).

Neill moved to Britain in 1980 and became a household name there as the 'daring' and 'sexually irresistible' spy in *Reilly, Ace Of Spies* (Thames Television, 1983) (Rook, 1983: 16–17). The latter established him as an actor with 'smouldering' sex appeal, which was (in the tradition of other English leading stars) downplayed by him in interviews.[4]

These different elements of Neill's public and acting persona were brought to bear on the role of Stewart and the audience response to it. For example, like Campion, Neill's interest in his own colonial heritage as a white (pakeha) New Zealander, his political sensitivity, his intelligence as an actor and his capacity to convey the right mixture of vulnerability and repressed anger made him an apt choice for the role of the handsome and awkward, buttoned up nineteenth-century colonial landowner.

Harvey Keitel as George Baines

There was a mixed response to Keitel's performance as the lover, Baines, and this may have been related to preconceptions of Keitel's own image through numerous Hollywood films. When *The Piano* was released, Keitel was best known for his image as a macho and rather tortured moody star, and for his tough roles in violent films. For example, in the same year as *The Piano,* Keitel took on roles in *Reservoir Dogs* (1993) and *The Bad Lieutenant* (1993), which could not be more different to the role of Baines in *The Piano.* Keitel's Hollywood film career took off alongside Robert De Niro in Martin Scorsese's *Mean Streets* (1973). Since then, his film roles have included the pimp in *Taxi Driver* (1976), Judas in *The Last Temptation of Christ* (1986) and the sympathetic cop in *Thelma and Louise* (1991) and a gangster in *Sister Act* (1992). In interviews, Keitel likes to remind us that he is an 'actor' not a 'star' and his repertoire has in fact been broad and varied, including less known international art-house films (Clinch, 1993: 28). The film critic David Thomson believes that

> Keitel's face carries burdens of resentment, mistrust, coldness intractability, selfishness, stubborn wilfulness and unalloyed solitary meanness of spirit without which he would not, could not, be the remarkable actor he is today.
>
> (1993: 20)

Both De Niro and Keitel are actors of the Method school, but journalists argue that they differ in the ways they use it in their performances. Mackenzie suggests that 'Method is a catholic, and whereas De Niro uses it to transform his entire body and become somebody else, Keitel 'transforms himself from the inside', and works with his character in an interactive way, merging part of the character he is playing with himself (1999: 10). Some detect a masochism in the lengths Keitel is willing to go in order to expose aspects of himself for the part he is playing (Mackenzie, 1999: 10) and Thomson has discussed the self-sacrificial aspect of Keitel's acting method: 'He gives himself to the screen helplessly. It is his one streak of generosity' (1993: 20).

In publicity terms, statements such as these also reinforce the public myth of Keitel's psychological depth and emotional integrity and create an aura that helps to shape the spectator's response to Keitel as Baines on the screen. Keitel's ability to combine in his acting a particular macho (active) quality of emotional fearlessness, alongside a more passive and needy 'helplessness', is something that reportedly attracted Jane Campion to Keitel as an actor and she has called him her 'muse' (Mackenzie, 1999: 10). For Campion, Keitel manages to combine the 'physical, very masculine' qualities of traditional male heroes with a gentleness that audiences rarely get to see in Keitel's films (Andrews, 1993a: 26). Campion had no doubts about his suitability for the role of Baines and is recorded as saying that the character is a 'female fantasy projection of a man, animal and yet sensitive' (Mackenzie, 1999: 10).

In order to explore further the emotional impact of Neill and Keitel's roles within the film's jealousy narrative, it is necessary to turn to questions of representation and the meanings and emotions that are evoked through the aesthetic qualities of the film text.

The jealous *mise-en-scène:* the otherness of the film's landscape

The *mise-en-scène* of *The Piano* provides an evocative setting for the triangular dramas that are enacted on the screen. This includes Nyman's eerie and minimalistic piano score, which was based on a Scottish folk tune (to evoke Ada's Scottish background) and was played by Holly Hunter, who reportedly is an accomplished piano player (Johnston, 1993: 56). In a discussion of the costumes, Bruzzi (1995) explores the way that the characters' clothes work as extensions of their characters. For example, Ada's clothes are used to seduce, and yet the hooped structures and stays of her dress and petticoats also work as a form of protection, guarding her against unwanted attention. Baines's minimal attire signifies his sexual freedom and the marks on his face also convey that he has 'gone native', reinforcing the stereotype of his sexual otherness in relation to the 'norm' of colonial white British masculinity. By contrast, Stewart's clothes are too tight and convey his uptightness and repressed positioning within the jealous triangle.

There has been criticism that the darkly lit landscape that evokes the mysterious and increasingly tangled emotional web of the narrative, also reproduces colonial discourses that equate darkness with the 'dark forces' of sexual transgression and unconscious desire (Margolis, 2000: 25). A number of film studies writers argue that the film's dramatic *mise-en-scène* also reproduces a trite and patronizing view of the Maori people as 'exotic people' in an 'exotic landscape' (Hardy, 2000: 76). Hardy suggests that the polarity between black and white is used metaphorically throughout the film, to connote among other things, order versus disorder, clarity versus confusion, virtue versus sexual desire (Hardy, 2000: 77).[5] Dyer (1997) argues that whereas in Western colonial discourse whiteness is taken for granted and perceived as 'normal', blackness is positioned as other and different, sometimes idealized and treated as special with exotic associations, or denigrated and demonized. From this perspective, *The Piano's* jealous *mise-en-scène* contributes to a set of associations between the jealous 'stranger', illicit desire and infidelity and non-European otherness. This is particularly the case in relation to the character of Baines, whose aesthetic closeness to the Maori natives links his seemingly uncomplicated sexual freedom with the colonial trope of the seemingly uncomplicated Maori people.

One can, however, also argue that the connotations of the racialized jealous *mise-en-scène* are more complex than that. Bruzzi (1995) suggests that the colonial polarity between black and white is implicitly challenged throughout *The Piano*. She explores the way in which the taken-for-granted whiteness of the European protagonists is problematized throughout the film by accentuating or by making 'strange its presumed signification' (Bruzzi, 1995: 263). Bruzzi discusses various examples of this, as in the 'inconsistent' use of whiteness as a signifier, something that is particularly the case in relation to 'sex and sexuality'. This includes the 'unaestheticized pallor' of Ada's face, the image of whiteness as 'aggression' with its associations of 'colonial invasion', the 'potential sensuality' of the white colonial body as represented through the close-up shots of Baines and Stewart. As Bruzzi goes on to argue:

> whiteness (like the colonial master Stewart) is shown to be ineffective rather than omnipotent: the Maoris scorn Stewart for offering them buttons rather than money, and they refuse to exchange their land for blankets and guns.
>
> (Bruzzi, 1995: 263)

This complexity has implications for the representation of male jealousy, as from Bruzzi's perspective the film does not take white heterosexual masculinity as given, but instead problematizes its universality, and shows its differences and inconsistencies. Stewart's right to jealous possession is undermined, and the masquerade of phallic masculinity and its emotional costs made apparent.

Ada as an object of jealousy and exchange

The jealousies of the different protagonists occupy a central theme throughout the film and help drive the narrative along to its conclusion. Sometimes, jealousy is conveyed to audiences through the character of Flora, who is jealous firstly of Stewart and then of Baines's relationship with her mother. The male characters express their contrasting jealousies in relation to Ada and each other. When Ada first begins to play the piano on the beach as Baines looks on, she takes off her wedding ring, an act which implicates the piano and Baines in her transgressive desires. The triangular structures that underpin the relationships on screen thus also include the piano, which, as Ada's preferred object of desire, causes friction between Ada and Stewart from the moment they first meet. A major difference between Baines and Stewart is that, whereas Stewart is rivalrous with the piano, Baines identifies with it pleasurably, as the object of Ada's pleasure and desire. In contrast to the traditional scenario of active, possessive Oedipal masculinity, Baines more 'passively' wants to *be* what she desires.

The film's triangular dramas are closely bound up with the representation of the possession and exchange of goods and commodities. Ada is in effect a mail-order bride, and the film's portrayal of the colonial ownership of land and Maori servants symbolically reinforce her status in this respect.[6] Irigaray's work is applicable here, as from the beginning of the film, Ada is positioned as 'the merchandise' which gets exchanged between men within patriarchal societies (Irigaray, 1977: 105). First, her father arranges her marriage to Stewart, a man she has never met. When Stewart meets her, he treats her in the way one might a disappointing package, commenting that she looks 'stunted'. Later, without Ada's consent, Baines makes a deal with Stewart and exchanges land for Ada's piano. As part of the deal, Stewart, without Ada's consent, also lends out his wife as a piano teacher. The deal that Baines instigates with Ada, in which she exchanges her body for piano keys and ultimately the piano, has been seen by feminist writers as further illustrating Ada's exploitation within the patriarchal system described by Irigaray (Dyson, 1995; Gordon, 1996).

However, another view has been put forward, which provides a more positive reading of the bargain as a process of active and pragmatic negotiation on Ada's part. Here, it is argued that Ada is not a passive party, but largely sets the terms of the bargain and reduces the number of visits to the number of black keys. As Gillett argues:

> This man has her piano and she wants it back. But choices always do take place within certain limits. The fact that these limits are patriarchal in their nature does not necessarily equate the events that take place with rape. As uncomfortable as this may be for audiences, Ada does make a choice, a measured choice. It is possible for her to leave. Importantly, she is not powerless; even whilst she is not standing on equal ground with this partner, Ada is not conquered.
>
> (1995: 286)

Later on, as Baines becomes increasingly attached to Ada, he breaks off the bargain and returns the piano to *her* – not Stewart – something that by implication challenges the patriarchal system of exchange as defined above.

Masculinity, melodrama, and a different kind of ending

The Piano contains many of the generic features associated with melodrama. In psychoanalytic terms, the psychic narrative power of cinematic melodramas lies in the Oedipal dramas that get played out on the screen (Mulvey, 1975, 1981). It is often argued that female melodramas instead invite modes of unconscious identification associated with fantasies of the pre-Oedipal mother in which the dilemmas of separation and desire are symbolized in relation to her (Modleski, 1982). However, even when such melodramas follow a female Oedipal journey and thus challenge the heroic male narratives of classic realist texts, the endings may nevertheless result in the woman being punished and the law of the father being re-established (Mulvey, 1975). Some feminist writers have argued, in a negative vein, that Ada's narrative also follows this feminine pattern of female melodrama. For example, Stewart's jealous revenge has been cited by feminists as a symbolic castration and a feminine Oedipal lesson in accepting sexual difference and lack (Dyson, 1995; Gordon, 1996). Here it is suggested that, following her rebellious affair, Ada is punished, learns her lesson and ends up somewhat conventionally (and passively) in happy domestic bliss, married to her lover George Baines.

This negative account of Ada's journey has implications for the representation of masculine jealousies. It implies that, despite the film's apparent feminist themes, it merely ends up reinstating in traditional fashion the patriarchal law and its jealous authority.

However, the film does not end with Stewart's jealous revenge, but instead the narrative moves on to show the possibility of a different kind of settlement. Just as Ada rejects the tragic, hysterical fate of drowning with her piano, Stewart also rejects the hysterical acting out of narcissistic male jealousy, and instead acknowledges Ada's difference and lets her go. After confronting his rival with a gun, the pointlessness of his jealous actions becomes apparent to him, and the audience experiences his disillusionment. In coming to terms with the disappointments of jealous loss in this way, Stewart also conveys a sense of 'good enough jealousy' as the projections fall away from his rival and his wife. As with Ada, who breaks her symbiotic tie with the piano and finds she has the will to change her life, Stewart also learns he doesn't have to perform masculinity as it is traditionally defined. Through the film's narrative, the portrayal of Stewart's jealousy moves from voyeuristic curiosity, through jealous rage, and finally to good enough jealousy, thus enacting for us a shift from narcissism to psychic complexity.

A different vision of rivalrous masculinities

A theme of this chapter so far has been the way in which *The Piano* illustrates both the notion of heterosexual masculinity as 'difference' and its emotional complexity, which is a feature of 'good enough masculinities'. The concept of 'difference' has a number of meanings in relation to the film's depiction of male jealousy. The most obvious example of this is seen in the differences between what one critic describes as the 'rough' and illiterate lover, Baines, and the landowner husband, Stewart (French, 1993: 4). As in the study of *A Perfect Murder*, the depiction of class differences in this film symbolizes men's different emotional subjectivities and their relationship to the woman in the triangle. On the one hand, the repressed Stewart is governed by possessive material interests, on the other, Baines is depicted as the 'noble savage', closer to nature and more attuned to the otherness of Ada and her wild desires (Pihama, 2000: 126). The differences between the two men are also encoded racially. For example, the Maori tattoos on Baines's face 'mark' him as different and 'other'. As mentioned earlier, the portrayal of Baines's identification with the Maoris has been caustically received by those who argue that the role reinforces old colonial stereotypes.[7] As Pihama argues:

> The character of Baines, like those played by Daniel Day-Lewis in *The Last Of The Mohicans* (Michael Mann, 1992) and Kevin Costner in *Dances with Wolves* (Kevin Costner, 1990), is the antithesis of the uptight, colonial, controlling white man epitomized by Stuart. These characters are promoted as the consciences of white colonial society, the colonizers' 'Jiminy Cricket'.
>
> (2000: 126)

Although on the face of it, Baines and Stewart represent two very distinct types of (racially encoded) masculinity, one can argue that, at other levels, the distinction between Stewart and Baines is not as clear cut as Pihama and others suggest. For example, both characters are portrayed as having complex emotional subjectivities, which are vulnerable at various moments in the narrative. The depiction of their vulnerabilities, which contributes to the feminization of the characters, destabilizes the certainties of the jealous triangle, providing insights into the potential complexities of emotional masculinities.

For obvious reasons, there has been criticism of Baines's 'opportunism' regarding the bargain that he strikes up with Ada over her piano (Pihama, 2000: 126). As Gillett points out, watching Baines barter with Ada over the piano and her visits is 'disturbing' and 'cannot be condoned' (1995: 283). However, although Baines may have initially bought Ada's piano, and in effect Ada too, the depiction of his power is undermined in a number of ways. As discussed above, this includes Ada's active role in the negotiation of the bargain, and also Baines's eventual refusal of it. As Gillett argues, 'Contravening the Oedipal logic of desire, Baines comes to the realization that his desire crucially has the passive aim "normally" allotted to woman' (1995: 282), and this is central in marking the 'gender ambiguity' of his character. Baines's refusal provides a different imaginary space for his and Ada's relationship, beyond the binary structures of sexual difference. Baines's identification with the otherness of Ada's creativity is powerfully conveyed in the scene when he first hears Ada play, and the image of Ada and Flora's androgynous seahorse shell design on the beach, explicitly mirrors the Maori markings on his face. From the moment Baines hears her play, he listens to and identifies with her desire, and this is a crucial difference from Stewart whose narcissism, until the final scenes of the film, prevents him from 'listening' to Ada and comprehending her 'other' voice. Atwood (1998) argues that Baines has a 'listening desire', which facilitates a receptive space for the spectator to create meaning. Compared to Stewart, the character of Baines is feminized in his desire 'to be what she desires', and to identify with the source of her creativity. In contrast to Stewart's possessive voyeurism, his character evokes a pleasurable identification with her exhibitionism as a performer and as producer of music.

Baines often makes uncomfortable viewing as the object (but also the subject) of Ada's lust and desire. Dyer (1982) has argued that male nakedness on screen is rare, as the penis can never 'live up to' the fantasy of the phallus. The shots of Baines's nakedness potentially feminize him through the objectification of his body in ways more usually reserved for women. The sarcastic comments from reviewers (discussed below) perhaps testify to this. This is one of the ways in which the spectator's expectations of the jealous triangle are made less secure.

The character of Baines opens up a space for Ada, who appears to have a will of her own and is clearly a separate person to Baines and Stewart, and not merely an object of exchange between them and a projection of male fantasy.

The differences between the two men are made apparent partly because of the vulnerability that Neill's subtle and sympathetic portrayal of Stewart exudes. Stewart's repressed and ultimately violent jealous behaviour is mostly interpreted by film studies academics unproblematically, as confirming him as a violent, patriarchal bully (Dyson, 1995; Gordon, 1996). However, Neill's performance also invites a more complicated response, which at different moments includes both sympathy and revulsion. Neill is particularly skilled at using different physical mannerisms to convey Stewart's vulnerability and jealous confusion in relation to Ada and her rejection of him. These mannerisms include his hesitant body language, his fluttering eyelids, the hair that keeps falling in his eyes, and the way that he is unable to meet the eyes of those who speak to him. Neill's sensitivity to the role is summed up in his description of Stewart:

> I see Stewart as being someone who is rather vulnerable. There are certain sad things about him: loneliness. What happens to him I think, is that this hell – a carapace that Victorian men could assume, is cracked and disintegrated by the power of his feelings for Ada, leaving him very exposed. I think of him as being a man that's lost his skin.
>
> (BFI, 1993)

As with the character of Baines, Stewart is also feminized in the way the camera lingers on his body, which is lit in a sensual peach/orange light. A memorable example of this is when Ada initiates a sexual encounter with Stewart, but won't allow him to touch her. The roles are reversed and he becomes the passive object of desire, something that in contrast to Baines, Stewart appears to find intolerable. The uncomfortable feelings aroused in this scene are also echoed in the press reviews, which sympathized with Stewart, finding the adulterous Ada's active lust for her husband incomprehensible.

From the beginning of the film, Ada appears to be for Stewart an object of 'fascination and shame' (Atwood, 1998: 90). He attempts to use Ada narcissistically, as a mirror to reflect back a positive image of himself, to mask his vulnerability and lack. The early scene where Stewart goes to meet Ada for the first time and uses a portrait of her anxiously as a mirror to check his appearance and straighten his hair, provides a poignant example of this. But Ada fails to reassure and proves an ineffective mirror in this respect. Stewart's narcissistic behaviour towards Ada evokes the mirroring role assigned to women in patriarchy and suggests that Stewart is attempting in the early part of the film to masquerade his masculinity defined as heteronormative sameness, but that Ada's response to him makes this unworkable and this plunges him into his jealous rage. She has a 'will' of her own and refuses the fantasy of male ownership and the projections that underpin it. Throughout the film, this representation is reinforced by the camera's refusal of the male gaze; Ada is not glamorized in any way. Stewart's attempts to impose the male gaze are often made explicit and problematized for the spectator through the technique and *mise-en-scène* of the film, as during the wedding photo scene, where our gaze is turned back on Stewart's gazing eye through the camera lens. Stewart's jealous voyeurism is ridiculed as he stares through a crack at the couple making love, as the dog licks his hand and then a button falls on his face (Hardy, 2000: 80). There is a comic parallel between this and the earlier scene cited above, when Stewart licks his fingers to straighten his hair. Hardy notes that even his attempt to cut off her hand has a cruel comedic and clumsy element to it, as in a blind rage he only manages to cuts off half a finger instead (2000: 80).

The projection of hate and desire on to the rival and the beloved is a key element in destructive narcissistic jealous rivalries. The Freudian implication of scenarios such as these is that the narcissistic jealous subject turns the rival into a mirror on to which he can project his own fantasies of the forbidden other (Freud, 1910, 1922). In *The Piano*, the impression is given that Stewart's narcissistic anxieties about the other initially have a number of outlets in terms of their projection on to the 'exotic' body of the New Zealand landscape and its Maori inhabitants, and on to the enigmatic Ada and her body, which is forbidden to him. Once it becomes clear that Baines has made him a cuckold, Baines becomes an object of rivalry and even sexual fascination for Stewart as he watches Baines and Ada make love.[8] The effect of this is to make Stewart appear simultaneously foolish, vulnerable and bullying, which undermines further his authority as a patriarch.

Until the final scenes of the film, Stewart's actions depict his inability to acknowledge the separateness of Ada, something which, as discussed in previous chapters, more generally provides the basis of destructive male jealousy. But the film tracks the changes in Stewart's jealousy, which in the end turns out to be 'good enough'. After

Stewart's violent and foolish revenge when she lies weak and asleep in bed, he appears to be overwhelmed by sentimental feelings and sings to her like a child. At this point his actions are those of a bully who is moved by the vulnerability of the victim he has managed to cow into submission. He takes sexual advantage of the situation, but she wakes and stares intensely at him, communicating her fury and her desire to be free. For the first time, Stewart listens to her desire and decides to let her go.

The scene when Stewart goes to visit Baines with a gun is significant insofar as it provides us with an alternative vision of the ending of jealous rivalry between the two parties. At first, Stewart confronts Baines with the gun, which conforms to traditional narratives of male rivalry. But when Stewart looks into the eyes of his rival, it is as if he realizes the pointlessness of his actions and the emptiness of male rivalry and jealous possession. The shared moment when Stewart and Baines acknowledge hearing the 'unspoken' by/from Ada creates an understanding between the two men beyond narcissistic rivalry. As the projections fall away, Stewart conveys to us that 'his enemy is not his enemy after all' (Hardy, 2000: 81). Baines is no longer a threat, Stewart no longer hates him and he just wants to be free.

I have argued that a component of 'good enough' jealous behaviour is the capacity to experience loss without resorting to omnipotent, narcissistic strategies to maintain possession. Stewart tries to assert his authority and fails, and consequently acknowledges the myth and 'illusion' of patriarchal masculinity (Hardy, 2000: 82). An important message of the film appears to be that only when Stewart acknowledges her difference and listens to her can he let her go (Atwood, 1998). The recognition of her separateness also frees him from the jealous doubts and narcissistic anxieties that have plagued him, and which have coloured his violent behaviour to her.

Images of masculinity, jealousy and otherness: the press response

The Piano received an enormous amount of international attention from both popular and academic critics.[9] Gender, jealousy, emotional repression and erotic passion are the recurring themes in the press reviews. The reviewers also use the Freudian discourse of 'repression' to analyse the underlying psychological tensions of character and plot.[10] Davenport's review is typical in the way it cites the film's 'hidden influence of a certain Dr. Freud':

Strange certainly, to sniff out old Sigmund's trail in the muddy tracks of the colonial New Zealand ... Her means of self expression, the piano, is more than a musical substitute for her lost voice or a safe outlet for inner intensity of feeling.

(1993a: 20)

Popular and academic reviews cite positively the powerful portrayal of the central character Ada and her psychological and emotional journey, which is central to the film's narrative.[11] The appeal of the film for female spectators, and the emotional tones of the reviews, can also be explained psychoanalytically, in terms of the film's associations with the pre-Oedipal, feminine psychic register. Ada's non-verbal, yet very assertive physical methods of communication (through her piano and her sign language) have been analysed in terms of the film's evocation of the semiotic and the maternal body (Irigaray, 1985; Kristeva, 1974).[12]

However, as mentioned earlier, the evocation of the feminine other in *The Piano* is also accompanied by the possibility of another kind of masculinity, mainly through what Atwood (1998) has identified as a non-possessive 'listening desire' on the part of the 'hero' Baines. The notion of the active 'feminine' reader in this instance goes beyond identifying with Ada's feminine otherness, as it also includes the pleasures and anxieties of identifying with a different, less possessive kind of masculinity, as identified in the earlier chapters. The concept of the feminine reader does not necessarily exclude men. Instead, it implies that the text in question opens up spaces for responses in the reader that can be characterized as 'feminine', precisely because of its openness and the unconscious fluidity between the semiotic and symbolic psychic registers and their associated modes of identification. Many of the male reviewers were also ecstatic about the film and the following is a good example:

The Piano is about disorientation. But more, it's about emotional free-fall; about the fateful plunge we humans go on willingly risking – in music, sex, passion, in almost every profound human transaction – from first diffident address to ultimate self-offering or self immolation.

(Andrews, 1993b: 21)[13]

It should be said that there was not universal critical praise for *The Piano* in the UK press reviews, and some dismissed the film as pretentious and overly melodramatic: '*The Piano* is a faux literary film for people who haven't read a book since leaving university' (Norman,

1994: 12). In contrast to the positive reviews cited earlier, which find the film's feminine and feminist themes exciting, anxieties about the film's excesses reflect, perhaps, a deeper set of anxieties about the other and irrational femininity. These same critical reviews are more sympathetic to Stewart's jealous plight than to the characters of Ada and Baines (Tookey, 1993: 40–1). Although Stewart's jealous revenge is universally recognized as violent and shocking, there is criticism that the husband was not jealous enough and his lack of 'suspiciousness over the affair is implausible' (Walker, 1993: 41).

This unease about the representation of the husband is suggestive of the potential difficulties for the spectator when witnessing the humiliating spectacle of the cuckolded husband. Neill's portrayal of Stewart is an extraordinary mixture of shyness and repressed, confused anger. It may be that, for some, Neill conveys a vulnerability that is difficult to watch. There is a widespread sympathy in the reviews for the character of Stewart, and some are critical of Ada's character and her irrational and unrealistic demands upon him regarding her piano:

> My problem with Ada – and I don't think it's because I am a man – is that I found her not sensitive but hard, not spunky but passive. It seems grossly anachronistic that a woman of her era would not feel some gratitude to a man who has given her and her daughter a new life.
>
> (Tookey, 1993: 40–1)

The shamelessness of the adulterous Ada and the image of her treating her husband as a sex object proves too much for this reviewer, who writes disparagingly about the way in which the men appear 'like marionettes under the control of a whimsical puppet-mistress' (Tookey, 1993: 40–1).

The sympathy for Stewart is largely related to Neill's performance and may also have been reinforced by his star profile as discussed earlier. Derek Malcolm's review is typical in its praise of Neill's performance:

> Neill too has seldom been better as the husband, as stiffly furious with his own vulnerable insufficiency, as with his wife's adultery and her ensuing treatment of him as an object once her desire has been fired.
>
> (1993: 4)

In contrast to the universal praise that Neill receives for his performance (alongside a sympathy for the character's role as the cuckolded husband), there is a mixed reaction from the press in relation to the performance of Harvey Keitel as Baines. There is praise (particularly from female journalists) for Keitel's erotic, if unconventional, portrayal of Ada's lover (see Francke, 1993a: 224–5). Some male journalists also find his interpretation of the role convincing: '[Keitel as Baines] has an unrelenting greedy stare, a brutalized yearning that is incredibly powerful' (Thomson, 1993: 20).[14] In terms of Baines's role in the triangle, many reviewers believe that he had not manipulated Ada in an overly exploitative manner, but instead, that she was the forceful figure in the triangle.

However, some journalists are more sceptical about the casting of Keitel for the part of Baines and find him to be an unconvincing lover. Most criticisms are related to perceptions of Keitel's crude Scottish accent, together with an embarrassment about his Maori markings and his apparent readiness to take off his clothes: 'Harvey Keitel seems completely out of his depth: his accent, along with the little girl's, seem to alter from scene to scene' (Tookey, 1993: 41).[15] For some, it is odd, not to say inexplicable that Ada would fall for what one critic calls (in an ironic vein) 'this rough and illiterate fellow' (French, 1993: 4). Another comments on the 'strangeness' and ill-defined nature of his character (Malcolm, 1993: 4). This may be partly due to the problems of Keitel's performance, but it may be that much of this criticism is also because he doesn't measure up to more traditional masculine images of the heroic or wicked lover. The binary discourse of the 'primitive' versus 'civilized' is often used unproblematically in reviews to describe the romantic appeal (or not) of Keitel's portrayal of 'the near savage' Baines (Davies, 1993: 44–5). For some reviewers, the strangeness of Baines's masculinity is related to the depiction of his 'going native with his Maori face tattoos' (French, 1993: 4). This reflects the film's problematic mode of address in relation to 'race' and colonialism more generally.

Conclusion

The Piano provides alternative narrative and aesthetic strategies for representing masculine jealousies to mass audiences at the cinema. The film is partly a sexual and a colonial allegory, and the film's subtext is also enriched through its reference to European fairy tales such as *Blue Beard* and *Red Riding Hood*. As Atwood points out, 'the beastliness' of the men in these fairy stories who 'mete out punishment' to the women are rarely 'problematized or questioned ... husbands must be obeyed and wolves are simply wolfish' (1998: 90). But in the case of *The Piano*, the woman ceases to be positioned as the projected object of shame and male lack. As the mock Bluebeard figure, Stewart's authority loses its mystique and his jealous voyeurism is ridiculed and made explicit. Ada survives Bluebeard's chopping block and does not dissolve into the sea like the Little Mermaid.

The film evokes a number of feminist issues related to the heroine Ada and the feminized portrayal of Baines and Stewart. However, as a number of film scholars have argued, the film is often more successful in its portrayal of gender than of Maori subjectivities and colonial relations. The progressive aspects of the film's depiction of gender and sexual difference contrasts with those such as *The End of The Affair,* where the more feelingful and reflexive representations of the male protagonists are represented at the expense of the female characters who are often marginalized or punished for their adultery. For example, in the *End of The Affair,* the two men achieve a way of tolerating a less rivalrous, more ambiguous relationship with each other (but not with God) at the expense of the enigmatic Sarah. Destructive rivalry is about the inability to live with not knowing and uncertainty, and in both the *End of the Affair* and *The Piano,* the jealous protagonists struggle with rivalry and come closer to less destructive solutions for dealing with it. However, in *The End of the Affair,* the heroine has to die for this to happen, whereas in *The Piano* Ada finds a different kind of ending for herself.

Some feminist scholars imply that the story would have been more transgressive had Ada died at sea with her piano. But perhaps this betrays an overly possessive view of her on the part of these writers, who want her to resist the patriarchal forces of the symbolic and view the ending as a kind of feminist 'cop-out'. Instead, Ada's narrative continues, but in an ambiguous vein. To disapprove of the ending is to deny, perhaps, the possibility of an alternative kind of settlement between the parties concerned and also the potential differences implicit in heterosexual masculinity. As Gillett argues, *The Piano* illustrates that heterosexual masculinities are not 'substitutable' and that one husband is not necessarily the same as another (1995: 281). Ada may have settled for a different vision of Oedipal domesticity with Baines, one within which she can learn to speak. But this vision is not divorced from the unconscious pre-Oedipal forces of the piano, which she revisits at night:

> it's a weird lullaby so it is, but it is mine. There is a silence where hath no sound. There is a silence where no sound may be in the cold grave under the deep sea.
>
> (Ada, *The Piano*)

9
Unfaithful: A Tale of Female Infidelity and the Jealousy of a Good Husband (*A. Lyne, USA/France, 2002*)

Introduction

Unfaithful (2002) is a Hollywood erotic thriller that depicts the emotional and moral dilemmas of a husband who responds jealously to his wife's adulterous affair. The film is based on Claude Chabrol's 1968 film *La Femme Infidèle* ('The Unfaithful Wife')[1] and was directed by Adrian Lyne, the director of the 1987 film *Fatal Attraction*. Just as *Fatal Attraction* pushed a number of cultural buttons in the 1980s about the dangers of marital infidelity, this film also captures a number of contemporary anxieties about the sexual politics of the family, marital fidelity and the loss of faith in the traditional model of the bourgeois nuclear family.[2] As one reviewer put it: 'Lyne [provides a] contemporary exploration of bourgeois adultery and its consequences in the Noughties' (Norman, 2002: 55).

As in *Fatal Attraction* (1987), the theme of the family and the betrayal of its members through marital infidelity provide the main focus for *Unfaithful*.[3] In Lyne's earlier film, the husband (Michael Douglas) was the adulterous character and the jealousy belonged to the now infamous figure of the 'bunny-boiler' mistress played by Glenn Close. In *Unfaithful*, however, the gender of the jealous characters changes, as it is the wife, 'Connie' (Diane Lane),[4] who has the affair with 'Paul' (Oliver Martinez) and it is the husband, 'Edward' (Richard Gere), who experiences the jealousy. In this respect, the film can be said to adopt a somewhat liberal 'take' on the dilemmas of modern marriage and the frustrations for women of settling for the middle-class dream of bourgeois family life. Nevertheless, the representation of the wife's affair and the husband's jealousy in *Unfaithful* is in many ways politically ambiguous and is arguably more conservative than it might first appear. For example, the threat to the family is not depicted as being related to the murderous instincts of the jealous husband, but rather to the wife's wayward sexuality. Thus, as with *Fatal Attraction*, it is the unruliness of female desire that is shown as posing the greatest threat to the stability of the family.

This chapter focuses on *Unfaithful* to explore the themes of sexual fidelity and the fantasy of the virtuous jealous husband and father who may, as with Edward in *Unfaithful*, find himself at the mercy of forces beyond his emotional control. I argue that the jealous dilemmas of the husband represented in this film also symbolize a broader set of cultural anxieties about the loss of paternal authority within the family, where competing definitions of what it means to be a husband and father struggle for hegemonic dominance. This hegemonic struggle is also linked to a conservative desire to recuperate cultural spaces made by feminism, and to present a version of femininity that is ultimately non-threatening for male spectators and the male gaze. In contrast to the other film case studies in the book, this chapter gives greater consideration to the feminine object of desire and jealousy, the wife and mother, Connie. Given that masculinity and femininity are shaped in relation to one another, the projections regarding the feminine figure of the unfaithful wife pictured in this film can tell us about fantasies of masculine jealousy and anxieties about the perceived loss of paternal authority and the fragmentation of the nuclear family as a Western ideal.

The chapter begins by discussing the film's director Adrian Lyne, whose significance lies in his track record of directing films that have caught the public mood and which have evoked popular controversy as a consequence.

The contradictions of Adrian Lyne: an *auteur* on the themes of sex, love and betrayal

Interviews with Lyne indicate that he is a very determined, 'hands-on' opinionated director, whose intentions played a considerable role in the shaping of *Unfaithful* as a finished product. As the film's producer points out, by the end of the film 'we had all been Adrian-ized' (Brown, 2002). In his account of the film's directorial process, Gere (2002) states: 'Adrian's very clear about what he wants ... no, he's not very clear, he's more bulldog-like. He just bites down and shakes it till he gets what he wants'. Yet, despite the rather macho connotations of this approach on set, Lyne says that he is interested in making films about 'the small picture', the domain of triangular relationships and family melodrama:[5]

> I've never really wanted to make *Robocop* or, I don't know, films involving hardware. I've always been interested in relationships and, in particular, people on the edge – and that's often expressed sexually.
>
> (Delingpole, 1998: 1)

Lyne is a British director who began his career in advertising and then in the 1980s and 1990s went on to make a number of commercially successful Hollywood films, in which psychological drama and sexual relationships played a central part. His films have often been the subject of controversy and whilst attracting large audiences, have been less well received by critics who tend to see his work as carrying the sensationalist and superficial values of advertising: 'he is a trickster who is all style and no substance' (Bygrave, 1987: 11). Lyne has also been accused of misogyny for his clichéd portrayal of women in so-called 'raunchy' sex scenes',[6] capturing the power-obsessed image of the 1980s and early 1990s in films such as *91/2 Weeks* (1986), *Fatal Attraction* (1987) and *Indecent Proposal* (1993) and also for providing an uncritically sexualized portrayal of the young Lolita in his 1997 adaptation of Nabokov's book.[7]

Journalists argue that his films show a particular preoccupation with the themes of 'sex, power and betrayal' (Macaulay, 2002: 18). Jealousy and adultery are key themes in two of his most well known films *Fatal Attraction* and *Indecent Proposal*, and *Unfaithful* perhaps works as the third film in a trilogy in that respect. Critics of Lyne point to the non-too-subtle way that his films preach a certain kind of reactionary morality that reinforces the myth of the American dream embodied through the perfect image of the happy nuclear family (Craving, 2002: 138). The moral message of these films arguably serves as a warning that adultery and the betrayal of one's family come at a price. In *Fatal Attraction*, the price of the husband's adultery was the murderous jealousy of the unhinged mistress; in *Indecent Proposal*, the price of the wife's infidelity for money was literally one million dollars and the potential destruction of a marriage; and in *Unfaithful*, the wife's infidelity leads to the husband taking jealous revenge with disastrous consequences for all parties concerned.

If a recurring theme of those films is the danger posed to the family by adultery, then another is the danger of female sexuality, and also, as in *Fatal Attraction*, the fearful and pathological nature of female jealousy, thereby invoking, if in a contemporary guise, the traditional patriarchal values of the sexual and emotional double standard for men and women.[8] Thus, despite the explicit eroticism of Lyne's films, a moral pattern emerges, which promotes the romantic image of the family under siege from dangerous feminine forces.[9] The latter can be found in the guise of the 'bunny-boiler' mistress played by Glenn Close in *Fatal Attraction*; in *Indecent Proposal*, it is the wife who, like Eve in the Garden of Eden, succumbs to temptation and sleeps with Robert Redford's character for a million dollars and in *Unfaithful*, it is the wife who becomes obsessed with a younger man.

As already mentioned, the moral contradictions of Lyne's films have not gone un-noticed by critics; yet in contrast to his previous films, *Unfaithful* is more positively received in the press as a departure from the sensationalism of his earlier work:

> For years Lyne was a classic unrepentant commercials director: over-lighting, over art-directing ... *Unfaithful* still has its visually arch moments – the newspapers swirling around Lane during her fateful first encounter, the fetishistic close-ups of kitchen-ware – but mostly Lyne is trying to observe the grey areas of real life.
>
> (Macaulay, 2002: 18)

Inspired by Chabrol's (1968) film *La Femme Infidèle*, Lyne nurtured the idea of making *Unfaithful* for a number of years (Lyne, 2002). The plot and story-line of the contemporary version clearly hold many similarities to *La Femme Infidèle* and are influenced by it. In this respect, whilst *Unfaithful* borrows from the tradition of French art-house cinema and so potentially points to its mixed status as a cross-over picture, much of its content, economic backing and promotion arguably classify it as a mainstream Hollywood film. However, the focus on the woman's sexuality and the ambivalence of her feelings for her role as a wife, invoke a more complicated picture of female sexuality than is often the case in Hollywood cinema. As one journalist argues, *Unfaithful* 'offers both the titillation of upscale soft-core sex and the cleansing serious-ness of high-minded drama' (Macaulay, 2002: 18).

There is general agreement amongst critics that *La Femme Infidèle* is a cinematic 'masterpiece' (Time Out, 2002: 379) and so in artistic terms is a hard act to follow. *La Femme Infidèle* does not focus on the wife's point of view and the details of her affair, but rather on the jealous husband, whose murder of the rival is carried out with a seemingly cold ruthlessness that recalls Hitchcock's *Dial M for Murder* (1954) and also the tradition of French existential cinema. Lyne's film clearly wishes to acknowledge the debt owed to the original. However, whilst containing the predictable, stylized, melodramatic tropes that we have come to expect of Lyne's work, *Unfaithful* is also more sexualized than the original, focusing more on the emotional and erotic details of the wife's affair. *La Femme Infidèle* was based on Flaubert's novel *Madam Bovary* (1857), although in contrast to the centrality of the heroine in that book, Chabrol's narrative focuses more on the husband and his story of morbid jealousy.[10]

By contrast, Lyne restores the centrality of the female figure to the forefront of his film, depicting her dissatisfaction with life as the bourgeois wife and mother. Another major difference between the two films is that in *La Femme Infidèle*, the ending is left more uncertain and ambiguous than in Lyne's, and hints that the husband may get away with the murder and continue to live out the life of the dutiful husband and father, thus exposing in a cynical and witty fashion the hypocrisy of bourgeois family life. However, as I discuss later, this is not the case in *Unfaithful*, as the underpinning morality of the film demands that the family must pay in some way for the murder of the wife's lover. In order to do this, Lyne includes an extra scene at the end of the film, giving greater emphasis to the moral dilemma faced by the couple as they wait undecided in the car outside the police station.

There is also a marked difference in the image of the husband in the two films, as Michel Bouquet's plump, formal appearance in the 1968 film contrasts with that of Richard Gere, who, despite playing against type in this instance, inevitably carries for audiences the aura or memory of his former 'playboy' image as a sex symbol. As Lyne points out: 'I'd always associated him with a kind of swagger ... and we did everything to avoid what he'd been before' (2002). Interestingly, it is reported that Lyne was so keen to provide an alternative image of Gere as the respectable, homely cuckold that he kept sending 'cookies and ice-cream' over to Gere with instructions to grow more 'podgy' for the role. Unsurprisingly perhaps for a man famed for his narcissism and physical self-control, Gere refused, 'did the opposite and worked out' instead (Wenn, 2006).

It is fascinating that a stand-off between the two men is constructed in the press through Lyne's apparent insistence in positioning Gere as the dull, disempowered cuckolded middle-aged husband, thus extending the rivalrous dynamics of the jealousy narrative beyond the film text itself, to the sphere of publicity and the consumption of film reviews. Gere's public image as a star has attracted much attention over the years and it clearly played a role in the promotion of the film. Given this significance, I now turn to the relationship between the construction of Gere as a star and his role as the cuckolded husband in *Unfaithful*.

Richard Gere, from playboy to family man: a jealous hero for the post-Clinton/Blairite era

> This is Gere's Picture after all; anyone who thinks otherwise might care to note a credit sequence that includes a costumer for Mr. Gere, make-up artist for Mr. Gere and hairstylist for Mr. Gere, but none for his leading lady.
>
> (Kerr, 2002: 45)

When *Unfaithful* was released, the role of the cuckolded husband was not one usually linked with Richard Gere. For many, his identity as a film star was still closely associated with his many film roles as the lover (for example, in *An Officer And a Gentleman* (1982) and *Pretty Woman* (1990)) and with his desirability as a narcissistic sex object, first established through films such as *American Gigolo* (1980) and *Breathless* (1983). Despite taking on those roles, Gere has always been keen to distance himself from the trivializing connotations of his physical glamour, and has developed a reputation as a moody, humourless interviewee, something that has not endeared him to journalists.[11] Like Lyne, then, Gere has a poor relationship with the press and, as with that director, he also made his name in the 1980s, where the focus on his body and his preening, narcissistic self-awareness in films such as *American Gigolo* appeared to capture the *zeitgeist* of that image-conscious decade.[12] Quotations from the tabloid press in the 1980s remind us how popular he was when he first emerged as the new Hollywood heartthrob:

> They call him King Of The Kissers. He is tall, dark and handsome ... he's made the girls gasp again.
>
> (Grosz, 1983: 14)

> He has a mixture of sexuality and vulnerability that's rare ... He has all the devastating magnetism of a new Valentino.
>
> (Churcher, 1983: 20)

The 'mixture of sexuality and vulnerability' cited in reviews provides a clue as to his appeal for many women, who, if some female reviewers are to be believed, want to mother him: 'Women don't just want to go to bed with him, they want to be his mother or his sister' (Churcher: 1983:

20). According to reports, Gere has always been uncomfortable with the feminized connotations of his image and clearly, he was – and is – also an object of desire for men too, as endless descriptions from male reviewers of his physical fascination imply: 'Pretty Man: Vain, taut, edgy, sexually aggressive, unforgettable in bed' (Leith, 1998: 4). His concern about the rumours about his sexuality led to the infamous denial in the papers about the break-up of his marriage to the supermodel Cindy Crawford: 'We are heterosexual and monogamous and take our commitment to each other very seriously' (Macaulay, 2001: 16).[13]

As if to counter the cultural associations of superficiality associated with his feminized identity as a sex object, Gere has been keen to emphasize the notion of his cultural awareness and emotional integrity. The latter is central to Gere's current mode of masculinity and also provides the key as to why the jealousy of his character in *Unfaithful* evoked sympathy from audiences. The idea that Gere has hidden emotional and cultural depths is a recurring theme of his interviews, together with his much publicized commitment to Buddhism,[14] Gere tells us he is a man who takes himself and his (method) acting seriously: 'An Actor is like a puppet; they are the same word in Hindi. It's a licence to be, to feel. Emotions are my oil paintings' (Gere, 2001: 5).[15]

Such a stance complements the development of his acting style, which over the years has increasingly conveyed a serious, 'taut' physicality, which is meant perhaps to mask a tortured soul hidden underneath (Leith, 1998: 4).[16] It is said that Gere's performances on screen are often characterized by periods 'of being motionless' and then 'quick, intense bursts of activity' – as for example – when suddenly making love or eating (Lane, 2002: 35), which perhaps is meant to convey to audiences a sense of emotional spontaneity and the authenticity of his engagement with the drama of existential forces beyond his control. All these qualities are brought to bear in his role as the husband in *Unfaithful*, where his performance contains the physical trademarks of what has so far been discussed, including the appearance of a serious and thoughtful stillness, as the husband with a repressed emotional life, linked perhaps to the apparent suddenness of his jealous response.

The construction of Gere's public persona through films and surrounding publicity clearly has implications for issues of spectatorship, and for the sympathetic identification with Gere's character of the jealous husband. As we have seen, Gere's image has developed considerably from his roles in the early stages of his career, when he was the strutting, feminized narcissistic object of desire for men and women. Through films such as *Pretty Woman*, and literally in *First Knight* (1995) (as Lancelot), his image took on the heroic connotations of the handsome knight in shining armour with emotional and moral integrity. More recently he has sought to emphasize his heterosexual credentials as a happily married family man: 'I'm a normal family guy myself' (Gere, 2002), 'I want to put my son to sleep and kiss my wife goodnight' (Pearce, 2003: 21). The discovery of Gere as the good father and husband makes it less surprising, then, that he was cast in the role of the apparently decent, but jealous husband and father in *Unfaithful*.

One can detect another similarity with Lyne through Gere's ethical stance to life and the development of his moral, public persona as a caring family man. This stance regarding the moral importance of the traditional family has implications for the depiction of jealousy in the film and its relationship to its moral stance regarding the jealous protection and sanctity of the family as the American Dream. In *Unfaithful*, Gere's public persona and role as the husband converge to produce a fantasy of masculinity that fits well for a post-Clinton/Blairite era, where decent, white, liberal-minded men raise families and strive for material comfort through hard work, but who may find themselves at the mercy of forces beyond their control.[17] Interestingly, a journalist spotted Gere's potential as the family man in 1997 when Blair was first elected:

> ... think *Pretty Woman*, Gere as an ambitious man in a suit, poised for huge upheaval, all serious intent. It's obvious to me: Tony Blair the movie.
>
> (Richards, 1997: 16)

Gere's model of masculinity has thus shifted from a feminized sexual object of desire in the 1970s and 1980s, to one today that is more in line with the law of the father – albeit with a moral and social conscience and a Blairite desire to change the world in the face of dangerous forces. Interestingly, as I go on to discuss, the danger in *Unfaithful* is symbolized through the guise of the wife's failed domestic femininity and wayward sexual desires.

Contemporary dilemmas of a good husband and father and the protection of the family

> I gave everything for this family ... you threw everything away – for what?
>
> (Edward to Connie in *Unfaithful*)

Gere's performance as Edward, the cuckolded husband and father in *Unfaithful*, should be seen in the light of recent anxieties about the fragmentation of the family in Europe and post-Clinton America. As discussed in Chapter 1, social, political and cultural changes have contributed to what some have defined as a Western 'crisis of masculinity'. Whether or not such changes, largely associated with the economic and social shifts of a post-industrial and globalized economy, actually constitute a 'crisis' has been the subject of much debate in sociology and cultural studies (Bainbridge and Yates, 2005; Segal, 1990). However one defines such social and cultural shifts and their consequences for the construction of masculinity and the lives of men (and there is agreement that some kind of shift has occurred), the *perception* of a crisis is evident in the proliferation of popular and academic discourses that have emerged around the so-called 'problem' of masculinity.

Throughout the 1990s and early 2000s, the family and, in particular, the emotive symbol of the beleaguered husband and father, have become a nexus for such anxieties and have been most forcefully articulated by an international fathers' rights movement. Threatened by social and economic developments, the gains made by feminism and the perceived loss of male authority in the home, they utilize what Collier (1996) has defined as a 'father-rights discourse' to construct a particular idealized image of familial masculinity as represented through the image of the hardworking family man who is both the breadwinner and a responsible father. Today, however, from the perspective of father-rights discourse, this model of the good father has been eroded, as men are increasingly at the mercy of hostile social and political factors over which they have little say.

The notion of 'father-rights' may sound rather extreme and reactionary in its nostalgia for a lost patriarchal authority within the family. Yet the anxieties that underpin its demands also resonate with much popular discussion of masculinity and fatherhood in the media and its representation in popular culture. To return a moment to the figure of Tony Blair and the liberal, chino-panted model of masculinity he represents, we can see that it is inextricably bound up with the notion of fatherhood as breadwinner and 'hands-on' fatherhood.[18] Today, just as politics is as much to do with marketing as its policies, voters in the United Kingdom are appealed to as members of 'hard-working families' and masculinity is defined in terms of being a 'good father' (Patterson, 2006: 16).[19] The ubiquity of images of fatherhood can also be found in the press, as in the marketing of 'Father's Day', where alongside numerous websites about 'fatherhood',[20] the topic of 'How To Be A

Great Dad' can even be found on the covers of special supplements attached to more 'serious' UK broadsheets (Anon, 2006: 1–5).

The ideology of 'Christian family values' is of course not confined to Europe and the United Kingdom,[21] but is perhaps most clearly exemplified through the US image of the hardworking family as the aspirational lynchpin of the American Dream, This relationship was satirized in the film *American Beauty* (1999), where the pointlessness of working long tedious hours for consumer goods one no longer wants or needs and the hollowness of a marriage built on that desire was explored.[22] The image presented in that film invoked the description of the American men in Faludi's book *Stiffed* (1999), whose role as husband and father have been undermined by consumerism and changed patterns of employment against a post-industrial landscape.

Discourses about the role of the husband often converge with those that articulate a backlash against the gains made by feminism within popular culture, and thus underline the significance of father-rights discourses and related representations regarding the loss of paternal control and possession for the preservation of hegemonic masculinity. As Collier (1996) argues, the construction of masculinity which underpins the notion of the 'good father and husband' within father-rights discourse is predicated upon a series of binary oppositions, in which masculinity is constructed through the 'disavowal of the feminine other'. This construction is linked to 'an incipient anti-feminism' and the perception that a loss of male authority within the family has occurred in conjunction with a loss of control over women's sexuality within the home (Collier, 1996: 19). Collier argues that a primary concern of fathers' rights organizations throughout the 1990s was 'the men's legal rights in relation to women, children and property ... what is sought is greater authority *over* relationships with women and children, not a qualitative shift in these relationships *per* se'.[23]

Representations of the father and the changing role of the husband within contemporary family life have been a recurring theme of films throughout the late twentieth and early twenty-first centuries. *Kramer Versus Kramer* (1979) is often cited as an early example of father-rights discourse being played out in the movies. Throughout the late 1980s and 1990s, representations of fathers played a significant role in signalling the arrival of 'new' caring masculinities (Jeffords, 1993). In films such as *The Full Monty* (1997), mothers were often marginalized or represented as inadequate and second best in relation to the sensitive new father. The backlash against mothers and feminism can be explained as a narcissistic fantasy of families without mothers, and even signals an envious desire to colonize the maternal role. One can apply the feminist post-Kleinian work of Maguire (1995) and Minsky (1998) to argue that such hostility towards mothers also signifies an unconscious envy of the feminine capacity to give birth in the first place.

A more overt example of this envious hostility towards mothers and their legal parental rights are the rightwing 'pro-family' men's groups in the United States and the United Kingdom. Perhaps what lies at the root of such groups is a longing for the restoration of the good father and the sense of containment that such a fantasy represents in an uncertain world.[24] However, part of that wish for the good father may also be the desire for the restoration of a sense of entitlement that, in the eyes of some, has been eroded over the years in the face of feminist demands. Given such anxieties, the jealousy of the beleaguered husband and father can be seen as a reactionary wish to jealously guard what's his against the forces of the late modern world, where the familial rules of entitlement are less certain. In the United States (and in Hollywood cinema), the fantasy of the family as the bulwark of the American Dream becomes a symbolic arena where wider national struggles and anxieties about identity, difference and otherness may be mirrored and tested. The American Dream has been defined as the belief that 'just by working hard enough, you can make it' (Harwood, 1997: 16). An essential part of this aspiration or belief is to observe the moral codes of family and nation. Against a post-9/11 backdrop, where Western liberal values of reason and tolerance have been tested,[25] the jealous fear engendered by the fantasy of the rivalrous interloper takes on a particular symbolic significance in this context.

Unfaithful is a film about the precariousness of the nuclear family and the instability of gendered family relations and parenthood within the late modern world as seen from the male point of view discussed above. *Unfaithful* was marketed as an erotic 'psychological thriller', but its focus on family relationships and the home draws on some of the generic conventions associated with family melodramas. The latter are characterized by the depiction of heightened emotions and Oedipal drama, and often reproduce in symbolic form, through the lenses of family relationships and the domestic setting, the social and political dramas of society more generally (Rodowick, 1982). Following on from this, one can see that *Unfaithful*, with its themes of feminine betrayal and beleaguered masculinity, provides an apt case study to explore further the depiction of masculine jealousy and its relationship to fatherhood and the precariousness of family life.

To explore the film's meaning in more depth, it is necessary to turn from the film's *context*, to the film's *text* and its systems of representation, which include its aesthetic pleasures and its conscious and unconscious modes of address.

The *mise-en-scène* of jealousy and the collapse of family boundaries

Edward: She likes it here?
Paul: More exciting than the suburbs I guess

Throughout the film, the fragility of the bourgeois family as a symbol of the American Dream is apparent. The idealized model of the Western nuclear family which emerged in the nineteenth century traditionally rested upon a gendered split between the private and the public spheres, between the domestic, feminized world of home and the masculine territory of the city and of paid work. The sexual double standard was linked to the division of these two spheres, an arrangement that was not only about men being able to have extra-marital sex; it also rested on an emotional division of experience based on the understanding that the wife should repress any feelings of jealousy (as in the long-suffering wife in *Fatal Attraction*).[26] However, in *Unfaithful*, it is the wife who commits adultery and the rational, respectable husband who tries to curb his feelings of irrational jealousy.

The tensions of this situation and the collapse of the gendered boundaries that previously defined roles and relations of the family are evoked throughout the film's *mise-en-scène*. The film begins with a montage of images (a huge white suburban house, gardens and lake, a boat, a bike, wind-chimes, a shutter banging and a dog) that are meant to signify the so-called 'ordinariness of everyday family life' (Gere, 2002).[27] The scarlet letters of the film's title then alerts us, by way of contrast, to the themes of infidelity and sexual betrayal that are to come. The montage of idealized affluent family images continues as the film progresses and we are introduced to Edward, Connie and their 8-year-old son, Charlie, as they get ready to leave for work and school. The family montage, with its stereotypical associations of the two spheres described above, is reinforced through the image of her waving goodbye at the window within the affluent 'safe' leafy suburban setting that contrasts with the urban location of her affair. Issues of race and ethnicity may not seem immediately relevant to the analysis of this film, yet as Dyer (1997) reminds us, that is because whiteness in

Western culture is so taken for granted. In *Unfaithful*, the image of safety conjured up by the family home is overwhelmingly white, from the light- and cream-coloured furnishings of the house to the people themselves who, with the exception of the black maid, are also white. The contrast between the calm lightness of the home and the darkly lit environment of the warehouse apartment where they make love reinforces the connotations of the colonial duality of black and white, linking it to the otherness of Connie's sexual desire beyond the domestic sphere.

As in the film *A Perfect Murder*, Connie's adulterous affair takes place in Paul's bohemian warehouse apartment in New York. His Frenchness (his Gallic accent, his looks and lifestyle) conveys, in a rather clichéd way, the exotic nature of her encounter with something 'other' that provides an escape from the boredom and safety of her suburban American life. Perhaps the mutual political animosity between France and the United States is meant to add an extra frisson to the depiction of the affair and the symbolism of Pauls's transgressive status as Connie's lover. The warehouse signals, again in a somewhat clichéd fashion, a fantasy of French 'old Europe' with antique Eastern carpets, bendy tulips in a vase, French books and intriguing sculptures and *objets d'art*. The scene of his flat depicts a land without trainers, computers and modern coffee-makers, in which ridiculously handsome men (like Paul) with their black floppy hair wear tweed coats and Guernsey jumpers, drink red wine and smoke copiously in between making love. The Gallic theme (perhaps with conscious reference to the film's French origins in *La Femme Infidèle*) is signalled throughout the film via the tinkley background piano music in the style of the French composer Eric Satie. There is also the lovers' visit to a Jacques Tati film, and the understated 'chic' style of Connie herself (often seen wearing a cream mackintosh), which is meant to convey the 'look' of French film stars. The muted lighting in Paul's apartment further reinforces this sense of 'the old world', a land which, in this romantic vision, is somehow closer to nature – and therefore to the 'natural' forces of jealous passion, because it has yet to be flattened and rationalized by the forces of modernity. Even the café they visit across the street appears French and sells cigarettes.

The two spheres of Connie's world (the suburban home and the transgressive sphere of Paul's warehouse apartment in town) are mediated by a third space which is depicted as the potentially hostile world 'outside', and which exists between those two locations. It is represented as the journey from the home to Paul's apartment and as the hostility of the weather outside her front door and outside Paul's apartment in the windy New York street. The train journey home after she first makes love with Paul was much commented on by reviewers, who enjoyed watching her recall her memories of making love. The Freudian connotations of the train as a phallic object are fairly obvious. However, one can also read that journey as symbolizing an erotic liminal me/not-me space and the pleasures of being engulfed by pre-Oedipal forces beyond one's control. Throughout the film, the wind is a recurring motif of chaos and danger and reminds us in a none-too-subtle way of the external and internal forces that may exist beyond our control. We first encounter the wind in the opening scene when Edward and Charlie leave the house for work and school, signalling the danger of the world beyond her front door and cueing us as to what will happen next. The wind is also largely responsible for Connie's first meeting with Paul outside his apartment, when they literally blow into each other.[28]

As discussed earlier, the psychological investment in the two spheres of family life has played a key role in the hegemonic preservation of a patriarchal familial ideal and the cultural divisions of gender.[29] In anthropological terms, they are associated perhaps with the symbolic values of the sacred and the profane and thus should be kept apart at all costs. The precariousness of maintaining the fiction of that division is represented as throughout it, the separateness of the two worlds becomes increasingly harder to maintain. This occurs when Connie bumps into friends from her suburban life, when visiting Paul, and when she forgets to pick up her child from school. Eventually the two worlds collide when Edward goes to visit Paul. The chaos of that collision is once more symbolized through the motif of the wind, through the glass globe of the Windy City (a tourist souvenir from Chicago) that Edward finds in Paul's flat and uses to kill Paul. It later transpires that Edward gave Connie the globe as a present and so, like Connie, it belongs at 'home'. In giving the snow globe to her lover, the separation between the two spheres collapses and Edward presumably feels a loss of control; he is emotionally overwhelmed by a form of morbid jealousy and feels compelled to act to resolve the contradiction. Later, when Edward dumps Paul's body in the landfill site, the wind blows again, evoking chaos as birds circle above them, and we see the old scraps of rubbish and plastic bags stuck to a fence that is falling down, giving the appearance of the torn sails of a shipwreck or broken borders of a battlefield.

The implication of that scene is that Edward, Paul's murderer, is also a victim, albeit one of circumstance and morbid jealousy. To explore the implications of this further, the chapter now turns to the film's depiction of choice and ethics in relation to jealousy and gender.

The sexual politics of blame and jealousy as an innate condition

> *Connie*: I think this is a mistake.
> *Paul*: There is no such thing as a mistake. Only what you do and don't do.
> *Connie*: Tell me what you did.
> *Edward*: You tell me what *you* did.

The moral culpability of the characters has already been touched on in relation to the sexuality morality of Adrian Lyne's films. The latter would seem to resonate with the recurring generic trope of melodramas, in which the transgressive, strong female character is usually punished in some way for her sins. Melodramas have historically placed strong female heroines at the centre of their narratives (Gledhill, 1987). The first half of *Unfaithful* follows in that tradition as we watch the progression of Connie's affair with Paul. However, the melodramatic narrative switches to the husband Edward as he appears increasingly marginalized by his wife and attempts to claw back his place within his wife's heart, thereby reflecting fantasies of the role of the displaced husband within society more generally.

As Edward's jealous suspicion develops, the film's narrative point of view moves from wife to husband, and this narrative fluidity is reflected in the film's sexual politics of blame, which becomes more ambiguous, as the ending makes clear. According to Lyne (BFI, 2002), the film is driven by Connie's adultery and Edward's wish for revenge. The morality of the characters and the sexual politics of blame are symbolized through the choices they make or don't make.[30] Whereas Connie is shown as impulsive, actively choosing to follow her instinctual desires, her husband is represented as passive, measured and slow to act, yet when he does so, the results are catastrophic, as he appears to react to emotional forces beyond his control. The lover is depicted as romantically innocent, lives in the moment and, like a child, appears to bear no responsibility for anything. In each case, then, they theoretically have choices, but cannot make them because in different ways, they become governed by their passions.

The discourse of innate passion is there in interviews with Lyne and Gere when talking about the motivations of the jealous husband. The wrongness of the husband's jealous revenge is not condemned by them, as, according to Gere (2002): 'we all have impulses ... the dark side can take over.' The film's director Lyne (2002) also had this in mind:

> I think all of us have a breaking point, where we could potentially be pushed over the edge. What does it take to bring us that far? ... This is a story in which it may actually be easier for the audience to forgive a murderer than an adulteress, which is insane of course!

The alleged sympathy for the husband may be 'insane', but one can also locate such sentiments both generically within the cinematic tradition of melodrama where the women is punished for transgressing the law (of male jealous possession), and also in Connie's taboo status as a bad mother. As discussed earlier, one can see the fantasy of the bad wife and mother represented through the discourse of father-rights. As a backlash phenomenon, this is arguably related to a profound fear and envy of women in an increasingly feminized society, where the fantasy of male loss may be matched by the perception of feminine entitlement and sense of 'having it all' (Yates, 2000). Whilst this may provide an extreme example of misogyny in action, it may nevertheless articulate concerns that find expression in films such as *Unfaithful* and in culture more generally. Such anxieties evoke fantasies of the engulfing mother, whose danger and otherness have their roots in very early pre-Oedipal projections and psychical defence mechanisms discussed by the psychoanalyst, Melanie Klein.[31]

A recurring theme of this book has been that whilst femininity has historically been constructed as the cultural and psychical other of masculinity, those binary divisions are now less certain. The collapse of the old boundaries has produced new possibilities for men and women and also new spaces for the production of fantasy and the creation of less reactive modes of masculinity and femininity. Fears, determined by the return of the (repressed) bad phallic mother, can be seen in this light.[32] They also resonate with the tone of moral indignation expressed by Lyne regarding Connie's betrayal of her family: 'The idea that this supposedly happily-married woman with a child should go and have an affair with this man is horrifying' (BFI, 2002). Connie's implied status as the 'bad mother' is reinforced through scenes which show her draped over the naked Paul in various states of disarray, surrounded by all the classic signifiers of debauchery including over-spilling ashtrays, half-drunk glasses of red wine, low lighting and the unmade bed. The latter is then contrasted with the image of her son Charlie, sitting on the steps outside his school, waiting to be picked up by his mother who has forgotten all about him. The scene when Connie meets her women friends in a café reinforces this cautionary message of the perils of infidelity, as one of the women tells how her greatest regret was cheating on her husband.

Throughout the film, Connie's culpability in the jealous murder of Paul is reinforced by the choices she is seen to make in order to actively pursue her love affair; from refusing the taxi so she can visit Paul's flat, to then calling him up and her final reluctance to end the affair.[33] When Connie does finally end it, the film allows her no credit for finally making the 'right' choice. The wish-fulfilment scene at the end of the film, when Connie imagines getting into a cab instead of agreeing to going upstairs with Paul to his flat, reinforces the old myth that women are governed by their desires and can only dream of doing 'the right thing'.[34] Edward hears Connie's tearful message ending the affair on the answer machine after he has killed her lover, thus reinforcing his helplessness in the face of her actions, emphasizing the pointlessness of his jealous murder. The implication appears to be that whilst it was Connie's choice to begin the affair and then seemingly end it at whim, Edward, in the classic manner of the helpless cuckold, can only react, thus possibly evoking further sympathy for his predicament.

Jealous bodies and the incestuous mother

> *Edward*: I can't do this
> *Paul*: What?
> *Edward*: I don't feel well.

The dilemmas of the sexual triangle are inscribed through the bodies of the three main protagonists. Connie's body is very expressive and there are numerous shots of her body quivering with guilty pleasure and desire, thus connoting in a fairly stereotypical romantic fashion the instinctive, feminine basis of her actions and desires and also her closeness to nature.[35] The contrasting nature of Connie and Edward's jealous responses are instructive as to the gendered depiction of jealousy in popular cinema. Her jealousy of Paul's new girlfriend provokes an immediate, furious, irrational, emotional response from her, which contrasts with her husband's slow-burning jealous response to the knowledge of her affair.

As discussed earlier, Gere was encouraged to change his body language, to play down his usual swagger and adopt what he sees as a more 'normal', 'everyman' quality to his appearance (Gere, 2002). The body of the rival, Paul, is clearly more handsome, lively and expressive in this film than that of the husband Edward, thereby reinforcing the victim status of Gere's character as the cuckolded husband. Edward's body becomes more expressive only when his emotions get the better of him and he murders the rival. But even the murder is presented in the manner of a sudden illness and as an unexpected shocking response to forces beyond his volition. This powerlessness is reinforced by Edward's glasses, which give him a slightly helpless quality and, interestingly, become tinged with a green light from the moment he goes to confront Paul.

The child-like qualities of the two men are also emphasized at different points in the film, which has the effect of reinforcing Connie's maternal role in relation to each of them. There is something powerless and even childish about Gere in this film when his actions are mirrored by shots of the son doing similar playful gestures and movements, as in the first scene when Edward and Charlie leave the house. However, it is the youthful lover, Paul, who is depicted as the most childlike and innocent and is very much positioned as the 'younger man' in relation to Connie.[36] Scenes of Connie laughing and joking with Paul are also interspersed with those of Connie playing with her son. Edward comments on his youth when he first meets him, when he gasps in amazement: 'How old are you?' Later, when he confronts Connie with the knowledge of her affair, he exclaims: 'you threw everything away – for what? He's a ... kid!' The implication here is that Connie has been doing something particularly taboo, perverse even, evoking erotic Oedipal fantasies of the bad incestuous mother who shares her love with both father and son (see Freud, 1910). Freud and, later, Seidenberg (1952) argue such jealousy may be underpinned by the pleasures of imagining the (maternal) love object with the other man, who in narcissistic fantasy represents the jealous subject as a small boy, triumphing over the powerful father. The voyeuristic pleasures of this imaginary scenario, which, of course, recalls the 'primal scene', also have implications for the pleasures of spectatorship, as the spectator's gaze is able to identify in a mobile fashion, with the different characters and fantasies enacted on the screen (Cowie, 1984). For some, such fantasies may also be influenced by the pleasure of seeing Richard Gere, the former sex symbol, being superseded by the handsome Oliver Martinez, as the current object of desire.

However, the ambivalent nature of desire means that such fantasies are also accompanied by the un-pleasures of loss and wounded narcissism.

The snow globe that gets exchanged between Edward and Connie and then Connie and Paul also symbolizes the carelessness with which Connie shares her love and, as discussed earlier, provides an important clue as to why Edward's jealousy emerges with such force. From the psychoanalytic perspective of Klein (1957), the snow globe represents the maternal breast, which is the object of desire for the pre-Oedipal child, and must be possessed at all costs. When Edward restores the globe back to their home, it is as if the rights of possession have been restored, the third party has been removed and Connie and he are reunited once more.[37]

Oedipal rivalry of father and son

The implied culpability of Connie in provoking Edward's murderous jealousy displaces our attention from the rivalrous context of the two men and the jealous fantasies that are stirred up in that scenario. As we have seen, Edward defines Paul as a 'kid', thus, from a psychoanalytic perspective, Edward becomes positioned as the father who fights with his son for the possession of the mother. The jealous aggression experienced by fathers towards their sons is a recurring theme of sociological and clinical case studies (Baumgart, 1990; Day Sclater and Yates, 1999). When considering the Oedipus complex and its implications for jealous rivalry, classical psychoanalysis has focused less on the murderous feelings of the father than on the son's (Freud, 1913). Benjamin (1990: 143–4) traces this omission back to Freud, who in his later formulations of the Oedipus complex focuses more on the murderous feelings of the son (Oedipus) towards his father (Laius) than vice versa. However, in his earlier work, Freud points to the inherent rivalry and aggression experienced by the father towards the son, who he knows one day will inevitably surpass him (1900: 290).

The individual and cultural idealization of the father as a defensive hegemonic mechanism against the fear of such aggression can also be seen in this light. Arguably, the displacement of guilt on to the woman through cinematic narratives such as *Unfaithful* provides an example of these hegemonic strategies in action, where such images work in a historically specific way to preserve the myth of the good husband and father as a cultural ideal at a time where such ideals are apparently under threat.[38]

As discussed in earlier chapters, such hegemonic struggles over the meanings of masculinity and, in particular, masculine jealousy may also be expressed beyond the film text, in the post-cinematic context of film reviews and the chapter now turns to that sphere of analysis.

The press response to *Unfaithful*: disappointment at the 'lack-lustre' cuckold

The press response to *Unfaithful* was mixed. In contrast to Lyne's previous films, some critics are quite complimentary about it:

> It's long been fashionable to deride Lyne's films for being both exploitative and ... morally reactionary. What's harder to fault is the care he lavishes on their design, which here at least, is a lot more than glossy. His images are as precise and thoughtful in their relevance to action and character as they are seductive in their own right.
>
> (Robey, 2002: 23)

Yet despite such praise, there is the familiar criticism of Lyne as a director who continues to reproduce in this film the values of advertising (Nathan, 2002: 12) and there are unfavourable comparisons made between Lyne and Chabrol, the director of *La Femme Infidèle*:

> Chabrol was (still is, at 73) the coolest, most formal *Nouvelle Vague* director. Lyne, on the other hand, is a gifted filmmaker, who learnt (in Keats's phrase) to load every rift with ore during the great days of television commercials, and his picture is somewhat cluttered.
>
> (French, 2002: 7)

The unfavourable comparisons to Chabrol imply that despite the film's pretensions as a cross-over film containing both French art-house and populist elements, the latter won out to the detriment of the film as a whole. Nevertheless, it is also widely agreed that the ambiguity of the characters do not conform to populist Hollywood stereotypes. This is not necessarily seen as a good thing by those who showed irritation about what they perceived to be Gere's 'lack-lustre' performance as the cuckolded husband. Such reviews imply that Gere's model of the hesitant, ordinary and vulnerable husband do not allow for the usual pleasures associated with the Hollywood model of active, vengeful masculine jealousy.[39]

As we have seen, in the film text of *Unfaithful*, the hegemonic struggle to defend the moral authority and cultural idealization of the father is expressed by the projection and displacement of anxiety onto the feminine object of desire (Connie). However, such hegemonic strategies are not reproduced in the press as reviewers universally praise the performance of Diane Lane and show sympathy for the dilemmas of her character 'Connie' (Nathan, 2002: 12).[40] Instead, many express considerable frustration with the 'passive', 'Spock-like detachment' of Gere's character 'Edward', who fails to live up to the ideal of the good husband and father (Kerr, 2002: 45). Whilst some critics appear to enjoy seeing Gere's character humiliated by his wife's infidelity (reflecting, perhaps, their dislike of the star more generally), they nevertheless express the un-pleasures of watching the 'wearily disconnected' performance of Gere as the 'hapless cuckold' who needed to act sooner to stop his wife's infidelity (Andrews, 2002: 20). Such criticism, is not only related to a dislike of Gere's performance, but to the passivity of his character Edward, whose inaction (until the murder) as the cuckolded husband is too uncomfortable to watch and appears to signal his failure as a model of familial masculinity.

Unsurprisingly, perhaps, the difficulty of identifying with the cuckold's dilemma is gendered; the female critics are far more positive about Gere and his character and also the film as a whole. For example instead of criticizing Edward's apparent procrastination in the face of his wife's infidelity, this journalist argues:

> He loves Connie too much to confront her: we see a decent agonized man, rendered almost creepily vulnerable by his need for his wife.
>
> (McCartney, 2002: 9)

Another highlights the un-pleasurable aspects of the film for male spectators:

> Women will most certainly dig the story and the arty sex scenes, while men will likely be too disturbed by the tables turned a bit.
>
> (Shiware, 2002: 9)

It may be then, that whilst Lyne's film fails to match the existential complexities of Chabrol's 1968 'masterpiece', he may – possibly despite himself – have succeeded in 'turning the tables' of the sexual double standard within Hollywood depictions of the family through a vision of the male cuckold as flawed, vulnerable and uncomfortable to watch.

Conclusion: family fictions, jealous loss and the lack of a happy ending

Unfaithful is a film about the precariousness of the Western nuclear family and marital relationships at a time when the old fictions of family stability are unravelling. This loss of faith, which is related to the social and political realities of social change, is also linked to the collapse of the cultural binary divisions of gender that once defined the gendered boundaries of the family and psychosocial family relations. Such changes have undermined the symbolism of the husband and father as a flawed ideal. This awareness is also linked to an acknowledgment of the fallibility of the myth of paternal authority more generally. Against this backdrop, competing definitions of masculinity within the family struggle for hegemonic dominance in different spheres of popular culture and, as ever, the resulting picture is complex and contradictory. Alongside the model of the liberal, enlightened father and husband, there is also a more reactionary model that seeks to re-establish the old essentialist binary oppositions of patriarchal masculinity and define itself in opposition to femininity. An important aspect of the latter is often the fascination and distrust of the 'other' and of feminine sexuality, including the notion of same-sex relationships as taboo. As Collier (1996: 31) and others remind us, research has shown that such anxieties are often expressed through fears of the 'engulfing phallic woman' who cannot be trusted or controlled sexually, and the 'unruly mother' who puts her own needs before those of the children. The controlling, fearful elements of this second model of the husband and father have clear implications for fantasies of masculine jealousy, based on a distrust of the other and a refusal to acknowledge the differences that come with social change.

Elements of both models of fatherhood identified above (reactionary and good enough) are represented in *Unfaithful* through the character of Edward. This chapter began by citing Lyne's earlier film *Fatal Attraction* and its status as a metaphor for 1980s anxieties about the threat to the family through AIDS, and also the powerful, feminist career woman as symbolized by the predatory phallic female mistress. Whereas Glenn Close's bunny-boiler evoked cries of 'kill the bitch' from audiences (Harwood, 1997: 2), Richard Gere's jealous murder in *Unfaithful* was, given the circumstances, depicted as reasonable and as an understandable jealous response to forces beyond his control. The roles may have been reversed since *Fatal Attraction*, but it is still the woman who is depicted as threatening the stability of the marital home.

However, as the reviews of the film imply, the desire to identify with narcissistic fantasies of the possessive husband are undermined by aspects of Gere's performance as Edward, whose vulnerability and awkwardness as the cuckold challenges more romantic and reactionary images of the wounded, jealous husband and thus attracts a less sympathetic identification from some male critics. From a critical perspective, such a response has potentially positive implications for issues of spectatorship and the forms of fantasy opened up by the film's narrative and mode of address. For example, the ambiguous ending does not provide the pleasures of closure that one might expect from a Hollywood film and its open-endedness does potentially create space within the film's mode of address for audiences to work through the psychological and ethical dilemmas of Edward's jealous revenge. However, the representation of jealousy and its psycho-cultural mode of address are not 'good enough', as the guilt appears to be projected back to the wife who in the end must carry it for both of them.

The ambiguity of the film's ending also has implications for what the film says about the family and its relationship to society and the fantasy of the American Dream. As discussed earlier, *Unfaithful*, with its emphasis on powerful family relationships, contains generic elements associated with family melodrama, including its function to symbolize social and cultural anxieties more generally. In the past, melodramas have been characterized by a utopian 'modernist' belief in progress and the future, one that would be passed on to the next generation through the male line (Harwood, 1997: 142). Male jealousy narratives, which imply the threat of a cuckoo in the nest, clearly test this fantasy more than any other and show the potentially precarious nature of patriarchal inheritance and its preservation through those means.[41] Harwood argues that in such films, children are meant to have a 'redemptive quality', as symbols of a better future (1997: 142). However, in *Unfaithful*, the son 'Charlie' is unable to resolve the contradictions and failures of his parents. When at the end of the film they debate their predicament and whisper in hushed, emotional tones about escaping to Mexico, Charlie lies asleep in the back of the car. His presence functions to underscore the significance of Connie and Edward's roles as parents and guarantees that they will make every effort to preserve the fantasy of their relationship as a symbol of the American Dream. Yet, Charlie's vulnerability also symbolizes their failure to look after him and do the right thing. Unfaithful to each other and unsure what to do next, their moral predicament also signals, perhaps, the failure of the American Dream to keep this couple, and others like them, safe.

10
Conclusion: Towards an Understanding of Masculinity, Jealousy and Cinema

The psycho-cultural shaping of masculinity and jealousy

A central question of this book is whether there has been a cultural shift away from narcissistic formations in favour of what might be called 'good enough' modes of masculinity, which are less defensive and better able to cope with emotional loss and the complexities of difference. Chapter 1 set the scene for those discussions by examining the alleged 'feminization' of society. That chapter presented the case that a shift is occurring in Western societies that is undermining dominant modes of hegemonic masculinity and the sense of patriarchal entitlement that underpinned it. Not surprisingly, the cultural response has been mixed. The idea that Western societies are increasingly 'feminized' has given rise to cultural anxieties for those who regard it as a negative development, inscribing a male loss as the cause of a crisis of identity for men. Such fears may be regarded as a backlash against feminism, or even as a cultural repudiation of difference and the otherness of femininity. But there have also been contrary responses which allow for the creation of less defensive and more reflexive states of mind, and thus for less rigid spaces for new masculinities to emerge.

In order to explore these contrasting aspects of cultural change in more detail, I identified two broad categories of masculinity that can be seen as 'ideal types', occupying opposite ends of a theoretical spectrum. 'Reactive' masculinities, defined as rigid, narcissistic and overly defensive, were contrasted with a reading of 'good enough' masculinities as connoting a reflexive capacity for deconstruction, and an ability to cope with psychic complexity and difference. Both positions are theoretical constructs and the duality implied by such a model should not obscure the continuities between the two extremes. Such continuities

164

were illustrated in the film case studies in Chapters 5 to 9, where the ambiguities and contradictions of contemporary masculinities were discussed in detail.

Psychoanalytic theory, with its emphasis on the conflictual nature of subjectivity and fantasy, is useful to explore the relationship between masculinity and jealousy today. Yet, in the past, male jealousy has largely been taken for granted within psychoanalytic theory, and women have tended to receive the most attention as the 'jealous sex' (Freud, 1933; Jones, 1929).[1] When male jealousy has been addressed, it has tended to be encoded as feminine, and derided as a hysterical feminized condition (Jones, 1929; Mullen, 1991). As Mitchell (2000) argues, such a strategy stems from a desire to mask male loss and vulnerability, and may result in the projection of jealousy on to women, who are perceived as hysterical and overly possessive. In addressing male jealousy, one aim of this book has been to challenge such projections, to turn the gaze away from the 'problem' of femininity, towards the 'problem' of masculinity and its jealous insecurities.

Chapter 2 explored the psychical relationship between jealousy and masculinity using three models. Two psychoanalytic models suggested a defensively driven relationship between male subjectivity and the unconscious, linked either to the pre-Oedipal mother or to the fearful castrating father. Such masculinities are most likely to be accompanied by envious, paranoid and narcissistic jealousies. These narcissistic models of jealous masculinity can be placed at the reactive end of the reactive/ good enough spectrum of masculinities. They imply that the subject is unable to tolerate emotional ambivalence and instead is likely to respond in an overly defensive, rigid manner to the uncertainties of contemporary culture.

The third model of masculine jealousy provides a less pathologizing reading of the relationship between jealousy and masculinity. The concept of a 'good enough' masculinity, as built upon multiple identifications with the Oedipal couple, presents a less persecutory understanding of ordinary male jealousy in contemporary society. Developing the ideas of Bollas (1992), which draw on the insights of Freud, Klein and Winnicott, it is possible to imagine the possibilities for less rigid and more reflexive forms of masculinity, which are less split and where possession of the desired object is less destructively driven. This third model of 'good enough' jealousy is not theorized idealistically as a sign of romantic love, but rather the term acknowledges the precariousness of 'normal' everyday jealous feelings as always resting ambivalently between love, the impulse for possession and the wish to ward off loss.

The place of masculine jealousy in contemporary culture

The sense of loss which underscores the experience of jealousy and its related fantasies resonates more broadly with descriptions of late modern culture, which has been characterized in terms of risk and the experience of uncertainty.[2] Theories of subjectivity and culture agree that the kind of psyche needed to handle the contradictions of late modernity and to live creatively with its tensions is one that can live with paradox and emotional ambivalence (Elliott, 1996; Yates, 2000).[3] The emotional capacity to cope with ambivalence and the differences that constitute the world of object relations provide a litmus test for how one is able to cope with the contradictions and uncertainties of late modernity more generally. As jealousy involves *both* love and hate, it tests this capacity more than any other emotion.

One can relate the changing cultural fortunes of male jealousy to the anti-jealousy discourses in Western societies that have emerged over the last 200 years (Stearns, 1989). The alleged demise in the social acceptability of male jealousy may, particularly in the latter half of the twentieth century, be linked to the 'crisis of masculinity' more generally, and several researchers have drawn attention to the anti-jealousy discourses of masculinity that pervade contemporary culture (Stenner, 1992; Van Sommers, 1988). Just as there has been a plurality of responses in popular culture to the supposed 'crisis' in masculinity, so also are the popular discourses around jealousy mixed, a situation that undoubtedly reflects the contradictions of contemporary masculinities more generally. Films and the extra-textual media and publicity that surround them provide a good yardstick of such shifts in popular values, as my film analyses have made clear. The film case studies illustrate that representations of jealousy contain elements of both these anti- and pro-jealousy positions.

The unfashionable status of male jealousy which gained ground, particularly in the latter half of the twentieth century, is related largely to the feminist critique of patriarchal masculinity. Another contributing factor was the Western counterculture of the 1960s and 1970s, which promoted the notion of individual personal rights and the importance of sexual freedom (Mullen, 1991). The desire of some men, past and present, to adopt alternative, less possessive attitudes than their fathers, can be seen in that politically progressive context (Segal, 1990). Yet, the adoption of anti-jealousy discourses can also be linked to the individualism of consumer culture, and may also signal a refusal to acknowledge the experience of loss and emotional dependency that often accompany jealous feelings (Lasch, 1979).[4] Whilst for some men, expressions of jealousy imply a shameful form of (feminine) weakness, it would seem that real incidences of destructive male jealousy might actually be on the increase.[5]

The phenomenon of stalking, which contains many of the possessive and voyeuristic traits of jealous behaviour, has also become an increasingly common feature of contemporary social and cultural life (Nicol, 2006). Nicol links this to the rise of celebrity culture, where the boundaries between self and other are continually erased and a sense of 'artificial intimacy' is created in the contemporary media through celebrity magazines such as *Heat* and *Closer*. Nicol relates the overly possessive attitudes of the infatuated stalker to the 'unrealistic' portrayal of love in popular culture, where the persistent male lover, who won't take 'no' for an answer is finally rewarded with the adoration of the woman concerned. Citing films such as *Pretty Woman* (1990) and *Il Postino* (1994), where the narrative of masculine rescue take place, Nicol argues that such images contradict the actual shift in the social codes of courting and sexual behaviour today, where obsessive pursuit of a man or woman is often read in less romantic terms as harassment. Yet films such as *Sleeping With The Enemy* (1991) and more recently *Enduring Love* (2004) provide examples of critical interpretations of the stalker, where its mode of address allows for sympathetic identification with the victim.

Noting that most stalkers are male and their victims female, Nicol cites the rise of new technology where, as in the film *A Perfect Murder*, it enables the jealous subject to track the movements of his victim in ways that were unavailable previously. Thus, just as the expression of jealous behaviour has become more socially taboo, the opportunity to pursue the fantasy of jealous possession has increased and is possibly even encouraged through the use and availability of new technology. As Stearns argues (1989), the pleasures of pornography and its widespread use in contemporary culture can also be seen as an example of the narcissistic jealous imagination at work today. Whilst there is now a widespread market for the female consumption of erotica and pornography, the dominant fantasy of the pornographic gaze still tends to be a masculine one (Frank, 2002; Green and Mort, 1996). The availability of masculine subject positions and the tendency to overlook the space of difference is also a theme in the history of jealousy where patriarchal codes of masculine entitlement have been dominant.

Jealous sensibilities and sexual difference

Questions of femininity and female jealousy have not been the focus of this book, and yet, given that masculinity has traditionally been defined in opposition to femininity, it is necessary to address the implications of the gendered duality of jealousy and jealous entitlement for masculinities and cultural change. Historically, sexual jealousy has been socially and legally sanctioned in Europe as the male prerogative and used to defend the integrity of men. Mastery over themselves and their emotions has in the past been socially, politically and culturally condoned for Western white men (Hall, 1992). The protection of property, including oneself, one's house, wife, country and empire, has long been encouraged and supported by law (Kennedy, 1993). The uproar when UK farmer Tony Martin was imprisoned for killing a 'trespasser' indicates the extent to which this set of beliefs about the right to protect one's property continues to enjoy popular support, even whilst the law seeks to place limits on the legitimate means by which this may be done (Biressi and Nunn, 2002).

Female possession has not been supported or condoned in the same way as male possession. In her discussion of the history of the male cuckold, Baumgart believes it is significant that there is no equivalent term for a deceived jealous woman (1990: 111). Women were not ridiculed in this way because they were already lacking in social status and so had nothing to legitimately jealously guard.[6] Just as women lacked the honour accorded to men, they have also been seen as 'active sources of potential dishonour' (Van Sommers, 1988: 114). God's jealous fury at Eve for her betrayal with the serpent in the Garden of Eden has served as a powerful allegory in Western culture for the weakness and corruptibility of women. Her subsequent role in the Fall of Adam provides a potent illustration of her fatal corrupting charms. In certain representations of this female archetype, the deadly *femme fatale* intentionally uses her seductive powers to corrupt men; in others, corruption is her innate state and as such invites the carnal desire of men whether she means it or not (Hughes-Hallett, 1990).

Until the late twentieth century, when concepts of emotional unhappiness received more professional attention, and were accorded more respect, female jealousy was regarded in a derisory way as 'only psychic' and pathologized as a mad, vengeful passion (Mullen, 1991).[7] Numerous representations of the destructive, jealous female in literature from *Medea* onwards testify to this (Baumgart, 1990: 111). However, the gendered double standards relating to entitlement have been challenged and have gradually changed over the years.[8] Today, the fact of female possession is less frowned upon, yet the connotations of greed and selfishness associated with female possession may still exert their influence.

From a psychoanalytic perspective, the patriarchal fear of female possession may be rooted in the psychic development of men as described in Kleinian and Object Relations psychoanalysis in terms of maternal ambivalence and fantasies of the persecutory mother (Maguire, 1995). Lacan and Freud also use the language of possession to describe the differences between the sexes and take the view that the possession or non-possession of the phallus marks out one's place as a man or a woman (Mitchell and Rose, 1982). Following Lacan, it is possible to speak of a jealous sensibility on the part of men, where the imagined possession of the fantasy phallus has played a central role in the shaping of defensive masculinities and the negation of femininity as other. Lacan refers to a phallic economy of having or being (the fantasy penis), whereby women are doomed to experience their lives from a position of lack. From this perspective of feminine non-possession, women are simply not entitled to get jealous, as they have nothing to lose in the first place (Moi, 1987).

A cultural crisis of masculinity

Yet, today, these relations of possession are changing; women are no longer 'the goods' of men (Irigaray, 1985). Instead of losing themselves in the gaze of men, they are actively looking back and daring to be jealous. As Moore reminds us, the language system has become unhinged from the 'transcendental signifier (the phallus, God, Man)', and meaning systems are refusing their fidelity to the old patriarchal order (1988: 177). This cultural shift provides the context for the development of masculine sensibilities where overly possessive jealous ways of perceiving the world and oneself might now be changing towards something more positive. Contemporary feminists have argued that in the late twentieth and early twenty-first centuries, late modernity has facilitated new cultural spaces for reflexive masculinities and a potential shift in the traditional gendered duality of emotional experience (Bainbridge and Yates, 2005; Minsky, 1998). However, the backlash to feminism and the ontological uncertainties of contemporary cultural life have also provoked a more negative defensive cultural response.

As we have seen, it is often argued that many men are finding it hard to cope with cultural and socio-economic changes, together with the shifts in gender and the changing relations of men and women (Day Sclater and Yates, 1999; Faludi, 1999). Such anxieties engendered by such changes are arguably key to the cultural crisis of masculinity, where the themes of jealousy, betrayal and the loss of possession often structure those representations of contemporary social and emotional predicaments of men. The envious fantasy that women are 'having it all' at the expense of men, appears in many guises in contemporary life (Minsky, 1998).

However, alternative images of masculinity and jealousy have also emerged which are better able to capture the emotional complexities and losses of masculinity (Bainbridge and Yates, 2005). As in the film *Brokeback Mountain* (2005), such representations challenge the old masculine subject positions, and are able to facilitate a more complicated response from spectators. In *Brokeback Mountain*, the film's mode of address allows space for the spectator to identify both with the love affair of the two men and with the jealousy of the two wives. Yet, as feminist research into contemporary cultural masculinities suggests, the depiction of emotional masculinities is too often at the expense of representations of woman, whose presence may be marginalized as a result. As with 'new fathers' (discussed in Chapter 9 in relation to the film *Unfaithful*), representations of the feelingful and nurturing 'new' man may enviously colonize the cultural space of sexual difference formerly occupied by women. Thus the image of the exaggerated suffering of the jealous man can be read as a mimicry of femininity and as a hysterical defence against loss and difference (Bainbridge and Yates, 2005; Mitchell, 2000).[9]

Representations of jealousy in mainstream cinema often reflect the cultural lack of faith in the traditional fictions and narratives of masculinity more generally (Butler, 2000; Owens, 1985). This perception of a shifting balance of power can be found in representations of masculinity and jealousy in the Hollywood cinema over the last 30 years. Masculinity is now portrayed as a more ambiguous gender category than previously, where the possessive gaze of the hero and the emotional and moral outcomes of jealous triangles are often less certain than in classic realist texts of the earlier Hollywood era. Alongside questions of representation, cinematic images of the jealous man also have implications for issues related to spectatorship and the therapeutic relationship between masculinity and affect. A psychoanalytic theme of this book has been the need to learn with emotional ambivalence and loss and the experience of watching a film may help us to do this. Narratives of certain films provide a therapeutic opportunity for the creative working through of feelings of mourning, rather than a melancholic denial of loss and its associated anxieties. Alongside the personal and psychic connotations of this for individual spectators, there are also broader cultural implications for the relationship between emotional cinematic texts and the unconscious fantasies about masculinity that circulate through society.

Such arguments can be usefully applied to the theme of masculinity in crisis. As discussed in Chapter 1, one definition of the crisis of masculinity is that it is about coming to terms with loss and a more flawed sense of itself. A film's capacity to evoke modes of identification that challenge male narcissism would seem to be a key feature of a more fundamental shift. In psychoanalytic terms, the challenge to male spectatorial narcissism implies a capacity to tolerate difference and the fallibility of the symbolic father (Cook, 1982; Neale, 1982). As we have seen, narratives of masculine jealousy are helpful to explore such themes, because wounded narcissism and the dilemmas of lack and loss often lie at the heart of male jealousy and its depiction on the screen. The ways in which spectators engage with such representations are significant, as their responses to jealousy scenarios provide a marker of their capacity to tolerate the losses of masculinity more generally.

The film *Nil by Mouth* (1997) provides an excellent, if harrowing, exploration of wounded masculinity and the repressed vulnerability that may fuel the violent bullying behaviour of the jealous husband. Shot in the mode of a realist drama with hand-held camera shots, the film depicts the most extreme, reactive forms of jealous masculinity, albeit with some hints of reparative masculine behaviour at the end. Yet, as an object of spectatorship and cultural analysis, the film's critical reading of masculinity and its depiction of the cycle of deprivation between father and son as being partly the cause of jealousy, refuses any of the narcissistic subject positions associated with more flattering and consoling interpretations of masculinity and fatherhood, as, say, in the *Full Monty*. Alongside the disturbing portrayal of domestic violence, the film's affective mode of address allows the spectator to experience both the poignant and destructive force of masculinity and its jealous fantasies in equal measure, forcing the subject to acknowledge the fallibility of the father and the costs of maternal envy.

Images of masculine jealousy and new spaces for spectatorship

The possibilities of the emergence of cultural spaces for alternative, 'good enough' images of emotional masculinities were explored through five film case studies. All the films contained images of male jealousy and so provided a means to explore the broader question regarding the potentiality of emotional masculinities today. In each case, the aims were: firstly, to examine narrative images of jealous masculinity; secondly, to explore the relationships between stardom and jealous masculinity; and thirdly, to understand the historical and cultural context and reception of those films and images of male stars, as documented through the publicity and press reviews. The case study methodology facilitated an exploration of the ways in which cultural discourses and fantasies of male jealousy were reproduced in three areas: narrative, stardom and press reviews. The focus on male stars and the fantasies engendered by their publicity, contrasts with studies that have tended to examine the star purely as a text, thereby ignoring the significance of the star for the analysis of spectatorship, fantasy and pleasure within a historical context. The attention given to the male star in the case studies also reflects the current preoccupation with celebrity and the meanings attached to public figures for any given audience.

Where possible, the cases studies were historicized to provide comparisons with earlier, or generically similar, versions of the film (as in *A Perfect Murder* and *Dial M For Murder* and *The End Of The Affair*), to construct an analysis of films and their stars and their accompanying reviews. The aim was to provide in-depth, historically layered accounts of the social, cultural and psychic dynamics of the films in question, and thus to explore the implications for changing formations of masculine jealousies in the late twentieth and early twenty-first centuries.[10]

Following the analysis of the five film case studies, what can be said about the potential in contemporary culture for representing the complexities of emotional masculinities and sexual difference, and how are these represented through masculine jealousy? Do those images of masculine jealousy suggest the emergence of new, expressive modes of emotional masculinity, which are less narcissistic, and better able to cope with loss, emotional ambivalence and the complexities of difference? Or do such images of masculine jealousy and male rivalry suggest a more defensive hegemonic response to change and otherness, where the threat of difference is dealt with through the reworking of narcissistic strategies associated with the dominant Hollywood cinema?

These questions are not simply answered, as the films analysed point to the complexities, contradictions and ambiguities of contemporary masculinities. Masculinities, it seems, retain elements of both reactive and good enough characteristics. Often, the 'progressive' aspects of the films, which included less rigid images of masculinity, were countered hegemonically in the field of consumption through the reviews. For example, in *Taxi Driver*, the film's critical message about alienated mas-

culinity and the violence of the rescue romance fantasy, is partly countered and defended against in the press by those male reviewers who,
in both 1976 and 1996, were seduced by Travis's mock-heroic narrative
of jealous chivalry.[11] Likewise, the problematization of the relationship
between history, nation and emotional masculinity in *The End of the
Affair* is countered by English reviewers who responded to threatening
aspects of the narrative by jealously defending the imagined territory
of Graham Greene for themselves.[12]

The relationship between films and their reviews in this context, suggests the value of film for an understanding of culture through reference to unconscious psychic mechanisms. The defensive psychic
processes that are stirred up when engaging with cinematic narratives
and articulated in the film reviews reflect, perhaps, both the lure of the
text and a desire to resist its pleasures. One can also apply the work of
Winnicott to emphasize that relationship as a creative therapeutic
space, where subjectivities are made and remade through the imaginative process of affective spectatorship and reflection. The writing of
reviews and the engagement of audiences with those reviews (through
the press and the Internet) invoke recent work done on the relationship between consumption of cinema and Winnicott's (1971) theory of
'transitional phenomena'.[13] They also reflect current discussions about
the therapeutic nature of contemporary culture, where new spaces of
consumption are created to work through and explore different facets
of subjectivity and its relationship to visual culture (Bainbridge and
Yates, 2007).

The 'therapeutic turn' within contemporary cultural life is fascinating when applied to the alleged feminization of masculinity and the
more emotionally expressive forms of masculinity today. Thus, alongside the complex and contradictory images of men in the films and the
engagement with those images in press reviews, the quality of emotions represented is also of interest. The portrayal of male jealousy in
the 1998 film *A Perfect Murder* provided a good example of the alleged
emotionalization of masculinity today when compared to the 1954
version *Dial M for Murder*. In many ways, Michael Douglas's image of
emotional masculinity exemplifies the recent cultural trope of masculinity in crisis, as his acting style connotes the flawed vulnerabilities
of white hegemonic masculinity. The expressive style of Douglas in his
depiction of Steven, the cuckolded husband in *A Perfect Murder*,
together with the response of the reviews, which relish his emotional
style, contrasts with the more repressed jealousy of Ray Milland in the
earlier version of the film, which at the time evoked a homophobic

response in sections of the press. In *Dial M For Murder*, one can detect parallels between the objectification of the woman and repressed homoerotic jealousy, both in the depiction of the husband played by Ray Milland and in the reviews.

Douglas's portrayal of the husband's sexuality in the modern version appears less repressed and is more emotionally expressive than Milland's. However, the melodramatic jealousy conveyed by Douglas also implies nostalgia for an earlier age of patriarchal masculinity, resonating with Jameson's critique of emotions in postmodern culture as empty pastiche (1991).[14] What is distinctive in this film is the treatment of the female object of jealousy. For example, the greater sexualization of the jealous triangle in the 1998 film and the heightened melodrama of the *mise-en-scène* are depicted at the expense of the female character played by Gwyneth Paltrow, who receives a misogynistic, envious response in the press. Despite the greater independence of her character, in comparison to the wife, played by Grace Kelly in the earlier version, she fails to evoke sympathy in the press as the female object of jealousy, and the 'progressive' aspects of her character are countered in the film by an appeal to older discourses of jealousy and the law.

One can also relate the more reactionary aspects of *A Perfect Murder's* depiction of jealousy to its generic status as a mainstream Hollywood thriller. The melodramatic representations of jealousy in *The End of The Affair* are, by contrast, not so nostalgic and more complex. As a crossover film with more art-house influences, it is able to convey a greater range of emotions in its male characters, and reflexively evoke the ugly complexities of jealousy as an ambivalent state of mind.[15] The film also shows an alternative way of imagining the resolution of jealous rivalry between the two men, which is less homoerotically repressed. However, for this to happen, and for the projections between the two men to fall away, the woman has to die: it is as if the text is unable to contain the contradictions of sexual difference.

The Piano represents an alternative reading of masculine jealousies, where the narrative opens up new spaces to imagine the plurality of masculinities and the different kinds of jealousies that may exist. This plurality disrupts the binary divisions of gender and sexual difference, which traditionally underpins hegemonic masculinity, and the contrasting images of the husband Stuart and the lover Baines illustrates the differences and sameness between masculinities. In this film the object of jealousy has a will of her own, and rejecting the traditional narrative trope of the tragic dying woman, she chooses to live instead.

The Piano thus shows the possibility of providing alternative, feminist narrative strategies for representing masculine jealousies to mass cinema audiences and a new way of imagining a good enough way of living with difference and the potential conflicts of jealousy.

As explored in earlier chapters, the representation of class, race, ethnicity and nation all play a role in the film case studies, symbolizing the differences between the male characters and the shifting positions within the hierarchy of the various jealous triangles. Nevertheless, femininity is often the central metaphor for all forms of difference represented in the film case studies, echoing Freud's (contentious) insistence on jealousy as a gendered construct. Whilst such a view is slightly problematic in the light of work in film studies that prominences other modalities of difference such as class or ethnicity in the construction of subjectivities, there is something about jealousy which invites this kind of reading.

One can see this at work in *A Perfect Murder*, where the representation of class occupies an important place in the narrative. Interestingly, however, the lover, who is a down at heel artist, does not evoke sympathy, whereas Douglas as a rich and powerful businessman does, and provides a hugely pleasurable performance as the murderous husband, thus negating our perception of him as an aging cuckold past his prime. From the perspective of the patriarchal husband, the threatening 'other' is symbolized less by the lover, and more by the economic and cultural forces of globalization which lie beyond his control. However, the wife, Emily, also becomes aligned with those global others in her job as a translator, and so it is she who most clearly signifies the greatest threat to the husband and the authoritarian jealous masculinity he represents. The danger of femininity is also a central theme in *The Piano*. The rivalrous differences between the husband and the lover are partly encoded through their relative class positions and also through Baines's identification with the Maories. Yet, ultimately, it is Ada's sexual infidelity that is portrayed as the greatest threat for the husband Stewart, and her second 'marriage' at the end of the film also goes someway towards removing that threat for Baines.

The theme of feminine sexuality is also central to the depiction of masculine jealousy in the film *Unfaithful*. A popular, liberal feminist discourse of domestic frustration informs the portrayal of the wife's desire to embark on an affair, and for half of the film the narrative belongs to her. Yet this 'progressive' aspect of the narrative is countered by the perception of her culpability in provoking the murderous jealousy of her husband. In many ways, the uncertainty and vulnerability of contemporary Western, white middle-class masculinity is exemplified through the image of Gere as the apparently well-meaning, yet hapless cuckolded husband and father. Perhaps the bewilderment of Gere's character in the face of the wife's betrayal also signals the failure of the family as symbolized through images of the American Dream, and in particular the betrayal of the good mother to protect the hegemonic status of paternal authority and all he represents for society. The failure and moral ambiguity of Gere's character is also signalled through the uneasy symbolism of the law and its capacity to bring them to justice, as Gere's character appears unable to accept responsibility for his actions. Interestingly, the weakness implied by his indecision upset Gere himself, who apparently thought the ending was 'bad Karma' (Wenn, 2006) and the same is true for the male critics who find his passivity in the face of his wife's infidelity too painful to watch. Despite the obvious pleasures of a film such as this that include the high production values of a Hollywood thriller, the challenges presented by the sight of Gere as the unhappy cuckold signal the poignancy of jealousy as a symbol of lost masculinity. The act of jealous vengeance in this film appears to stem more from an act of pathology than the traditional and romantic trope of manly revenge.

Transitional, good enough masculinities, jealousy and cultural change

A key theme of discussions in this book has been the notion that the alleged 'feminization' of culture has engendered new cultural spaces for modes of masculinity to emerge, and it is interesting to speculate upon the quality and content of such spaces. On the one hand, invoking negative descriptions of today's 'therapy culture', one can argue that they are being filled up with superficially emotive, sentimental images of masculinity which work to deny the contradictions and messiness of emotions in all their complexity (Craib, 1994; Furedi, 2004). The jealousies associated with such spaces are likely to have a hysterical, fetishistic quality, and may be used to deny the psychic losses of masculinity. The latter invokes those critiques which discuss the alleged cultural crisis of masculinity in negative terms (Butler, 2000), and suggests that late modern culture creates 'fetishistic' spaces for identification, rather than 'transitional' ones which imply movement and creativity (Bainbridge and Yates, 2005).

So far, the Hollywood depiction of masculine jealousy in the early twenty-first century has contained both fetishistic and transitional spaces, and the film *King Arthur* (2004) perhaps falls into the fetishistic end of the spectrum (Bainbridge and Yates, 2005). *King Arthur* is a reworking of the Camelot myth, which in the past involved the triangular sexual jealousies associated with courtly love and the domestic dramas of Guinevere and King Arthur's court.[16] However, the latest film adaptation is a departure from that tradition and disinvests the myth of the masculine losses associated with the jealousies of the traditional story. In this version, the chivalrous dynamics are not directly played out in relation to the woman in the domestic setting of Camelot, but rather the object of desire is symbolized in terms of the quest for 'freedom' and identity through male homosocial bonding against the enemy in battle. However, the film's depiction of jealousy contains the ambiguities of contemporary masculinities in its refusal to work with the traditional cultural tropes of male chivalry and romance. The quest for freedom and the triangular dynamics that underpin its heroic narrative can also be found in films such as *Troy* (2004). Just as in 1976, when *Taxi Driver* evoked the Vietnam War, *Troy* and *King Arthur* also reference the recent war in Iraq. However, whilst in *Taxi Driver*, Travis's desire to guard the woman jealously against the 'enemy' works ironically as a critique of heroic jealous masculinity, the hero in *King Arthur* (Clive Owen) takes himself and his identity crisis far more seriously and his role ultimately works in a more concrete fashion to reinforce a fantasy of heroic noble jealousy.

In psychoanalytic terms, the film *King Arthur* recalls the Freudian Oedipal narrative of the male hero searching for his identity. The recent jealousy narrative of the film *Basic Instinct 2* (2006), in which Sharon Stone reprises her role as the deadly *femme fatale*,[17] reflects more the fantasies of the pre-Oedipal phallic mother discussed by Melanie Klein. The film revolves around Stone's character, Catherine Tramell, who sets out to trick and entrap the psychoanalytic shrink, Michael Glass, played by David Morrissey. She sets him up as the murderer and he ends his days in a mental hospital, where she pushes him around in the grounds in his wheel chair. The last shot is of her taunting him about her victory and that his downfall was related to his male jealousy. In this reading, then, recalling the genre of *film noir* masculinity in crisis films of the 1940s and 1950s, male jealousy becomes a signifier of male lack in relation to the phallic superiority of Woman, and it is interesting that this fear is being renewed again in the contemporary climate.

In contrast to films such as *Basic Instinct 2*, however, there is, the potential for cultural spaces to emerge, in which emotional ambivalence can be tolerated, facilitating the kind of good enough jealousies described throughout this book. As discussed in earlier chapters, the latter is not a romanticization of jealousy, but rather it connotes the precariousness of emotional subjectivity, where the desire for possession coexists with the dilemmas of living with difference and the psychic complexities of object relations. It connotes a less idealized, grandiose model of gendered subjectivity and masculine fantasy, where alongside feelings of aggression and loss, the other is tolerated and held in mind. In cinematic terms, one can cite such films as *Closer* (2004), where the contrasting jealousies of both male protagonists Dan (Jude Law) and Larry (Clive Owen), represent this complex of jealous feelings, whilst their differences remind us of the plurality of masculine jealousies. The film's mode of address facilitates a complicated set of identifications for spectators as the jealous bodies of the two men promise the pleasures of narcissistic identification, yet simultaneously provide a reminder of male lack. One can argue that such contradictions have always existed in relation to Hollywood masculinities. Yet in this case, alongside the complex representations of masculinity where the certainty and pleasures of jealous possession are problematized, there is also the presence of Natalie Portman's character, Alice, the object of jealousy. Her playful and elusive femininity refuses the projections of the jealous character, Dan, thus opening up for audiences new spaces for identification and complex object relating not premised on the negation of the feminine other.

One can argue, then, that within contemporary Western culture, there is an interesting mixture of transitional and fetishistic spaces (often within the same film), and how men and masculinities are positioned in relation to these depends upon issues of context and biography. A key aspect of more positive accounts of masculinity and jealousy is the capacity to live with difference without resorting to destructive, rivalrous subject positions when faced with the complexity of the other. Such strategies have implications beyond the lived individual experience of everyday life, as they also contribute to the shaping of fantasies that circulate through culture, which in turn mediate the male subject's psychocultural sense of himself and his relationship to the world.

Appendix: Case Study Film Synopses

Taxi Driver (M. Scorsese, USA, 1976)

Taxi Driver tells the story of ex-marine, Travis Bickle (Robert De Niro), who suffers from insomnia and drives a cab at night in the most seedy areas of New York. Travis is an unhappy, social misfit who is lonely and psychologically fragile. He becomes increasingly angry at the degenerate surroundings of the city and the people who occupy the streets. We follow Travis's vision through the windscreen of his cab, one that also mirrors his increasingly psychotic and alienated state of mind. Travis becomes obsessed with the beautiful Betsy (Cybil Shepherd), a presidential campaign-worker whom he barely knows, but idealizes as he watches her at work from his cab across the street. He eventually plucks up courage to speak to her and takes her out for coffee. Later he takes her to a porn film, and she reacts angrily and rejects him. At first he cannot accept her rejection and then he grows angry and decides she is a bad person 'like all the others'. Meanwhile, Travis meets the young prostitute Iris (Jodie Foster), whom he wants to save from her pimp Sport (Harvey Keitel). Travis has an encounter with a jealous husband in the back of his cab (Martin Scorsese), who speaks of the 44 magnum gun as being the best weapon for his jealous revenge. Travis then decides to buy such a gun and he ends up buying a virtual arsenal of guns and weapons. After an unsuccessful attempt to kill the politician Pallantine, he kills Iris's pimp Sport instead and carries out his massacre of the men in Iris's house. At the end of the film, we learn that Travis has been made a hero, and Iris's father writes to thank him for returning his daughter to him. The last scene is of Betsy getting a lift and Travis now rejects her invitation to meet up again. But we are not given a happy ending with Travis driving off into the sunset. Instead, the music jars and the eyes of the jealous man appear briefly in his mirror to remind us that Travis is by no means at peace.

A Perfect Murder (A. Davis, USA, 1998)

A Perfect Murder tells the story of a ruthless and powerful businessman, Steven Taylor (Michael Douglas), who plots to kill his wife Emily Bradford Taylor (Gwyneth Paltrow). She works as a translator for the UN, and is having an affair with struggling artist David Shaw (Viggo Mortenson). Unbeknown to his wife, Steven finds out about the affair, meets David and blackmails him about his criminal past. Steven says he will tell no one if David kills his wife for a million dollars. Steven appears to be motivated by sexual jealousy and the desire to obtain her trust fund when she dies. Steven is in dire financial trouble and Emily's money would save him from bankruptcy.

David agrees to do this and at a later meeting at his palatial apartment, Steven gives him instructions on how to carry out the murder. The plan is that Steven will go to his club to play cards and will phone Emily at home from his mobile phone. In the meantime, Steven will leave a key for David who will let himself in. She will answer the phone in the kitchen, David will kill her and then leave, giving the impression of a random intruder having attacked his wife. This all goes according to plan – up to the point when Emily kills the intruder in the kitchen. When Steven returns, he discovers that the dead intruder is not David, but somebody else hired by David. The police arrive, headed by David Suchet as the American-Arab detective Mohamed Karaman. He strikes up a rapport with Emily who can speak Arabic.

David turns the tables and tries to blackmail Stephen about the murder plot, as he secretly recorded that conversation. The power struggle continues between the two men for the rest of the film. At one point, Steven tells Emily about David's criminal past and it seems that they may be reconciled. However, it gradually dawns on her that something is wrong when she finds that her key is missing. It transpires that Steven gave her key to David when planning the murder, and then when he found the body of the dead intruder, he mistakenly took the stranger's front-door key from his pocket, wrongly thinking it was Emily's, and gave it back to her. She tracks down the intruder's flat, finds that her key fits his lock and suspects that some plot has been hatched.

Steven meets David to give him his blackmail money. Steven then hides in the shower of the apartment in the train that David is to catch to Canada for his escape. David enters his carriage and with a nice Hitchcockian touch, Steven leaps out of the shower and kills him. Steven learns that David has sent Emily Steven's murder-plan instructions on a tape and hurries home to prevent Emily from playing it. However, while Steven takes a shower at home, she finds the tape and discovers her husband's plot to kill her. They fight and she shoots him dead. The sympathetic New York detective arrives to find that she has killed yet a second man in self-defence and comforts her, saying, 'What else could you do?'

Dial M For Murder (A. Hitchcock, USA, 1960)

The film takes place in one setting, the sitting-room of a Maida Vale flat in London. The husband (played by Ray Milland) is an ex-tennis player who is married to a wealthy and beautiful wife (played by Grace Kelly). She has an ex-lover visit her, and he becomes anxious that she will divorce him and that he will be left penniless. He contacts and blackmails a 'shady school chum' (Whitefait, 1954) into killing his wife. As in the modern version, he phones her up whilst she is alone in the flat, and she fights off and kills the intruder with the scissors from her sewing box. The husband then takes advantage of the situation and decides to get her hung for murder instead. He almost succeeds, as she is arrested and convicted of murder. However, at the last moment, on the eve of her execution, the Scotland Yard Inspector discovers the truth and saves her.

The End Of The Affair (N. Jordan, USA, 1999)

The film is set in London and the story moves back and forth between the years during and immediately after World War II. With one exception, when Sarah tells her side of the story, the film is narrated throughout from the point of view of the male jealous protagonist, Maurice Bendrix, in an angry diary 'of hate'. The diary is used throughout the film as a narrative device to guide us temporally and spatially back and forward between the events that take place. The diary – and the film itself – begins from the perspective of the present, and Bendrix's voice-over takes us back to the year after the end of World War II when he goes for a walk on the common. He bumps into an old acquaintance Henry, they go back to his house and he tells Bendrix that he thinks his wife Sarah is having an affair. Bendrix appears effected by Henry's jealousy and offers to go to a private detective on his behalf. Henry refuses, but Bendrix does so anyway, and later on in the film he confronts Henry with the results of what he believes to be Sarah's infidelity. In the meantime, we learn that the source of Bendrix's anxious curiosity about Sarah's infidelity is his own powerful jealousy, and this is his real reason for hiring 'Parkis', the private detective, to follow her.

Following the meeting with Henry, Bendrix's voice-over takes us back to an earlier scene in 1939, when he first meets Sarah and from then on, the film is largely taken up with their passionate and illicit love affair during the war. A bomb drops on the house where they have been making love and Bendrix is injured but survives; and Sarah mysteriously ends the affair. The portrayal of the affair is intercut with scenes of Bedrix's 'post-affair' encounter with Sarah, his visit to the detective agency and his dealings with the detective 'Parkis' and his son 'Lance'. At one point he confronts the distressed Henry with 'evidence' of his wife's infidelity and tells him of his own past love affair with Sarah. It is only when he obtains Sarah's journal/diary that both he and we are enlightened as to what has really been going on and why Sarah ended the affair. It transpires that she has not been having affairs with other men, but has taken up a committed Christian relationship with God. In the minutes immediately following what she believed to be Bendrix's fatal accident, she promised God that she would end the affair if he 'let' Bendrix live. When Bendrix did live, she was convinced that a miracle had taken place and had no choice but to keep her promise.

Following this revelation, Bendrix persuades her to leave Henry for him and they are briefly reunited as lovers in Brighton. However, Henry arrives in Brighton to tell them that following the results of the doctor's tests, Sarah only has weeks to live and together they all return to London. Henry asks Bendrix to move in with Sarah and him, which he does, and the two men nurse her until her death. Having insisted on a non-Catholic burial, Bendrix learns from Parkis that God/ Sarah is responsible for 'the miracle' of making the disfiguring birthmark on Lance's cheek disappear. For Bendrix, this perhaps is the final humiliation and evidence of God's 'cunning' in his battle to win over and convert souls. Thus by the end, Bendrix's rage is no longer aimed at Henry or Sarah, but at God for taking Sarah away from him. He refuses the 'comfort' of God and Roman Catholicism, and his final plea (to God) is just to be left alone.

The Piano (J. Campion, Australia/New Zealand, 1993)

The Piano is set in nineteenth-century colonial New Zealand. A mute Scottish woman, Ada, and her young daughter, Flora, are sent by her father to New

Zealand for an arranged marriage with a landowner, Stewart. She arrives from the rough seas with her daughter and her piano. After a night alone on the beach, Stewart and his estate manager (Baines) arrive with Maori servants to collect them. Stewart insists that they leave the piano behind and Ada is angry and upset. Later, she persuades Baines to take her and Flora back to the beach to play the piano. Baines then makes a deal with Stewart and exchanges some land for the piano on the beach. Part of the bargain is that Ada is to give Baines piano lessons. However, it transpires that he does not wish to learn to play, as instead he wants to listen to her play. Ada and Baines then strike up a new bargain (she negotiates one black note for every visit), whereby she can have her piano back if she allows him to caress her while she plays. She agrees and Flora is now told to wait outside while she visits Baines. Flora is jealous and unhappy about this.

In the meantime, Ada and Stewart are not getting on very well and sleep separately. They visit a local play (*Blue Beard*) and Baines sees Stewart and Ada holding hands and is jealous and leaves. On the next visit, Baines asks Ada to take off her clothes and lie with him. She agrees and Flora spies on them through a crack in the wall of Baines's hut. Later, Stewart punishes Flora for misbehaviour, and she tells him that Baines doesn't play the piano during his lessons. Meanwhile, Baines declares his love for Ada, he says that he wants to finish the lessons and he gives her the piano. Stewart is confused and annoyed about this, but the piano is sent back to Stewart's house.

Ada declares her love to Baines and they sleep together. Following Flora's revelations, Stewart's curiosity drives him to spy on Ada and Baines making love. Later, Stewart confronts Ada and locks her in the house and boards up the windows. Ada initiates some sensual encounters with Stewart, and later he unboards the windows and door. They hear that Baines has decided to leave the island. Ada promises Stewart that she will not visit Baines, but she breaks her promise by carving a message on a piano key and telling the reluctant Flora to take it to Baines. Flora betrays her mother by taking the key to Stewart instead. Stewart returns immediately in a rage, drags Ada outside and chops off her finger. He gives the finger to Flora to take to Baines. Stewart visits Baines and confronts him with a gun, but doesn't shoot him. He tells Baines that he wants to let Ada go and asks him to take her away. Ada, Baines and Flora leave the island with the piano. Ada changes her mind and tells them to cast the piano into the water. Her foot is caught in the rope attached to the piano and she nearly drowns, but to her surprise, she finds the will to live and manages to free herself. She goes on to make a new life with Baines and learns to speak, but can only do so in the dark. At night, she dreams of her piano at the bottom of the ocean with herself still attached to it.

Unfaithful (A. Lyne, USA/France, 2002)

Unfaithful tells the story of a seemingly 'perfect' marriage and family life that is disrupted by the infidelity of the wife and the jealousy of a husband who kills the male rival in a moment of jealous rage. The film begins by showing us everyday domestic scenes of the husband, Edward (Richard Gere), the wife, Connie (Diane Lane), and their young son in the idealized setting of affluent middle-class suburban family life. On a trip to town, however, Connie meets a handsome Frenchman, Paul (Oliver Martinez), who is a book dealer and lives in a converted loft. Unable to resist his charms, she soon begins a secret passionate affair with him, and her husband and child become increasingly displaced as the affair takes over her life. The husband grows suspicious and after hiring a private detective discovers her affair and goes to confront the lover in his warehouse apartment. In a sudden and unexpected fit of jealous rage, Edward hits Paul over the head with the glass snow globe (a gift first given to Connie by Edward. and then given to Paul by Connie).

Edward does his best to clean up the scene of the crime, rolls Paul's body up in a rug and drags it to the car and hides it in the boot. He manages to catch the end of his son's school performance and he cleans himself up in the school bathroom. Later he dumps the body at the rubbish tip and then tries to pretend nothing has happened. Eventually, the police turn up at the family home asking questions about the whereabouts of Paul, who is reported missing, and Edward tells Connie what he has done. She appears to forgive him and the rest of the film is about when and whether Edward should confess to the police. The closing shot is of the couple sitting in their car, with their son asleep on the backseat, outside the police station, discussing whether Edward should give himself up, or whether they should leave America and begin a new life elsewhere.

Notes

1 Setting the Scene: Masculinity, Jealousy and Contemporary Culture

1 There is a wealth of sociological literature on the topic of late modernity, and the meaning of the term itself is a much contested one. Most sociologists agree that contemporary culture is characterized by risk, uncertainty and fragmentation (Bauman, 2000; Beck, 1992; Giddens, 1991) and that such changes have implications for the shaping of subjectivities (Elliott, 1996a; Giddens, 1991). For some, such as Giddens (1991), late modernity has, in a potentially positive way, given rise to 'the reflexive self', whereas others emphasize the emptiness and superficiality of consumer culture and the regulatory encroachment of the state and the paranoid, narcissistic defences that individuals and organizations develop as a result (Craib, 1994; Lasch, 1979). See Elliott (1996a) for a useful summary of these debates.

2 Bainbridge and Yates (2005) have applied the language of the British psychoanalyst D. W. Winnicott to this third, ambiguous model of masculinity, naming it 'transitional masculinity'.

3 The terms *emotion* and *affect* are often used interchangeably today. Broadly speaking, the term *affect* can be defined as 'the repercussions of an emotional experience', that are linked psychically to unconscious processes. Whereas the term *emotion* has social connotations that point to the influence of social and cultural codes and feeling rules (see Stearns, 1989), the term *affect* is used in psychoanalysis to connote its unconscious roots (Laplanche and Pontalis, 1988: 14). Where possible, both terms are used throughout this book to reflect these different uses. For a discussion of the terms *emotion* and *affect*, see Music, 2001: 3–5; and for a psychoanalytic discussion of *affect*, see Laplanche and Pontalis, 1988: 13–14.

4 Studies that have examined the alleged narcissism of contemporary Western culture point to the proliferation of popular psychology and self-help books today (Craib, 1994) and this also extends to self-help books, magazine features and hypnotherapy sessions that address the 'problem' of jealousy, and inform consumers on how best to 'overcome it'. These include: Paul Hauk's *Jealousy; Why It Happens and How to Overcome It* 1993, ' How to Handle Your Jealous Heart', *Good Housekeeping*, 1996, 'Overcome Jealousy Now: Harley Street Hypnotherapy.

5 Following Kuhn (1994: 21), the term 'dominant cinema' is used to mean Hollywood or Hollywood influenced films.

6 See Chapter 6 for an in-depth discussion of Michael Douglas and *A Perfect Murder*.

7 See Chapter 4 for a discussion of these cinematic terms in relation to narratives of jealousy.

8 *Taxi Driver, The Piano* and *The End of The Affair* can be defined as 'crossover' films because they appeal to both popular and arthouse audiences

and, as I discuss later, aspects of the other two films (*A Perfect Murder* and *Unfaithful*) are, if indirectly, influenced cinematically by the independent film sector. Given the influence of the art-house/independent sector on these films, then they are arguably useful markers of the relationship between the radical potential of cinema and spectatorship, masculinity and cultural change. Yet since their release, all films have been commercial box-office hits and have continued to sell well on DVD. Details of their commercial box-office success can be accessed on http://www.Internetmoviedatabase.com./. All films chosen won major film awards in various categories, including Oscar and Bafta awards. On 8 November 2006, the Movie Database 'weighted average vote' from its users rated all the films no lower than 6.5 out of 10 and its gender differentiated popularity lists indicated that the five films were popular with men between the ages of 18 and 44, each scoring no less than 6.5.

9   This 'rescue narrative' and its relationship to male jealousy are explored in Chapter 5.

10   From a Freudian perspective, all heterosexual jealousies are psychologically related to (frustrated) Oedipal sexual desire (Freud, 1922), including bisexual desire.

11   The aim is therefore to refuse the essentialist implications of male jealousy as a timeless, innate emotion without difference.

12   The concept of the 'other' has a variety of connotations within the different psychoanalytic theories of subjectivity and the unconscious (see Evans, 1996; and Frosh, 1997; for further discussion of these theoretical differences). For Lacan, subjectivity is irrevocably formed in otherness, first through an imaginary relationship to the mother and then to the symbolic father and patriarchal language. Lacan distinguishes between the term ' the little other' and 'the big Other': the former is inscribed in the imaginary order, whereas the latter refers to the symbolic sphere of language and the law (Evans, 1996: 132–3).

13   For example, classical Freudian psychoanalytic explanations of masculinity have argued that masculinity is formed fearfully and competitively in relation to fantasies of the castrating Oedipal father, who may also be idealized as a defence (Freud, 1923; Jones, 1929), or to use the psychoanalytic approach first taken by Melanie Klein, as the outcome of earlier, pre-Oedipal fantasies associated with the phallic mother and the need to separate from her (Maguire, 1995; Minsky, 1998). See Chapter 2 for further discussion.

14   Alongside Winnicott (1971), this third model of masculinity and jealousy also owes much to Bollas's (1992) theory of the 'good enough Oedipus complex'. These ideas are expanded in Chapter 2. See also Yates (2000).

15   Jeffords argues that throughout the late 1980s and 1990s, 'fathering was a key characterization and narrative for displaying the "new" Hollywood masculinities' (1993: 254).

16   An example of such attitudes can be found with the UK Men's Movement, and the UK pro-family Cheltenham Group, who bemoan the loss of traditional, more distinctive gender roles of mothers and fathers in the family (Brosman, 1995; Collier, 1996: 24).

17   The growth of a commercial gay culture has been influential in challenging the necessary relationship between masculinity and heterosexuality by depicting men as objects of erotic desire (Gill, Henwood and Richards, 2000: 104).

18 For example, see Cohen and Jones, 'Are Men the New Women? Or why men are losing more than their dignity in the battle of the sexes'(2000: 1); Watson, 'Exit Macho Man: Are Men the New Women?' (2000: 27).

19 There are parallels here with the discussion earlier in this chapter about the representation of fatherhood and the absent mother in Hollywood movies

20 See Hammond (1993) for an extended discussion of contemporary male and female melodramas.

21 In the 1980s, when images of the 'new man' began to emerge, feminist writers asked whether representations of new masculinities in the media signified anything more meaningful for feminist politics than the late capitalist market readjusting itself to a popular feminist culture (Moore, 1988). These arguments echo debates in feminist film scholarship about the relationship between representations of new men and a broader backlash against feminism (Butler, 2000; Rowe, 1995).

22 The 'tragedy' of Shakespeare's *Othello* is often cited when discussing the enigma of masculine jealousy and the play has been adapted for cinema several times. See for example Lawrence Olivier's classical Shakespearian version in 1965 and the recent adaptation *O* (2001), which was represented as a High School drama. See Vaughan (1996) for an extended cultural history of *Othello*.

23 For instance, see Delingpole, 1996: 24; Grant, 1996: 58; and Peachment, 1996: 14.

24 The relationship between destructive morbid jealousy and homosexuality was also a recurring theme in twentieth-century medical discourses about jealousy and is related to the feminization of jealousy as a condition connoting weakness and over-dependency (Mitchell, 2000; Mullen, 1991).

25 Thereby also reproducing the stereotypical links between images of black masculinity and sexual potency. For further press reviews on this theme, see Malcom, 1996: 8–9; Shone, 1996: 6–7; and Walker, 1996: 32.

26 Press reviews and archive material for the films cited can be accessed at the British Film Institute Library, London.

Part I   The Psycho-Cultural Shaping of Masculine Jealousy

2   Psychoanalytic Understandings of Masculinity and Jealousy

1 For instance, see Cobb and Marks, 1979; De Silva, 1997; Dolan and Bishay, 1996.

2 Psychoanalytic theory argues that jealousy becomes problematic at the point that it interferes with love and work (Freud, 1917a: 289).

3 For instance, see Cohan, 1987; Freud, 1911, 1922; Jones, 1929; Klein, 1957; Lagache, 1938, 1949; Mollon, 2002; Riviere, 1932.

4 As I go on to discuss later in this chapter, the 'depressive position' refers both to an early psychic stage of development (one that follows the 'Paranoid Schizoid' position) and to a state of mind. The depressive position infers a capacity to acknowledge the goodness and separateness of the maternal object and also a capacity to cope with the losses and contradictions of object relations (Klein, 1952: 79).

5 Freud's tolerant tone perhaps indicates the extent to which he had come to terms with his own jealous feelings, first, in relation to the sibling rivalry he felt toward his younger brother Julius, who died at only eight months, and also his sister Anna, and second, during his courtship of Martha Bernays. The fact that it took him 40 years from that time to address jealousy indicates, perhaps, the extent to which he had to struggle with it (Baumgart, 1990; Houzel, 2001).

6 Freud suggests that a person's jealousy becomes a suitable case for treatment when the symptoms are 'accompanied by intense suffering and, as an objective fact, it threatens the communal life of a family' (1917a: 289).

7 For further discussion, see Fenichel, 1946: 513.

8 The mirror does not have to be literally a mirror. It can be a (m)other's face or reaction.

9 This psychic schism is reinforced when the subject enters the symbolic realm of culture, when the subject takes on his or her position within the language system. In learning to speak, culture enters the subject and structures its desires in relation to the phallus and patriarchal law (Lacan, [1953] 1977: 68)

10 The film is an adaptation of Christopher Hampton's 1985 stage play *Les Liaisons Dangereuses*, which was based on a scandalous eighteenth-century novel by Choderlos de Laclos. For a more recent film adaptation of the story set in contemporary America, see *Cruel Intentions* (1999).

11 There are similarities with Mitchell's (2002) argument that male hysteria vanished as a psychiatric illness because it was projected on to the 'problem' of femininity instead.

12 There are parallels to be drawn here between his use of the mask metaphor in relation to the notion of repressed homosexuality and Joan Riviere's 1929 paper on 'Womanliness as Masquerade', published in the same year.

13 For a discussion of this issue, see Gay, 1988; Maguire, 1995; Weeks, 1992. As Maguire points out, 'Homosexuality created an irresolvable and theoretical dilemma for Freud who argued against those who wanted to "abolish" it' (1995: 197). Freud's enlightened views of homosexuality were nevertheless qualified by his belief that homosexuality is related to 'arrested development (a refusal to acknowledge the social limits of Oedipal desire) and also narcissism, (seeking the self in the guise of another)' (Maguire, 1995: 198).

14 For further discussion, see Rose, 1987; Weeks, 1985.

15 See Neale (1983) for further discussion on this theme.

16 Her ideas were influenced by the work of Joan Riviere who in 1932 devoted an entire paper to the question of jealousy and its relationship to envy.

17 Melanie Klein spelt the term 'fantasy' 'phantasy' to denote its unconscious roots (see Hinshelwood (1991) for further discussion). I will use that spelling when referring to Klein's work.

18 See Bishop, 1996; and Riviere, 1932 for further discussion of these psychic processes.

19 For example, see Freud, 1911, 1913, 1917a, 1933; Klein, 1946, 1955; Lacan, 1991.

20 In cultural terms, the emphasis on lateral rather than vertical relationships may also reflect the turn from Oedipus as 'the myth of our time' and loss of

patriarchal social structures associated with it, to Narcissus (Benjamin, 1990).

21 The associations of romantic jealousy with what Shakespeare called 'the knawing worm of suspicion' and the voyeurism that accompanies it found more concrete expression in the naming of *jalousie* blinds in seventeenth-century France which had horizontal slats (Baumgart, 1990: 111). Given that romantic jealousy is often associated with Oedipal suspicion and the voyeuristic wish to spy on the unfaithful beloved, one can understand why the blinds were given their name, because they enabled a person to spy on another without being seen.

22 The emphasis given to the rivalry with the pre-Oedipal mother rather than the Oedipal father in the construction of subjectivities has become dominant in British psychoanalysis and can be traced back to the 1930s, when Melanie Klein and Ernest Jones first challenged the phallocentricism of Freud's theories (Maguire; 1995; Mitchell, 1975, 2000).

23 There is also an implicit analogy being made here between American foreign policy in Vietnam and the more recent American invasion of Iraq and the neo-conservative ideology that supported that invasion.

3   Theories of Masculinity, Cinema, Spectatorship and the Jealous Gaze

1 For example, see Cook, 1982; Neale, 1982, 1983.

2 Lacan argues that in terms of the child's changing perception of the world, the Symbolic follows the imaginary stage and is associated with the Oedipal crisis and the subject's acquisition of language and gendered identity and a submission to the law.

3 Feminist film-makers also became involved in producing an alternative women's cinema that challenged the old patriarchal images of femininity (Kuhn, 1994).

4 The character of Travis Bickle in *Taxi Driver* inspired John Hinckley to stalk Jodie Foster (who played Iris in the film) and in 1981 to attempt to assassinate Ronald Reagan. For a discussion of Stalking and its relationship to contemporary culture, see Nicol, 2006.

5 For an excellent summary of Freud's ideas on fetishism and their application to cinema, see Cook and Berninck, 1999: 347–9.

6 In 1981, following criticism about the absence of the feminine gaze in her analysis, Mulvey published 'Afterthoughts on Visual Pleasure and Narrative Cinema' inspired by *Duel In the Sun*, to acknowledge that women also read films in active rather than passive ways.

7 Mackinnon (2003) argues that the male gaze and the embodied male spectator are conflated in Mulvey's account and that Mulvey's theory fails to take account of the social spectator, and the social differences between men.

8 However, Dyer argues that there is more at stake for the male viewer, who, in terms of castration anxiety, has more to lose (1982: 269).

9 From a Lacanian perspective, learning to speak coincides with the castration complex and the acceptance of the symbolic father and his laws. Thus, the acquisition of language challenges the subject's narcissism.

10 Neale insists on the social influence of gender as a social and cultural formation (1983: 11).
11 Silverman (1980, 1988) explores the masochistic male gaze and focuses on the moments of rupture in the text where the power of the male gaze breaks down.
12 I am using the term 'Kleinian' to connote a school of psychoanalytic thought which includes the work of Karen Horney.
13 Klein spelt the term 'fantasy' with a *ph*(antasy) to distinguish it from conscious fantasy and to denote its unconscious roots.
14 See, for instance, Carveth and Gold, 1999; Creed, 1993; Gabbard and Gabbard, 1987.
15 See also Radstone (1995a) for a discussion of this approach.
16 See Cohan and Hark's 'Introduction' to their volume about masculinities in Hollywood cinema (1993: 3).
17 For instance, see Bainbridge and Yates, 2005; Kirkham and Thumim, 1993, 1995; *Screen* special issues on Trauma in 2001 and 2003.
18 Like Neale (1982), Radstone (1995a, 1996) focuses on the need to mourn and to come to terms with the fallibility of the idealized father.

4   Analysing Jealousy Texts from a Psycho-Cultural Perspective

1 A film's *mode of address* 'refers to the ways in which the text assumes certain responses, which may or may not be operative in different reception conditions' (Mayne, 1993: 29).
2 It is often argued that a feature of postmodern cinema is the nature of its ambiguous, less fixed mode of address (Hill, 1998).
3 One can argue that contemporary addresses to the Hollywood industry and its institutions are also a move away from the implied voluntarism of cultural studies audience research which emphasizes the role of negotiation over globalization and media institutions (Morley, 2002).
4 There is debate about the extent to which the content of such films are determined and influenced by the commercial considerations of the Hollywood industry (Wyatt, 1998). For example, Miramax is now a subsidiary company of Disney, which is a global leader in the entertainment industry. In backing low-budget art-house films in the independent sector, Miramax helped Disney reach out to new niche markets (for further discussion see Polan, 2001: 18; Wyatt, 1998: 81).
5 See also Dyer, 1998b: 35; Storey, 1996: 73.
6 For further discussion, see Staiger, 1993, 2005.
7 For example, as Crofts argues:

> As written texts, reviews offer detailed, condensed, and discursively rich evidences of readings of films ... They also have value as indicating broader community responses to film. Given that reviewers are both opinion leaders and responsible to the commonality of their readerships, conceived as broad market sectors with certain reading competencies and forms of cultural capital, reviews give indicative – not definitive – pointers to prevailing discursive assumptions among the communities of those who write and read film reviews.
>
> (2000: 154)

8 Dyer applies these categories to analyse the cultural construction of stars (1998b: 60).
9 For instance, see McDonald, 2000; Turner, 2004.
10 For instance, see Kirkham and Thumim, 1993, 1995; Minsky (1998).
11 It has been defined as 'all the elements placed in front of the camera to be photographed: the settings and props, lighting, costumes and make up, and figure behaviour' (Bordwell and Thompson, 1997: 480).
12 As in the earlier chapter on psychoanalytic understandings of male jealousy, the case studies do not only refer to the evocation of desires in a Lacanian sense, but also where appropriate they discuss the jealous wishes, anxieties and defences discussed in Kleinian and Object Relations theory.
13 A good example of this can be found in Radstone's (1995a) analysis of *Sea Of Love* (1989). Radstone draws on cultural and Lacanian psychoanalytic theories to chart the symbolic male Oedipal trajectory of the 'hero' played by Al Pacino, and his relationship to patriarchy and the symbolic father.
14 The case studies do not specifically dwell on the questions of genre in any depth; however, each of the films broadly contains generic elements common to melodramatic film dramas.
15 See also Lupton, 1998: 85; Walster and Rapson, 1996: 96.
16 There are certain parallels between what is being described in terms of affect and spectatorship and Linda Williams's work on ' Body Genres' (1991) in terms of the power to induce a physical response in spectators.
17 De Niro reportedly imagined being a crab as part of preparation for the role of Travis (Taubin, 2000).
18 The films analysed in these chapters are as follows: *Taxi Driver* (1976/1996), *A Perfect Murder* (1998), *The End Of The Affair* (1999), *The Piano* (1993) and *Unfaithful* (2002).

Part II Masculine Jealousy in the Movies

5 *Taxi Driver*: The Psychopathic Hero and the Rescue Romance: How Jealousy Drives the Narrative Along (*M. Scorsese, USA, 1976*)

1 Larsen (1999) cites its place in the American Film Institute's '100 films of all time'.
2 For instance, see: http://www.boxoffice.com/cgi/classicsearch.p1; http://www.All-reviews.commovie/ videoreview; www.imdb.com./taxidriver/ttoo75314/user-comments.
3 *Taxi Driver* is also a film about an attempt to assassinate a politician and the story was inspired by a real-life failed assassination attempt by Arthur Bremer on Alabama Governor George Wallis in 1972. The scriptwriter Paul Schrader was influenced by the journal of Bremer's *An Assassin's Diary* (1973). Following the film's release in 1976, John Hinckley Junior claimed that the film inspired his attempt to kill Ronald Reagan in 1981.
4 As Pam Cook notes, Scorsese is a renowned '*cinéphile*', and Scorsese refers knowingly to earlier films of the classic cinema, often to make a point about the present. As Cook argues: 'One of the characteristics of New Hollywood that marks it off from classic Hollywood is that it's produced and consumed by knowledgeable intellectuals. It sells itself on the basis of reflexivity, calling up classic Hollywood to differentiate itself from it' (1982: 40).

5 Approximately 1930–1960s.
6 De Niro's New York Italian street credentials are also emphasized in the studio publicity for his early films, where we are told that he grew up in 'New York's tough lower East Side, known as Little Italy' (BFI, 1979).
7 The most famous case of this was his preparation for the role of the boxer Jake La Motta, in *Raging Bull* (1980) where he gained several stones in weight to portray the character in his later years of physical decline.
8 Neale (1983) argues that given the social taboos about homosexuality, the male body can only be the object of the erotic male gaze at the cinema if it is depicted in an action scene, or scarred or wounded in some way
9 See also Cannon, 1997; Coleman, 1976; Damiani, 2000; Malcom, 1976, Shorter, 1976.
10 See J. Rice's (1976) discussion of Herrmann's score and his other musical film scores, which include *Vertigo* (1958).
11 See also Scorsese's *The Big Shave* (1967), which he made as a critique of the Vietnam war.
12 From the perspective of the psychoanalyst Melanie Klein, such splitting maintains the goodness of the primary object, in its most fundamental form, the breast. For Freud (1910), the 'prostitute'/madonna divide is related to Oedipal guilt and anxiety and reflects much more the divisions within the subject about the ideational content of their own sexuality.
13 There is a telling contrast here with films of the past when kidnapped and distressed young women were depicted as having a stronger sense of familial place and belonging. A good example of this is *The Searchers* (1956) as many of its narrative themes and images are re-worked (often consciously by Scorsese) in *Taxi Driver* (Buscombe, 2000; Taubin, 2000). In both films, the jealousy of the male protagonist occupies a central, if at times less obvious role in driving the narrative. In both cases, the hero is also located outside society and driven by a fear and hatred of the other.
14 See Berardinelli, 1998; Fox, 1996; Larsen, 1999.
15 For 1990s reviews, see Cannon, 1997; Ebert, 1996. 1976 reviews include: Blake, 1976: 4; Canby, 1976: 36; Christie, 1976: 10; Davis, 1976: 8; Rice, 1976: 109–23.
16 Past reviews include: Arnold, 1976; Blake, 1976: 4; Malcom, 1976: 61; Murf, 1976; Robinson, 1976: 7; Westerbeck Jn., 1976. For present reviews see: Berardinelli, 1998; Cannon, 1997; Henkel, 1999.
17 The work of director Tarantino, is most often cited here (see Butler, 2000).

6 Michael Douglas: Envy, Greed and Jealous Desire in *A Perfect Murder* (*A. Davis, USA, 1998*)

1 To illustrate this, I refer to the (mainly) UK press reviews of Douglas the star, before and during the film, alongside the reviews of the film itself.
2 For instance, see Andrews, 1998: 22; Sweet, 1998: 5; Williams, 1998: 9.
3 For instance, see Marshall, 1988: 14–15; Stanbrook, 1988: 18; Thomson, 1995: 22–3.
4 As in the piece in *Today* newspaper: 'My fatal attractions, by Michael Douglas' (Ambrose, 1988: 9). It was also widely reported that Douglas was being pursued by mistresses and obsessed fans, see Burke, 1988: 98–100; Marshall, 1988: 14-15.

5 It is reported that her father refused to attend the premiere of *Great Expectations* because of 'her passionate love scenes' (McDonald, 1998: 2).
6 For instance, see Sweet, 1998: 5; Queenan, 1998: 16–17.
7 Some of his later films represent a departure from his more macho image. See, for example, *The Wonder Boys*, (2000) and *Traffic* (2001).
8 See BFI press file on *A Perfect Murder* (BFI, 1998).
9 See Christopher, 1998: 44; Sweet, 1998: 5; Walker, 1998: 26.
10 Freud's (1913) account of the primal horde tells the story of a group of brothers who kill their father because of their resentment of his authority and their sexual rivalry. Their subsequent guilt is later warded off, by idealizing the memory of the powerful patriarch through totems, sacrificial objects and religious worship of God the father.
11 See, for instance, French, 1998: 6; Shone, 1998: 7; Walker, 1998: 26.
12 See also Bishop, 1996; and Weiland, 2000 for a psychoanalytic discussion of this type of love.
13 Hitchcock's films have in the past been the focus of much critical feminist attention and have played an important role in the development of feminist film theory (for example, see Modleski, 1988; Mulvey, 1975).
14 For instance, see Queenan, 1998: 16–17; Shone, 1998: 7; Berardinelli, 1998.

7 Englishness, Nation and Masculine Jealousy in *The End Of The Affair* (N. Jordan, USA/UK, 1999)[1]

1 An earlier version of this chapter was published in the *Journal of Cultural Research*, 10(3), July 2006, pp. 219–35.
2 Heritage films are by definition set in the past and contain a range of different generic elements that tend to draw on dominant notions of 'England's rich historical and cultural heritage' (Hill, 1999: 77).
3 The station café played a key role in *Brief Encounter* (1945) as the setting for the forbidden love affair between the characters of Celia Johnson and Trevor Howard. See Dyer (1993) for an extended analysis of *Brief Encounter*.
4 For details of his biography and acting career see Thomson, 2002: 286–7.
5 The construction of Fiennes as the epitome of well-bred Englishness dates back to 1992, when he first received national press publicity for playing T. E. Lawrence in a television film *A Dangerous Man – Lawrence After Arabia*, (ITV, 18 April, 1992). Headlines proclaimed him as 'the great white hope' (Gritten, 1992: 34–9). In 1992, Fiennes played 'Heathcliff' in a film re-make of *Wuthering Heights* (1992), where reviews chose instead to emphasize his Byronic 'black side' (Jones, 1992: 54). The different aspects of Fiennes's acting and film persona came together in his performance as Count Amassy in *The English Patient* (1996), where his reputation as an English heartthrob was confirmed.
6 See Spicer (2003) for a discussion of masculinity in British popular cinema.
7 For example, see Jones, 1994: 29–31; Gerrard, 1999: 30–4.
8 The maternal Oedipal sub-plot of Fiennes's life was publically reinforced in 1995 when he played a 'mother-obsessed *Hamlet*' at the Hackney Empire theatre in London, and reportedly fell in love with his co-star Francesca Annis, who played 'his' (i.e., Hamlet's) mother, Gertrude (Covenay, 1997: 20).

9 The notion of reflexive masculinity has much in common with descriptions of the late modern emotional subject, who can deconstruct his or her emotions as they are lived and experienced. For further discussion, see Giddens, 1991, 1992; Lupton, 1998.

10 See Lacan's *Encore*, cited in Benvenuto and Kennedy, 1986: 190.

11 Contrary to the book and the earlier 1955 version of the film, Bendrix is given an extra act within which to win back Sarah from God and take her away to Brighton for a romantic weekend. Sarah gives up her religious pact with God and falls back helplessly into his arms and the audience are saved from that particular jealous loss.

12 For instance, see Muller and Burke, 'Critic and Priest Discuss "The End Of The Affair"', 1955: 27–30.

13 For example, see *Mona Lisa* (1986), *The Crying Game* (1992), *Interview With The Vampire* (1994), *The Butcher Boy* (1997).

14 For coverage of the censorship controversy, see Billson, 2000: 10; Dawtrey, 2000: 18.

15 For instance, see Bradshaw, 2000: 2; Fisher, 2000: 37; Walker, 2000: 29.

16 See Bainbridge and Yates (2005) for further discussion of these themes.

8   *The Piano*: A Feminine Narrative of Masculine Jealousies (*J. Campion, Australia/New Zealand, 1993*)

1 This positive interpretation of *The Piano* as a feminist film is a contested position. Some feminist film scholars argue that *The Piano* pleasurably reproduces for the spectator old patriarchal subject positions, and also reinforces patriarchal relations of exchange between men and women (Gillett, 1995; Polan, 2001).

2 Many commentators on the film discuss feminist perspectives on *The Piano*. See, for example, Bruzzi, Dyson, Gillett in 'Reports and Debates' sections in *Screen*, 1995; and Gordon, 1996; Margolis, 2000; Coombs and Gemmell, 1999.

3 The James Mason tag was cited in newspaper articles about him throughout the 1980s. See, for example, 'The man they call the new James Mason' (Mann, 1984: 15); and apparently 'even Mason was impressed' by Neill (Taylor, 1989: 19).

4 For example, see Bamigboye, 1980: 15.

5 This includes the black piano notes, the whiteness of Ada's skin, the darkness of the forest where Baines lives and the whiteness of Flora's dress and her wings in her angel costume.

6 This illustrates the critique that the Maori cast are used merely as foils for the European characters (Hardy, 2000).

7 For bell hooks, 'Baines is the Tarzan of the Piano', who reinforces the nineteenth-century romantic myth of the heroic half native white man who protects the innocent 'happy go lucky' Maoris from the bad colonizers (Pihama, 2000: 126).

8 He even tries to mirror his rival Baines, when after watching Ada and Baines together, he unsuccessfully tries to rape his wife in the forest. See Hardy (2000: 80) for a discussion of this.

9 The breadth and content of the reviews reflect the film's cross-over between art-house and popular entertainment.

10   See, for example, Billson, 1993: 4; Errigo, 1993: 42; French, 1993: 4.
11   In this respect, as mentioned earlier, the film follows in the cinematic tradi-
     tion of 'the woman's film' and female melodrama, where strong female
     characters play a central role in the drama (Gledhill, 1987).
12   As Crofts (2000) argues, this explains the near ecstatic reviews of the film
     on the part of some female reviewers: 'For a while I could not think, let
     alone write about the Piano without shaking. Precipitating a flood of feel-
     ings, *The Piano* demands as much a physical and emotional response as an
     intellectual one' (Francke, 1993a: 224–5).
13   See also Billington, 1993: 30; Davenport, 1993a: 20; Mars-Jones, 1993: 26.
14   See also Brown, 1993: 37; Mars Jones, 1993: 26; Romney, 1993: 33–4.
15   See also Billson, 1993: 4; Dalton, 1993: 22; Malcolm, 1993: 4; Steyn, 1993: 46.

9   *Unfaithful*: A Tale of Female Infidelity and the Jealousy of a Good Husband (*A. Lyne, USA/France, 2002*)

1   For a summary of the plot-line and related web links and images for *La
    Femme Infidèle*, see: http://www.imdb.com/title/tt0064323/
2   See Harwood (1997) for a critical discussion of *Fatal Attraction* and also
    http://www.imdb.com/title/tt0093010/ for a synopsis of the film and
    related web links.
3   The names and jobs of the main characters in the film are laden with sym-
    bolic irony in this context as 'Constance' (Connie) is the name of the
    unfaithful wife (Diane Lane), the cuckolded husband Edward (Richard Gere)
    runs a security firm, the lover Paul, (Oliver Martinez) sells antique romantic
    French books, and the 8-year-old son Charlie dresses up in a rabbit costume
    for his school play, thus recalling the rabbit of bunny-boiling incident that
    so threatened the family in *Fatal Attraction* (Nathan, 2002: 12).
4   Diane Lane received an Oscar for Best Actress for her performance as
    Connie.
5   Profiles of Lyne reinforce his non-macho, high-powered director image. As
    one journalist recalls: 'with his long, straggly ginger hair and rumpled blue
    shirt, he doesn't look like a man who earned a billion dollars for the
    Hollywood studio system. Even his middle-class Home Counties accent
    seems all wrong' (Tabakoff, 1993: 17).
6   Thereby evoking Ariel Levy's (2005) feminist critique of 'raunch culture'.
7   And, of course, remake of Kubrick's 1962 film *Lolita*.
8   For further discussion of this double standard, see Lupton (1998).
9   Critics have likened Lyne to 'a whore posing as a moralist' (Macaulay, 2002:
    18).
10 *Madame Bovary* tells the story of a frustrated doctor's wife (Emma Bovary),
    who seeks to escape the boredom of her domestic life through love affairs
    and living beyond her means.
11 For example, one journalist, citing his notorious reticence, likens interview-
    ing him to 'interviewing a number 3 bus' (Lane, 2002: 3).
12 In the early stages of his career, Gere was often likened to John Travolta –
    who was first offered the role of the 'Armani-clad escort' in *American Gigolo*
    (Macaulay, 2001: 16). When Travolta pulled out of the film, Paul Schrader
    offered it to Gere instead. For an example of the kind of publicity where the

two stars are compared, see 'An Officer And A Gentleman Takes On A Disco Battle Of The Sexies!' (Connew, 1983: 16–17).

13   They divorced shortly afterwards.

14   Although caustically labelled 'The Dalai Luvvi' (Worrall, 1997: 8), his commitment to Buddhism appears genuine and he has been involved in the campaign to free Tibet from China.

15   Gere has a reputation for his enigmatic pronouncements. In 2003, Gere won the Plain English Campaign's 'Foot in Mouth' prize with the words: 'I know who I am. No one else knows who I am. If I was a giraffe and somebody said I was a snake, I'd think, "No actually I'm a giraffe"' (Anon, 2002: 29).

16   Reports say that Gere began a philosophy degree at the University of Massachusetts in 1967, but then dropped out of university to become an actor and then a hippy before turning to acting as a serious career. For an excellent summary of his life and early career, see Price's 1982 *Rolling Stone* interview with Gere (Price, 1982: 13–16).

17   In *Unfaithful*, such forces are represented as female desire.

18   The same can be said of the opposition leader David Cameron, who at the time of writing, is the Conservative leader of the Opposition party in the United Kingdom.

19   Indeed, to be a credible political leader, this appears to be an important criterion, as the publicity surrounding Gordon Brown's new family perhaps illustrates (Sands, 2006: 11).

20   For example, see: http://dir.yahoo.com/Society_and_Culture/Holidays_and_Observances/Father_s_Day/ Accessed 10 August 2006.

21   There are a 'record number of committed Christians' in the UK New Labour government, who are 'united in their family values' (Patterson, 2006: 16). It is interesting, then, that at the time of writing Deputy Prime Minister Prescott has kept his job, despite his much-publicized extra-marital affairs.

22   Such pressures were also feminized in the film and linked to the unreasonable demands of his neurotic, materialistic wife.

23   In 1991, a House of Lords ruling in the United Kingdom made 'marital rape' illegal (Collier, 1996: 19).

24   The fathers' rights group Fathers4Justice have staged a number of publicized stunts to promote the rights of fathers. They recently reformed as Real Fathers4Justice, see their website at: http://www.realfathersforjustice.org for an example of a US fathers' rights organization, see The Fatherhood Coalition at: http://www.fatherhoodcoalition.org/.

25   And, some might say, have been left wanting. For a discussion of these issues, see Clarke (2006).

26   For a discussion of these themes, see Moi (1987) and Stearns (1989).

27   Of course the affluence of the surroundings and the depiction of the black maid, the only black character in the film, makes it anything but ordinary, and signifies instead a particular vision of white middle-class America.

28   Evoking the scene in the famous adultery film *Brief Encounter* (1945), in which Celia Johnson's character gets grit in her eye and Trevor Howard helps her, Connie cuts her knee and Paul offers to clean it up for her.

29   Even though the symbolism regarding the cultural binary divisions of gender has outlived the reality of Western families, where women now mostly take paid work.

30 A point that is reinforced by Gere (2002) and Lyne (2002) who have discussed the motivations of the characters in relation to the film's alleged existentialism and the nature of choices made by the protagonists in relation to the jealousy triangle.

31 And which is explored in Chapter 2 of this book.

32 'The phallic mother' is a classical psychoanalytic concept from the Kleinian tradition. The concept has been defined thus: 'the latter is mainly a pre-Oedipal fantasy, that the woman (mother) is endowed with a phallus (external or internal). In later life, it is met in men who feel masochistic and submissive towards women' (Limentani, 1993: 282).

33 There are a number of episodes where Connie is seen to consciously initiate and pursue the affair with Paul. For example: when she first agrees to let Paul give her a plaster for her cut knee; when she later calls him from Grand Central Station and then agrees to go to his flat for coffee; and when she says she knows she must leave Paul's flat and go home, but does not.

34 As, for example, with Freud, who in his essay 'Female Sexuality' (1931) argues that because they anatomically lack the threat of castration, females have weaker super-egos than males and so by implication are more narcissistic and lack the moral conscience of their brothers. For a feminist discussion of Freud and femininity, see Benjamin, 1990.

35 Again, see Freud (1931).

36 Connie is meant to be in her late thirties and in fact looks quite youthful. Paul is meant to be in his early twenties and Edward in his forties.

37 When Connie discovers the photograph of Edward, Charlie and herself tucked into a compartment at the bottom of the globe, she also finds a rather corny message from Edward saying: 'To my beautiful wife, the best part of every day!'

38 The depiction of the rivalrous aggression between father and son is a recurring trope in the history of Hollywood cinema and can be found both in films, and in their various forms, such as John Wayne Westerns, *The Red River* (1948) and *The Searchers* (1956) and the idealization of the strong patriarch in *The Godfather* trilogy (1971, 1974, 1990). For an excellent, critical depiction of the morbidly jealous father, see Ray Winstone's performance as the violent husband in *Nil By Mouth* (1997) and for a powerful representation of sexual rivalry for the son's girlfriend, see *Damage* (1992).

39 As, for instance, with Michael Douglas in *A Perfect Murder* (1998).

40 As one reviewer puts it: 'You naturally warm to her. It makes for perfect casting. Lane's displays of self-disgust and excitement give her deviance a sympathetic arc: the cathartic release of a wife coming to realize her idyllic has run out of spontaneity' (Nathan, 2002: 12).

41 The film *Howards End* (1992) provides a good example of this.

10 Conclusion: Towards an Understanding of Masculinity, Jealousy and Cinema

1 See Moi (1987) for a useful discussion of this point.

2 As mentioned in earlier chapters, there is a substantial body of literature within psychosocial and cultural studies about the nature of contemporary culture and the implications of social and cultural change for the shaping of identities today; see Craib, 1994; Elliott, 1996; Giddens; 1991. There has, how-

ever, been less psychosocial research carried out into the relationship between gender, culture and society today. For exceptions to this, see Frosh, 1994; Jefferson, 1994.

3 Psychoanalytic theory defines emotional ambivalence as 'the holding of contradictory feeling states in the relationship towards one object' (Hinshelwood, 1991: 218).

4 In his study of jealousy, Stenner argues that the relationship between the 1960s discourse of permissive heterosexuality and anti-jealousy is still used by young men today, who utilize it in opposition to possessiveness and over-emotional femininity (1992: 122–3). The men in his study use a 'laddish' discourse of anti-jealousy to express their need for sexual freedom and independence. The 'permissive', 'laddish', anti-jealousy stance of the men in Stenner's study of jealous narratives, contrasts with the women in his research, who use a companionate, 'have and to hold' relational model of heterosexuality as a guide for their relationships. The 'have and to hold' discourse is associated with 1950s heterosexuality and emphasizes sexual fidelity and 'privileges love, security and romance'.

5 Throughout the 1990s, psychiatric and criminal reports of its actual incidences were as strong as ever and may continue to be on the increase (see Burton, Regan and Kelly, 1998; Kelly, 1997).

6 As Van Sommers argues, while in European 'honour' societies, men were encouraged to be 'active and competitive' and could win back their honour if it had been stolen, 'female honour and shame were, by contrast, passive and defensive and once lost could not be reclaimed' (1988: 114).

7 From a Freudian perspective, this is defined as an inevitable symptom of penis envy (Freud, 1931).

8 The Married Women's Property Act in 1882 can be seen as a key moment in this history.

9 See Chapter 7 for further discussion of this point in relation to the film *The End of The Affair* (1999).

10 One cannot, from such a small sample, make any definite conclusions about the nature of masculinity and cultural change. However, as with most cultural research in this field, the aim is not to provide some definite empirical 'proof', but rather to contribute to a greater understanding of developing trends and provide the basis for further research in the area. For useful discussions on the aims and strategies of film and cultural studies research, see Bordwell and Thompson, 1997; Gledhill, 1995; Nicols, 1985; Staiger, 2005.

11 Thus invoking my earlier discussion regarding the contemporary fascination with stalkers.

12 As discussed below, Richard Gere's vulnerable 'everyman' depiction of the cuckolded husband in *Unfaithful* also received a luke-warm reception from male critics.

13 Yates and Day Sclater define 'transitional phenomena' thus:

> Winnicott (1971) explicitly links his description of cultural experience in adult life to the 'transitional phenomena' of infancy and to the space that emerges between mother and child for play. He argues that the psychic significance of this space, in which subjectivity is constituted and re-constituted, remains throughout our lives.
>
> (2000: 137)

14 Throughout this book, I have used the term *late modernity* to describe the nature of the contemporary post-industrial world, where the old certainties have been lost, but where opportunities for a new reflexive awareness on the part of individuals, society and culture now exist alongside a negative and reactive potential for destruction. In contrast to the terms *postmodernity* and *postmodernism*, which denote a break with *modernism* and its goals as linked to the Enlightenment project, *late modernity* acknowledges both the psychosocial continuities and discontinuities with those modernist goals, social conditions and cultural aspirations. For further discussion of these terms and related cultural and sociological debates about modernism and postmodernism, see Giddens, 1991; Elliott, 1996.

15 The open-endedness of many 'New Hollywood' cross-over films suggest their potential as feminist texts, reflecting the feminization of popular culture more generally. Yet, as we have seen in relation to this and other films, there may be a number of narrative factors contained in a film and its publicity, which may undermine its status as a feminist text.

16 As made popular in the Lerner musical *Camelot* (1967), based on the T. H. White version of the myth, *Once and Future King* (1939).

17 Sharon Stone starred in the original 1992 version with Michael Douglas.

Filmography

91/2 Weeks, A. Lyne, USA, 1986.
A Perfect Murder, A. Davies, USA, 1998.
About a Boy, C. and P. Weitz, UK, 2002.
American Beauty, S. Mendes, USA, 1999.
American Gigolo, P. Schraeder, USA, 1980.
American Psycho, M. Harron, USA, 2000.
An Officer and a Gentleman, T. Hackford, USA, 1982.
Basic Instinct 2, M. Caton Jones, Germany/UK/USA, 2006.
Basic Instinct, P. Verhoeven, USA, 1992.
Beau Travail, C. Denis, France, 1998.
Ben Hur, W. Wyler, USA, 1959.
Billy Elliott, S. Daldry, France/UK, 2000.
Boiler Room, B. Younger, USA, 2000.
Bonnie and Clyde, A. Penn, USA, 1967.
Boogie Nights, P. Thomas Anderson, USA, 1997.
Breathless, J. McBride, USA, 1983.
Bridget Jones' Diary, S. Maguire, USA/GB, 2001.
Brief Encounter, D. Lean, Coward-Cineguild, GB, 1945.
Brokeback Mountain, A. Lee, USA, 2005.
Broken Flowers, J. Jarmusch, USA/FR, 2005.
Caché (Hidden), M. Haneke, France, 2005.
Camelot, J. Logan, USA, 1967.
Cape Fear, M. Scorsese, USA, 1991.
Captain Corelli's Mandolin, J. Madden, USA/France/GB, 2001.
Casino Royale, M. Campbell, USA/Germany/GB/Czech Republic, 2006.
Chariots of Fire, H. Hudson, GB, 1981.
Citizen Kane, O. Welles, USA, 1941.
Closer, M. Nichols, USA, 2004.
Cruel Intentions, R. Kumble, USA, 1999.
Damage, L. Malle, Germany/GB/France, 1992.
Dangerous Liaisons, S. Frears, GB/USA, 1988.
Dead Ringers D. Cronenberg, Canada/USA, 1988.
Death Wish, M. Winner, USA, 1974.
Dial M For Murder, A. Hitchcock, USA, 1954.
Dirty Harry, D. Siegal, USA, 1971.
Disclosure, B. Levinson, USA, 1994.
Duel In the Sun, K. Vidor, USA, 1946.
East Of Eden, E. Kazan, USA, 1955.
Easy Rider, D. Hopper, USA, 1969.
Enduring Love, R. Mitchell, GB, 2004.
Eternal Sunshine of the Spotless Mind, M. Gandry, USA, 2004.
Falling Down, J. Schumacher, USA, 1992.
Fatal Attraction, A. Lyne, USA, 1987.

Fight Club, D. Fincher, USA/Germany, 1999.
First Knight, J. Zucker, USA, 1995.
Forrest Gump, R. Zemeckis, USA, 1994.
Gaslight, T. Dickinson, GB, 1940.
Gilda, C. Vidor, USA, 1946.
Gladiator, R. Scott, GB/USA, 2000.
High Fidelity, S. Frears, USA, 2000.
Howards End, J. Ivory, GB/Japan, 1992
Il Postino, M. Radford, France/Italy/Belgium, 1994.
In The Company of Men, N. La Bute, USA, 1997.
Indecent Proposal, A. Lyne, USA, 1993.
Interview With The Vampire, N. Jordan, USA, 1994.
King Arthur, A. Fuqua, USA/Ireland/GB, 2004.
Kramer versus Kramer, R. Benton, USA, 1979.
L.A. Confidential, C. Hanson, USA, 1997.
La Femme Infidèle, C. Chabrol, France, 1968.
Lolita, S. Kubrick, USA, 1962.
Lolita, A. Lyne, USA/France, 1997.
Magnolia, P. T. Anderson, USA, 1999.
Mean Streets, M. Scorsese, USA, 1973.
Memento, C. Nolan, USA, 2000.
Mission Impossible 11, J. Woo, USA, 2000.
Mona Lisa, N. Jordan, GB, 1986.
Moulin Rouge!, B. Lurman, USA, 2002.
My Brilliant Career, G. Armstrong, Australia, 1979.
Mystic River, C. Eastwood, USA, 2003.
Nil By Mouth, G. Oldman, GB, 1997.
Notting Hill, R. Mitchell, GB/USA, 1999.
O, T. Blake Nelson, USA, 2001.
One Hour Photo, M. Romanek, USA, 2002.
Othello, O. Welles, France/USA, 1952.
Othello, S. Burge and J. Dexter, UK, 1965.
Othello, O. Parker, GB/USA/France, 1995.
Pearl Harbor, M. Bay, USA, 2001.
Pretty Woman, G. Marshall, USA, 1990.
Psycho, A. Hitchcock, USA, 1960.
Quiz Show, R. Redford, USA, 1994.
Raging Bull, M. Scorsese, USA, 1980.
Rebecca, A. Hitchcock, USA, 1940.
Rebel Without a Cause, N. Ray, USA, 1955.
Reservoir Dogs, Q. Tarrantino, USA, 1993.
Se7en, D. Fincher, USA, 1995.
Sex, Lies, and Videotape, S. Soderbergh, USA, 1989.
Shine, S. Hicks, USA, 1996.
Sister Act, E. Ardolino, USA, 1992.
Sleeping With the Enemy, J. Ruben, USA, 1991.
Spartacus, S. Kubrick, USA, 1960.
Taxi Driver, M. Scorsese, USA, 1976, re-released 1996.
The Bad Lieutenant, A. Ferrara, USA. 1993.

The Ballad of Jack and Rose, R. Miller, USA, 2005
The Big Shave, M. Scorsese, USA, 1967.
The Butcher Boy, N. Jordan, USA, 1997.
The Constant Gardener, F. Meirelleses, Germany/GB, 2005.
The Crying Game, N. Jordan, GB, 1992.
The Deer Hunter, M. Cimino, USA, 1978.
The Devil Wears Prada, D. Frankel, USA, 2006.
The End of the Affair, E. Dmytryk, USA, 1955.
The End of The Affair, N. Jordan, USA/Germany, 1999.
The English Patient, A. Minghella, USA, 1996.
The Full Monty, P. Cattaneo, USA/GB, 1997.
The Game, D. Fincher, USA, 1997.
The Godfather Part 2, F. Ford Copolla, USA, 1974.
The Godfather Part 3, F. Ford Copolla, USA, 1990.
The Godfather, F. Ford Copolla, USA, 1971.
The Graduate, M. Nichols, USA, 1967.
The Last Temptation of Christ, M. Scorsese, USA, 1986.
The Piano, J. Campion, Australia/New Zealand, 1993.
The Quiet American, P. Noyce, Germany/USA, 2002
The Red River, H. Hawkes and A. Rosson, USA, 1948.
The Road to Perdition, S. Mendes, USA, 2002
The Searchers, J. Ford, USA, 1956.
The Weather Man, G. Verbinski, USA, 2005.
The Wonder Boys, C. Hanson, USA/Germany/Japan, 2000.
Thelma and Louise, R. Scott, USA, 1991.
Three Men and a Baby, L. Nimoy, USA, 1987.
Three Men and A Little Lady, E. Ardolino, USA, 1990.
Traffic, S. Sodberbergh, USA, 2001.
Troy, W. Peterson, USA/Malta/GB, 2004.
Unfaithful, A. Lyne, USA/France, 2002.
Vertigo, A. Hitchcock, USA, 1958.
Wall Street, O. Stone, USA, 1987.
Wuthering Heights, P. Kosminsky, GB, 1992.

Bibliography

Ambrose, D. (1988). 'My fatal attractions, by Michael Douglas', *Today*, 22 February, p. 9.

Amidon, S. (1996). 'Lost romantics', *Sunday Times, Section 9*, 15 December, p. 4.

Andrews, G. (1993a). 'Grand entrance', *Time Out*, 20 October, pp. 24–26.

Andrews, N. (1993b). 'The touch of a virtuoso', *Financial Times*, 28 October, p. 21.

Andrews, N. (1998). '*A Perfect Murder*', *Financial Times*, 15 October, p. 22.

Andrews, N. (2000). 'War time adulterers keep the faith', *Financial Times*, 10 February, p. 18.

Andrews, N. (2002). '*Unfaithful*', *Financial Times*, 6 June, p. 20.

Ang, I. (1985). *Watching Dallas: Soap Opera and the Melodramatic Imagination*, London: Methuen.

Anon (1954). '*Dial M for Murder*', *Saturday Review*, 29 March, p. 20.

Anon (1995). 'The frame of a Dane', *Sunday Telegraph*, 5 March, p. 31.

Anon (2002) 'Well said, Mr. Gere', *Daily Telegraph*, 6 December, p. 29.

Anon (2006) 'How to be a great dad', *The Independent Extra*, 15 June, pp. 1–5.

Anthony, A. (1995). 'Singular white male', *The Observer Life Magazine*, 26 November, pp. 12–16.

Arnold, G. (1976). *Washington Post*, 10 February, BFI Press Cuttings Pack: *Taxi Driver*, London: British Film Institute.

Atwood, F. (1998). 'Weird lullaby; Jane Campion's The Piano', *Feminist Review*, 58 (Spring), 85–101. Manchester: Manchester University Press.

Austin, T. (2002). *Hollwood, Hype and Audiences; Selling and Watching Popular Film in the 1990s*, Manchester: Manchester University Press.

Bainbridge, C. and Yates, C. (2005). 'Cinematic symptoms of masculinity in transition: Memory, history and mythology in contemporary film', in *Psychoanalysis, Culture & Society*, 10(3), 299–318.

Bainbridge, C., Radstone, S., Rustin, M. and Yates, C. (eds) (2007). *Culture and The Unconscious*, Basingstoke: Palgrave Macmillan.

Bainham, A., Day Sclater, S. and Richards, M. (1999). 'Introduction', in Bainham, A., Day Sclater, S. and Richards, M. (eds), *What is a Parent? A Socio-Legal Analysis*, Oxford: Hart, pp. 1–22.

Bamigboye, B. (1980). 'Lucky Sam ... no macho man', *Evening Standard*, 17 January, p. 15.

Basuroy, S. Chatterjee, S. and Ravid, S. A. (2003). 'How critical are critical reviews? The box-office effects of film critics, star power and budgets', *Journal of Marketing*, 67, (October), 103–17.

Baudrillard, J. (1985). 'The ecstasy of communication', in Foster, H. (ed.), *Postmodern Culture*, London: Pluto Press, pp. 126–34.

Baudry, J. L. (1970). 'Ideological effects of the basic cinematographic apparatus', *Film Quarterly*, 28(2), Winter, originally written in 1970 then translated 1974 by A. Williams. Later reprinted in Baudry, L. and Cohen, M. (eds) (1999). *Film Theory and Criticism*, 5th edn, Oxford: Oxford University Press, pp. 345–55.

Baudry, J. L. (1975). 'The apparatus: Metaphysical approaches to the impression of reality in cinema', *Camera Obscura*, 1 (Fall), originally written in 1975 then translated 1976 by J. Andrews and B. Augst. Later reprinted in Baudry, L. and Cohen, M. (eds) (1999). *Film Theory and Criticism*, 5th edn, Oxford: Oxford University Press, pp. 760–77.

Baudry, L. and Cohen, M. (eds) (1999). *Film Theory and Criticism*, 5th edn, Oxford: Oxford University Press.

Bauman, Z. (2000). *Liquid Modernity*, Cambridge: Polity Press.

Baumgart, H. (1990). *Jealousy; Experiences and Solutions*, Chicago: University of Chicago Press.

Beck, U. (1992). *Risk Society: Towards a New Modernity*. London: Sage.

Benjamin, J. (1990). *The Bonds of Love: Psychoanalysis, Feminism and the Problem of Domination*, London: Virago Press.

Benjamin, W. (1992). *Illuminations: Edited and with an Introduction by Hannah Arendt*, trans. H. Zohn, London: Fontana Press.

Benvenuto, B. and Kennedy, R. (1986). *The Works of Jacques Lacan: An Introduction*, London: Free Association Books.

Berardinelli, J. (1998). See: http://www.cybernex.net/~berardin. Accessed 24 January 2000.

Berens, J. (1995). 'Fiennes time', *GQ*, March, pp. 116–19.

Berman, E. (1997). 'Hitchcock's *Vertigo*: The collapse of the rescue fantasy', *International Journal of Psychoanalysis*, **78**, pp. 975–96.

BFI (1979). 'Publicity for *The Deer Hunter*', BFI Press Cuttings Pack, London: British Film Institute.

BFI (1993). *The Piano, Production Notes*, BFI Press Cuttings Pack, London: British Film Institute.

BFI (1998). *A Perfect Murder*, Warner Brothers Publicity Notes, BFI Press Cuttings Pack, London, British Film Institute.

BFI (2002). *Unfaithful*, Twentieth Century Fox Production Notes, BFI Press Cuttings Pack, London: British Film Institute.

Billington, M. (1993). 'Harmony of key symbols', *The Guardian*, 6 November, p. 30.

Billson, A. (1993). '*The Piano*', *Sunday Telegraph*, 31 October, p. 4.

Billson, A. (1998). '*A Perfect Murder*', *Sunday Telegraph*, 18 October, p. 8.

Billson, A. (2000). '*The End of the Affair*', *Sunday Telegraph Review*, 13 February, p. 10.

Biressi, A. and Nunn, H. (2002). 'An Englishman's case', *Soundings: A Journal of Politics and Culture*, **20** (Summer), 37–45.

Bishop, B. (1996). 'Othello – faith and doubt in the good object', *British Journal of Psychotherapy*, **12**(3), 323–31.

Blake, J. (1976). 'Taxi driver on trip to mass murder', *Evening News*, 12 August, p. 4.

Bocock, R. (1993). *Consumption*, London: Routledge.

Bollas, C. (1992). *Being a Character*, London: Routledge.

Bordwell, D. and Thompson, K. (1997). *Film Art: An Introduction*, 5th edn, London and New York: McGraw-Hill.

Bowie, M. (1987). *Freud, Proust and Lacan: Theory as Fiction*, Cambridge: Cambridge University Press.

Bradshaw, P. (2000). 'An unholy communion', *The Guardian*, *G2*, 11 February, pp. 4–5.

Bremer, A.H. (1973). *An Assassin's Diary*, New York: Harper's Magazine Press.

Brosman, J. (1995). 'Men behaving sadly', *New Statesman and Society*, 4 August, pp. 16–17.

Brown, G. (1993). 'Campion finds an epic voice', *The Times*, 28 Ooctober, p. 37.

Brown, M. (2002). DVD 'Special Feature: Director's Commentary', *Unfaithful*, USA: Twentieth Century Fox Film Corporation.

Bruzzi, S. (2005). *Bringing Up Daddy: Fatherhood and Masculinity in Post-War Hollywood*, London: British Film Institute.

Burke, T. (1988). 'The *Fatal Attraction* of Michael Douglas', *Cosmopolitan*, January, pp. 98–100.

Burton, S., Regan, L. and Kelly, L. (1998). *Domestic Violence: Supporting Women and Challenging Men*, Cambridge: Polity Press, in Association with the Rowntree Foundation.

Buscombe, E. (2000). *The Searchers*, London: British Film Institute Publishing.

Buscombe, E., Gledhill, C., Lovell, A. and Williams, C. (1975–6). 'Psychoanalysis and film', in Screen (eds) (1992). *The Sexual Subject: A Screen Reader in Sexuality*, London: Routledge, pp. 35–46.

Butler, A. (2000). 'Feminist theory and women's films at the turn of the century', *Screen*, 41(1), 73–86.

Butler, J. (1990). *Gender Trouble: Feminism and the Subversion of Gender Identity*, London: Routledge.

Bygrave, M. (1987)'Mortal Friends', *Guardian*, 17 December, p. 11.

Cameron, I. (1976). 'Manhattan transfers', *Spectator*, 28 August, p. 19.

Canby, V. (1976). 'Flamboyant "Taxi Driver" by Scorsese', *New York Times*, 15 February, p. 36.

Cannon, D. (1997). '*Taxi Driver*', *Movie Reviews UK*, query@filmu-net.com.

Carroll, R. (2000). 'Scorsese tells Leo "life's not a beach"', *The Observer*, 22 October, p. 26.

Carter, A. (1995). *The Bloody Chamber and Other Stories*, London: Vintage.

Carveth, D. and Gold, N. (1999). 'The preoedipalizing of Klein in (North) America: Ridley Scott's *Alien* re-analyzed', *PSYART: A Hypertext Journal for the Psychological Study of the Arts*. http://www.clas.ufl.edu/ipsa/journal/1999_carveth03.shtml. Accessed 20 January 2007.

Case, B. (2000). 'Holy ghosts', *Time Out*, 12 January, pp. 20–2.

Cashin, F. (1976). 'A taxi ride to terror', *The Sun*, 21 August, p. 13.

Choderow, N. J. (1978). *The Reproduction of Mothering: Psychoanalysis and the Sociology of Gender*, Berkley: University of California Press.

Christie, I. (1976). 'The old alchemist stirs things up', *Daily Express*, 20 August, p. 10.

Christopher, J. (1998). 'Douglas sinks his teeth into another role', *Times*, 15 October, p. 44.

Churcher, S. (1983). 'The Gigolo becomes a gentleman', *Daily Mail*, 27 January, pp. 20–1.

Clanton, G. and Smith, G. (eds) (1986). *Jealousy*, London: University Press of America.

Clarke, S. (2006) *From Enlightenment to Risk: Social Theory and Contemporary Society*, Basingstoke: Palgrave Macmillan.

Clinch, M. (1993), 'Method in his madness', *Evening Standard*, 7 January, p. 28.

Cobb, J. P. and Marks, I. M. (1979). 'Morbid jealousy featuring as obsessive-compulsive neurosis: Treatment by behavioural psychotherapy', *British Journal of Psychiatry*, **134**, 301–5.

Cohan, S. and Hark, I. R. (eds) (1993). *Screening The Male: Exploring Masculinities in Hollywood Cinema*, London: Routledge.

Cohan, S. J. (1987). 'Pathological jealousy', *International Journal of Psycho-analysis*, **68**, 99–108.

Cohen, D. and Jones, D. (2000). 'Are men the new women?', *Indepemdent, Wednesday Review*, 16 February, p. 1.

Coleman, I. (1976). '*Taxi Driver*', *New Statesman*, 23 August, BFI Press Cuttings Pack, London: British Film Institute.

Collier, R. (1996). 'Coming together? Post-heterosexuality, masculine crisis and the new men's movement', *Feminist Legal Studies*, **IV**(1), February, 3–48.

Connell, R. W. (1995). *Masculinities*, Cambridge: Polity Press.

Connew, P. (1983). 'Battle of the sexies!', *Daily Mirror*, 31 May, pp. 16–17.

Cook, P. (1982). 'Masculinity in crisis?', *Screen*, **23**(3–4), 39–42.

Cook, P. and Bernink, M. (eds) (1999). *The Cinema Book*, 2nd edn, London: British Film Institute.

Coombs, F. and Gemmell, S. (eds) (1999). *Piano Lessons: Approaches to 'The Piano'*, Sydney, Australia: John Libbey.

Copjec, J. (1982). 'The anxiety of the influencing machine', *October*, 23 (Winter), 43–60.

Covenay, M. (1997). 'Top of the world', *Observer Review*, 16 February, p. 20.

Coward, R. (1999a). *Sacred Cows: Is Feminism Relevant to the New Millennium?*, London: Harper Collins.

Coward, R. (1999b). 'Men on the verge of feminist debate', *The Guardian*, 9 September, pp. 6–7.

Cowie, E. (1984). 'Fantasia', in Evans, J. and Hall, S. (eds) (1999), *Visual Culture: The Reader*, London: Sage, in association with The Open University, pp. 356–69.

Craib, I. (1994). *The Importance of Disappointment*, London: Routledge.

Craving, C. (2002). 'Lyne disease', *Village Voice*, 14 May, p. 138.

Creed, B. (1993). *The Monstrous Feminine: Film, Feminism, Psychoanalysis*, London: Routledge.

Creed, B. (1998). 'Film and psychoanalysis', in Hill, J. and Church Gibson, P., *The Oxford Guide to Film Studies*, Oxford: Oxford University Press, pp. 77–90.

Crichton, P. (1996). 'Did Othello have "the Othello syndrome"?', *Journal of Forensic Psychiatry*, **7**(1), 161–9.

Crofts, S. (2000). 'Foreign tunes? Gender and nationality in four countries: Reception of *The Piano*', in Margolis, H. (ed.), *Jane Campion's The Piano*, Cambridge: Cambridge University Press Film Handbooks, pp. 135–90.

Curtis, Q. (1996). 'A modest moor, with much to be modest about', *Independent on Sunday*, 18 February, p. 13.

Dalton, S. (1993). '*The Piano*', *New Musical Express*, 6 November, p. 22.

Damiani, C. (2000). *Archive TNT Rough Cut Movie Reviews*, at: david@roughcut.com

Davenport, H. (1993). 'Love for the love of Ada', *Daily Telegraph*, 29 October, p. 20.

Davies, C. (1993). 'Night of the hunter: The saga of erotic discovery that is women's movie of the year', *Mail On Sunday*, 24 October, pp. 44–5.

Davis, V. (1976). 'The master actor who's hailed by Hollywood, but wants to be alone', *Daily Express*, 25 May, p. 12.

Dawtrey, A. (2000). 'UK reins in "Affair"', *Variety*, 20 December, p. 18.

Day Sclater, S. (2000). *Families*, Oxford: Hodder & Stoughton.

Day Sclater, S. and Yates, C. (1999). 'The psycho-politics of post-divorce parenting', in Bainham, A., Day Sclater, S. and Richards, M. (eds), *What is a Parent? A Socio-Legal Analysis*, Oxford: Hart, pp. 271–93.

De Silva, P. (1997). 'Jealousy in couple relationships: Nature, assessment and therapy', *Behaviour Research and Therapy*, 35(11), 973–85.

Delingpole, J. (1996). 'Upstaged by the bad guy', *Daily Telegraph*, 16 February, p. 24.

Delingpole, P. (1998). 'Fatally attracted', *Daily Telegraph Arts*, 25 April, p. 1.

Dinnerstein, D. (1987). *The Rocking of the Cradle and the Ruling of the World*, London: Women's Press.

Dolan, M. and Bishay, N. (1996). 'The effectiveness of cognitive therapy in the treatment of non-psychotic morbid jealousy', *British Journal of Psychiatry*, 168, 588–93.

Downing, C. (1977). 'Jealousy: A depth-psychological perspective', in Clanton, G. and Smith, G. (1986), *Jealousy*, London: University Press of America, pp. 72–9.

Dyer, R. (1982). 'Don't look now: The male pin-up', in Screen (eds) (1992), *The Sexual Subject: A Screen Reader in Sexuality*, London: Routledge, pp. 265–76.

Dyer, R. (1993). *Brief Encounter*, London: British Film Institute Publishing.

Dyer R. (1997). *White*, London: Routledge.

Dyer, R. (1998a). 'Introduction to film studies', in Hill, J. and Church Gibson, P., *The Oxford Guide to Film Studies*, Oxford: Oxford University Press, pp. 3–11.

Dyer, R. (1998b). *Stars, New Edition*, London: British Film Institute.

Dyson, L. (1995). 'Reports and debates: The return of the repressed? Whiteness, femininity and colonialism in *The Piano*', *Screen*, 36(3), 267–76.

Ebert, R. (1996) 'Taxi Driver, Twentieth Anniversary Edition', 1 March, available at: http://rogerebert.suntimes.com/apps/pbcs.dll/article?AID=/19960301/REVIEWS/603010301. Accessed 6 June 1996.

Ebert, R. (2000). Movie Review database, *Chicago Sun-Times Review Archive*, *1085–2000*, June.

Eleftheriotis, D. (1995). 'Questioning totalities: Constructions of masculinity in the popular Greek cinema of the 1960s', *Screen*, 36(3), 233–42.

Elliott, A. (1996a). *Subject to Ourselves: Social Theory, Psychoanalysis and Postmodernity*, Cambridge: Polity Press.

Errigo, A. (1993). '*The Piano*', *Today*, 29 October, p. 42.

Evans, D. (1996). *An Introductory Dictionary of Lacanian Psychoanalysis*, London: Routledge.

Faludi, S. (1991). *Backlash: The Undeclared War Against American Women*, New York: Crown Publishers.

Faludi. S. (1999). *Stiffed: The Betrayal of the Modern Man*, London: Chatto & Windus.

Featherstone, M. (1991). *Consumer Culture and Postmodernism*, London: Sage.

Fenichel, O. (1946). *The Psychoanalytic Theory of Neurosis* London: Routledge & Kegan Paul. Reprinted 1990, London: Routledge.

Fielder, L. A. (1970). *Love and Death in the American Novel*, London: Paladin.

Fisher, N. (2000). 'A Fiennes romance', *The Sun*, 12 February, p. 37.

Flaubert, G. (1857) *Madam Bovary*, trans. G. Wall, Oxford: Oxford World Classics (2002 Edition).

Fox, M. (1996). *'Taxi Driver'*, *Movie Magazine International Review*, 14 February, p. 1. Also see: http://www.shoestring.org/mmi_revs/taxi-driver.html. Accessed 6 January 2001.

Francke, L. (1993). *'The Piano'*, *Sight and Sound*, November, 224–5.

Frank, K. (2002). *G. Strings and Sympathy: Strip Club Regulars and Male Desire*, London: Duke University Press.

French, P. (1993). 'Neither upright nor grand – but both at once', *Observer*, 31 October, p. 4.

French, P. (1998). 'Redial M for Murder', *Observer Review*, 18 October, p. 6.

French, P. (2002) 'Other films: *Unfaithful*' *Observer Review*, 9 June, p. 17.

Freud, S. (1900). 'The maternal and sources of dreams', in Strachey, J. S. (ed. and trans.), *The Interpretation of Dreams*, The Penguin Freud Library, 4, reprinted 1991, London: Penguin Books, pp. 247–377.

Freud, S. (1905). 'Three essays on the theory of sexuality', in Strachey, J. S. (ed. and trans.), *On Sexuality*, The Penguin Freud Library, 7, reprinted 1977, London: Penguin Books, pp. 33–171.

Freud, S. (1910). 'A special type of choice of object made by men (contributions to the Psychology of Love I)', in Strachey, J. S. (ed. and trans.), *On Sexuality*, The Penguin Freud Library, 7, reprinted 1977, London: Penguin Books, pp. 227–43.

Freud, S. (1911). 'Psychoanalytic notes on an autobiographical account of a case of paranoia (*Dementia paranoides*) (Schreber) (1910–1911)', in Strachey, J. S. (ed. and trans.), *Case Histories II*, The Penguin Freud Library, 9, reprinted 1991, London: Penguin Books, pp. 131–220.

Freud, S. (1913). *Totem and Taboo*, trans. J. Strachey, reprinted 1960, London: Routledge & Kegan Paul.

Freud, S. (1917). 'General theory of the neurosis', in Strachey, J. S. (ed. and trans.), *Introductory Lectures on Psychoanalysis*, The Penguin Freud Library, 1, reprinted 1973, London: Penguin Books, pp. 231–95.

Freud, S. (1921). 'Group psychology and the analysis of the ego', in Strachey, J. S. (ed. and trans.), *Civilization, Society and Religion*, The Penguin Freud Library, 12, reprinted 1984, London: Penguin Books, pp. 91–241.

Freud, S. (1922). 'Some neurotic mechanisms in jealousy, paranoia and homosexuality', in Strachey, J. S. (ed. and trans.), *On Psychopathology*, The Penguin Freud Library, 10, reprinted 1979, London: Penguin Books, pp. 196–208.

Freud, S. (1923). 'The ego and the id', in Strachey, J. S. (ed. and trans.), *On Metapsychology, the Theory of Psychoanalysis*, The Penguin Freud Library, 11, reprinted 1984, London: Penguin Books, pp. 339–40.

Freud, S. (1924). 'The dissolution of the Oedipus complex', in Strachey, J. S. (ed. and trans.), *On Sexuality*, The Penguin Freud Library, 7, reprinted 1977, London: Penguin Books, pp. 313–43.

Freud, S. (1925). 'Some psychical consequences of the anatomical distinction between the sexes', in Strachey, J. S. (ed. and trans.), *On Sexuality*, The Penguin Freud Library, 7, reprinted 1977, London: Penguin Books, pp. 323–44.

Freud, S. (1927). 'Fetishism', in Strachey, J. S. (ed. and trans.), *On Sexuality*, The Penguin Freud Library, 7, reprinted 1977, London: Penguin Books, pp. 345–57.

Freud, S. (1931). 'Female sexuality', in Strachey, J. S. (ed. and trans.), *On Sexuality*, The Penguin Freud Library, 7, reprinted 1977, London: Penguin Books, pp. 367–92.

Freud, S. (1933). 'Femininity'. Lecture 33, *New Introductory Lectures on Psycho-analysis*, SE22, Buckingham: Open University Press, 112–35.

Frosh, S. (1997). *For and Against Psychoanalysis.* London: Routledge.

Furedi, F. (2004). *Therapy Culture*, London: Routledge.

Gabbard, G. O. (ed.) (2001). 'Introduction', in Gabbard, G. O. (ed.), *Psycho-analysis and Film*, London: Karnac, pp. 1–14.

Gabbard, K. and Gabbard, G. O (1987). '*Alien* and Melanie Klein's Night Music', in Gabbard, G. O. and Gabbard, K. (1999), *Psychiatry and the Cinema*, 2nd edn., Washington: American Psychiatric Press, pp. 277–91.

Gallafent, E. (1988). 'Black satin: Fantasy, murder and the couple in "Gaslight" and "Rebecca"', *Screen*, **29**(3), Summer, 84–103.

Gay, P. (1988). *A Life For Our Time*, London: J. M. Dent & Sons.

Gere, R. (2001). 'Try to leave your ego behind', *Sunday Telegraph Review*, 7 October, p. 5.

Gere, R. (2002) DVD 'Special Feature: Interview with Richard Gere', *Unfaithful*, USA: Twentieth Century Fox Film Corporation.

Gerrard, N. (1999). 'It's Ralph', *Observer Magazine*, 14 November, pp. 30–4.

Gibbs, J. (2002). *Mise-En-Scène; Film Style And Interpretation*, London: Wallflower Press.

Giddens, A. (1991). *Modernity and Self-Identity*, Cambridge: Polity Press.

Giddens, A. (1992). *The Transformation of Intimacy*, Cambridge: Polity Press.

Gill, R., Henwood, K. and McLean, C. (2000). 'The tyranny of the six pack? Understanding men's responses to representations of the male body in popular culture', in Squire, C. (eds), *Culture In Psychology*, London: Routledge, pp. 100–18.

Gillett, S. (1995). 'Reports and debates: Lips and fingers: Jane Campion's *The Piano*', *Screen*, **36**(3), 277–87.

Gledhill, C. (1987). *Home Is Where The Heart Is: Studies in Melodrama and the Woman's Film*, London: British Film Institute.

Gledhill, C. (1995). 'Women reading men', in Kirkham, P. and Thumim, J. (eds), *Me Jane: Masculinity, Movies and Women*, London: Wishart & Lawrence, pp. 73–93.

Gordon, S. (1996). Reports and Debates: '"I clipped your wing that's all": Auto-eroticism and the female spectator in *The Piano* debate', *Screen*, **37**(2), Summer, pp. 193–205.

Grant, B. (1996). 'Astray on the moor', *Sunday Express*, 18 February, p. 58.

Green, N. and Mort, F. (1996). 'Visual representation and cultural politics', in Robertson, G., *The Block Reader in Visual Culture*, London: Routledge, pp. 226–42.

Greene, G. (1951). *The End of The Affair*, London: Penguin Books (reprinted 2000).

Gritten, D. (1992). 'The great white hope', *Daily Telegraph, Weekend Magazine*, 11 April, pp. 34–9.

Gritten, D. (2000). 'Film reviews: *The End of the Affair*', *Daily Telegraph*, 11 February, p. 29.

Grosz, R. (1983) 'King of the kissers', *The Sun*, 17, January, pp. 14–15.

Hall, C. (1992). *White, Male and Middleclass: Explorations in Feminism and History*, Cambridge: Polity Press.

Hall, S. (1977). 'Encoding/decoding', in Hall, S., Hobson, D., Lowe, A. and Willis, P. (eds) (1980), *Culture, Media, Language*, London: Hutchinson, in association with the Centre for Contemporary Cultural Studies, University of Birmingham, pp. 128–39.

Hammond, M. (1993). 'The historical and hysterical: Melodrama, war and masculinity in Dead Poets Society', in Kirkham, P. and Thumim, J. (eds), *You Tarzan: Masculinity, Movies And Men*, London: Lawrence & Wishart, pp. 52–64.

Hardy, A. (2000). 'The last patriarch', in Margolis, H. (ed.), *Jane Campion's 'The Piano'*, Cambridge: Cambridge University Press, pp. 59–85.

Harwood, S. (1997). *Family Fictions: Representations of the Family in 1980s Hollywood Cinema*, Basingstoke: Macmillan Press.

Hauck, P. (1993). *Jealousy: Why It Happens and How to Overcome It*, London: Sheldon Press.

Henkel, G. (1999). '*Taxi Driver*', DVD Review, June, pp. 1–2. Also see: http://www.dvdreview.com/fullreviews/taxi_driver.shtml. Accessed 20 January 2001.

Hill, J. (1998). 'Film and postmodernism', in Hill, J. and Church Gibson, P., *The Oxford Guide to Film Studies*, Oxford: Oxford University Press, pp. 96–105.

Hill, J. (1999). *British Cinema in the 1980s: Issues and Theories*, Oxford: Clarendon Press.

Hill, J. and Church Gibson, P. (eds) (1998). *The Oxford Guide to Film Studies*, Oxford: Oxford University Press.

Hinshelwood, R. D. (1991). *A Dictionary of Kleinian Thought*, 2nd edn, London: Free Association Books.

Hollway, W. (1987). '"I just wanted to kill a woman", Why? The ripper and male sexuality', Feminist Review (eds), *Sexuality: A Reader*, London: Virago.

Hollway, W. (1989). *Subjectivity and Method in Psychology: Gender, Meaning and Science*, London: Sage.

Hornby, N. (2000). *About a Boy*, London: Penguin Books.

Horney, K. (1926). 'The flight from womanhood: The masculinity complex in women as viewed by men and by women', in Kelman, H. (ed.) (1967), *Feminine Psychology*, New York: W. W. Norton, pp. 47–53.

Horney, K. (1932). 'The dread of woman: Observations on a specific difference in the dread felt by men and women for the opposite sex', in Kelman, H. (ed.) (1967), *Feminine Psychology*, New York: W. W. Norton, pp. 33–46.

Horrocks, R. (1994). *Masculinity in Crisis: Myths Fantasies and Realities*, Basingstoke: Macmillan.

Houston, D. (1954). '*Dial M for Murder*', Spectator, 23 July, BFI *Dial M For Murder* Press Cuttings Pack: London: British Film Institute.

Houzel, D. (2001). 'The "nest of babies" fantasy', *Journal of Child Psychotherapy*, 27(2), 125–38.

Howe, D. (1996). '*Taxi Driver*', Washington Post, 1 March, pp. 1–2.

Hughes-Hallett, L. (1990). *Cleopatra, Histories, Dreams and Distortions*, London: Bloomsbury.

Hutchinson, T. (1976). 'Those mean streets', *Sunday Telegraph*, 22 August, p. 10.

Irigaray, L. (1977). 'This sex which is not one', in Marks, E. and de Courtivron, I. (eds) (1981), *New French Feminisms*, Hertfordshire: Harvester Press, pp. 99–106.

Irigaray, L. (1985). 'Commodities among themselves', in Irigaray, L., *This Sex Which Is Not One*, trans. C. Porter, New York: Cornell University Press, pp. 192–7.

Jameson, F. (1985). 'Postmodernism and consumer society', in Foster, H. (ed.), *Postmodern Culture*, London: Pluto Press, pp. 111–25.

Jameson, F. (1991). *Postmodernism, or, The Cultural Logic of Late Capitalism*, London: Verso.

Jefferson, T (1994). 'Theorising masculine subjectivity', in Newburn, T. and Stanko, E. A. (eds), *Just Boys Doing Business?*, London: Routledge.

Jeffords, S. (1993). 'Can masculinity be terminated?', in Cohan, S. and Hark, I. R. (eds), *Screening the Male: Exploring Masculinities in Hollywood Cinema*, London: Routledge, pp. 245–63.

Johnston, S. (1993). 'Well, Holly would, wouldn't she?', *Independent*, 23 October, p. 56.

Johnston, S. (1999). *Sunday Telegraph Review*, 14 November, p. 7.

Jones, E. (1929). 'Jealousy', in Jones, E. (1950), *Papers on Psychoanalysis*, 5th edn, London: Bailliere, Tindall & Cox, pp. 325–40.

Jones, L. A. (1992). 'One more Arabian knight', *You Magazine, Mail on Sunday*, 29 March, pp. 54–8.

Kael, P. (1976). 'Underground man', *New Yorker*, 9 February.

Kaplan, E. A. (ed.) (1978). *Women in Film Noir*, London: British Film Institute.

Kaplan, E. A. (1990). 'From Plato's cave to Freud's screen', in Kaplan, E. A. (ed.), *Psychoanalysis and Cinema*, London: Routledge, pp. 1–23.

Kaplan, E. A. (1998). 'Classical Hollywood film and melodrama', in Hill, J. and Church Gibson, P., *The Oxford Guide to Film Studies*, Oxford: Oxford University Press, pp. 272–83.

Kelly, L. (1997). *Domestic Violence: Help, Advice and Information*, 2nd edn, London: Islington Council.

Kennedy, H. (1993). *Eve Was Framed: Women and British Justice*, London: Chatto & Windus.

Kerr, P. (2002). 'Low Gere', *New Statesman*, 25 May, p. 45.

Kingsley, H. (1976). 'Go on, take this nasty ride', *Sunday People*, 22 August, p. 15.

Kirkham, P. and Thumim, J. (eds) (1993). *You Tarzan: Masculinity, Movies and Men*, London: Lawrence & Wishart.

Kirkham, P. and Thumim, J. (eds) (1995). *Me Jane: Masculinity, Movies and Women*, London: Wishart & Lawrence.

Klein, M. (1945). 'The Oedipus complex in the light of early anxieties', in Klein, M. (1988a), *Love, Guilt and Reparation and Other Works, 1921–1945*, London: Virago, pp. 370–420.

Klein, M. (1946). 'Notes on some schizoid mechanisms', in Klein, M. (1988b), *Envy and Gratitude and Other Works, 1946–1963*, London: Virago, pp. 1–25.

Klein, M. (1952). 'Some theoretical conclusions regarding the emotional life of the infant', in Klein, M. (1988b). *Envy and Gratitude and Other Works, 1946–1963*, London: Virago, pp. 61–94.

Klein, M. (1957). 'Envy and gratitude', in Klein, M. (1988b), *Envy and Gratitude and Other Works, 1946–1963*, London: Virago, pp. 176–236.

Klein, M. (1988a). *Love, Guilt and Reparation and Other Works, 1921–1945*, London: Virago.

Klein, M. (1988b). *Envy and Gratitude and Other Works, 1946–1963*, London: Virago.

Kolker, R. P. (1998). 'The film text and film form', in Hill, J. and Church Gibson, P. C. (eds), *The Oxford Guide to Film Studies*, Oxford: Oxford University Press, pp. 11–30.

Kramer, P. (1998). 'Post-classical Hollywood', in Hill, J. and Church Gibson, P. C. (eds), *The Oxford Guide to Film Studies*, Oxford: Oxford University Press, pp. 289–310.

Kristeva, J. (1974). 'Revolution in poetic language', in Moi, T. (ed.) (1986), *The Kristeva Reader*, Oxford: Basil Blackwell, pp. 89–137.

Kristeva, J. (1991). *Strangers to Ourselves*, New York: Columbia University Press.

Kuhn, A. (1994). *Women's Pictures; Feminism and Cinema*, London: Verso

Kuhn, A. (2002). *An Everyday Magic: Cinema and Cultural Memory*, London: I. B. Tauris Publishers.

Lacan, J. (1949). 'Mirror stage as formative of the function of the I', in Lacan, J. (1997), *Écrits: A Selection*, trans. A. Sheridon, London: Tavistock, pp. 1–7.

Lacan, J. (1953). 'The function and field of speech and language in psycho-analysis', in Lacan, J. (1977), *Écrits: A Selection*, trans. A. Sheridon, London: Tavistock, pp. 30–113.

Lacan, J. (1958). 'The signification of the phallus', in Lacan, J. (1977), *Écrits: A Selection*, trans. A. Sheridon, London: Tavistock, pp. 281–91.

Lacan, J. (1977). *Écrits: A Selection*, trans. A. Sheridon, London: Tavistock.

Lacan, J. (1991). *The Four Fundamental Concepts of Psycho-Analysis*, trans. A. Sheridon, London: Penguin Books.

Lagache, D. (1938). 'A contribution to the study of ideas of homosexual infidelity in jealousy', in Lagache, D. (1993), *The Work of Daniel Lagache, Selected Writings*, London: Karnac Books, pp. 3–15.

Lagache, D. (1949). 'Homosexuality and jealousy', *International Journal of Psycho-analysis*, **31**, 24–31.

Lane, H. (2002) 'The Gere Hunter', *Observer Magazine*, 15 December, pp. 33–6.

Laplanche, J. and Pontalis, J.-B. (1964). 'Fantasy and the origins of sexuality', in Burgin, V., Donald, J. and Kaplan, C. (eds) (1986), *Formations of Fantasy*, London: Routledge, pp. 5–34.

Laplanche, J. and Pontalis, J.-B. (1988). *The Language of Psychoanalysis*, London: Karnac Books.

Larsen, J. (1999). *DVD Review: Internet Movie Database*, at: rec.arts.movies.reviews. Accessed 12 June 2006.

Lasch, C. (1979). *The Culture of Narcissism*, New York: Norton Paperback (reprinted 1991).

Lawrence, L. (1998). 'Very convincing love scene, Miss Paltrow', *Evening Standard*, 14 September, p. 7.

Lebeau, V. (2001). *Psychoanalysis and Cinema: The Play of Shadows*, London: Wallflower Press.

Lehman, P. (ed.) (2001). *Masculinity: Bodies, Movies, Culture*, London: Routledge.

Leith, W. (1998) 'Pretty Man', *Observer Life Magazine*, 19 April, pp. 7–8.

Lejeune, C. A. (1954). 'Lady killer', *The Observer*, 18 July, BFI Press Cuttings Pack, London: British Film Institute.

Levy, A. (2005). *Female Chauvinist Pigs: Women And The Rise of Raunch Culture*, New York: Free Press.

Limentani, A. (1993). 'To the limits of male heterosexuality: The vagina-man', in Breen, D. (ed.), *The Gender Conundrum: Contemporary Psychoanalytic Perspectives on Femininity and Masculinity*, London: Routledge and The Institute of Psycho-Analaysis, pp. 273–85.

Lley, C. (2006). 'The last hero', *The Observer Magazine*, 17 December, pp. 14–20.

Lupton, D. (1998). *The Emotional Self*, London: Sage.
Lury, C. (1996). *Consumer Culture*, London: Polity Press.
LWT (1999). Interview of M. Douglas on the *South Bank Show*, London Weekend Television, 15 February.
Lyne, A. (2002). DVD 'Special Feature: Director's Commentary', *Unfaithful*, USA: Twentieth Century Fox Film Corporation.
Macaulay, S. (2001) 'He's still prince of the charmers', *Published by who?* 4 June, p. 16.
Macaulay, S. (2002) 'Sex, lies and stereotypes', *Times, Section 2*, 13 May, p. 18.
Mackenzie, S. (1999). 'A man of feeling', *Guardian, Weekend*, 13 November, pp. 8–13.
Mackie, P. (1976) Untitled, *Sunday Times*, 22 August, BFI Press Cuttings Pack: *Taxi Driver*, London: British Film Institute.
MacKinnon, K. (1997). *Uneasy Pleasures: The Male As Erotic Object*, London: Cygnus Arts.
MacKinnon, K. (2003). 'Male spectatorship and the Hollywood love story', *Journal of Gender Studies*, 12(2), 125–36.
Maguire, M. (1995). *Men, Women, Passion and Power: Gender Issues in Psychotherapy*, London: Routledge.
Malcolm, D. (1976). 'Hell on wheels', *The Guardian*, 19 August, p. 61.
Malcolm, D. (1993). 'Undisputed Campion', *The Guardian, Section 2*, 22 October, p. 4.
Malcom, D. (1996). 'Bard to the bone', *The Guardian, Section 2*, 15 February, pp. 8–9.
Mann, R. (1984). 'The man they call the new James Mason', *Sunday Express*, 14 August, p. 15.
Margolis, H. (ed.) (2000). *Jane Campion's 'The Piano'*, Cambridge: Cambridge University Press Film Handbooks.
Mars Jones, A. (1993). 'Poetry in motion', *Independent*, 29 October, p. 26.
Marshall, W. (1988). 'Star of *Fatal Attraction* talks about sex, love and his wife', *Daily Mirror*, 22 January, pp. 14–15.
Martin, N. (1998). 'Romance, jealousy and the perfect relationship', *The Psychologist*, February, 81.
Martin, N. (2000). 'Greene and film sex scenes defended by Fiennes', *Daily Telegraph*, 1 February, p. 13.
Mathes, E. W. (1992). *Jealousy, the Psychological Data*, New York: University Press of America.
Matthews, P. (1998). '*A Perfect Murder*', *Sight and Sound*, 10 October, p. 49.
Mayne, J. (1993). 'Paradoxes of spectatorship', in Turner, G. (ed.) (2002), *The Film Cultures Reader*, London: Routledge, pp. 28–45.
McCartney, J. (2002). '*Unfaithful*', *Sunday Telegraph Review*, 6 June, p. 9.
McDonald, P. (1998). 'Gwyneth's mission impossible', *Evening Standard*, 5 June, p. 2.
McDonald, P. (2000). *The Star System: Hollywood's Production of Popular Identities*, London: Wallflower Press.
Mellen, J. (1977). *Big Bad Wolves: Masculinity in the American Film*, London: Elm Tree Books.
Metz, C. (1975). 'From the imaginary signifier: Identification, mirror'/'The passion for perceiving'/ 'Disavowal, fetishism', in Braudy, L. and Cohen, M.

(eds) (1999a), *Film Theory and Criticism*, 5th edn, Oxford: Oxford University Press, pp. 800–17.

Minsky, R. (1996). *Psychoanalysis and Gender*, London: Routledge.

Minsky, R. (1998). *Psychoanalysis and Culture*, Cambridge: Polity Press.

Mitchell, J. (1975). *Psychoanalysis and Feminism*, Harmondsworth: Pelican Books.

Mitchell, J. (2000). *Mad Men and Medusas: Reclaiming Hysteria*, London: Penguin Books.

Mitchell, J. and Rose, J. (eds) (1982). *Jacques Lacan and the Ecole Freudienne: Feminine Sexuality*, Basingstoke: Macmillan.

Modleski, T. (1982). 'Never to be thirty-six years old: *Rebecca* as female Oedipal drama', *Wide Angle*, 5(1), 34–41.

Modleski, T. (1988). *The Women Who Knew Too Much: Hitchcock and Feminist Theory*, London: Methuen.

Moi, T. (1987). 'Jealousy and sexual difference', in *Feminist Review* (eds), *Sexuality: A Reader*, London: Virago, pp. 136–48.

Mollon, P. (2002). *Shame and Jealousy: The Hidden Turmoils*, London: Karnac.

Moore, S. (1988). 'Getting a bit of the other: The pimps of postmodernism', in Chapman, R. and Rutherford, J. (eds), *Male Order, Unwrapping Masculinity*, London: Lawrence & Wishart, pp. 165–92.

Morel, G. (2000). 'Feminine jealousies', in Saleci, R. (ed.), *Sexuation*, Durham, NC: Duke University Press, pp. 157–69.

Morley, D. (1980). *The 'Nationwide' Audience: Structure and Decoding*, London: British Film Institute.

Morley, D. (1986). *Family Television: Cultural Power and Domestic Leisure*, London: Comedia.

Morley, D. (2002). Keynote address at the 'Language Communication and Culture' Conference, Evora, Portugal, 28–30 November.

Muir, S. (1997). 'Interview with M. Douglas', *Daily Telegraph*, 6 October, p. 15.

Mullen, P. E. (1991). 'Jealousy: The pathology of passion', *British Journal of Psychiatry*, 158, 593–601.

Muller, R. and Burke, J. (1955). 'Critic and priest discuss "The End of The Affair"', *Picture Post*, 2 April, pp. 27–30.

Mulvey, L. (1975). 'Visual pleasure and narrative cinema', in Baudry, L. and Cohen, M. (eds) (1999), *Film Theory and Criticism*, 5th edn, Oxford: Oxford University Press, pp. 833–44.

Mulvey, L. (1981). 'Afterthoughts on "visual pleasure and narrative cinema"', inspired by *Duel In the Sun*', in Kaplan, E. A. (ed.) (1990), *Psychoanalysis and Cinema*, London: Routledge, pp. 24–35.

Muncie, J. and Wetherell, M. (eds) (1995). *Understanding the Family*, London: Sage.

Murf, (1976). '*Taxi Driver*', *Variety*, January, 28.

Music, G. (2001). *Affect and Emotion*, Reading: Icon Books.

Nathan, I. (2002). 'Love in a cold climax', *Times, Section 2*, 6 June, p. 12.

Neale, S. (1982). '*Chariots of Fire*: Images of men', *Screen*, 23(3–4), 47–53.

Neale, S. (1983). 'Masculinity as spectacle – Reflections on men and mainstream cinema', *Screen*, 24(6), 2–16. Later reprinted in Cohan, S. and Hark, I. R. (eds) (1993), *Screening The Male: Exploring Masculinities in Hollywood Cinema*, London: Routledge, pp. 9–20.

Neale, S. (1986). 'Melodrama and tears', *Screen*, 27(6), 6–22.

Neale, S. and Smith, M. (eds) (1998). *Contemporary Hollywood Cinema*, London: Routledge.

Nichols, B. (ed.) (1985). *Movies and Methods, Volume 2*, London: University of California Press.

Nicol, B. (2006). *Stalking*, London: Reaction Books.

Norman, N. (1994). 'The film that's dividing London's dinner parties', *Evening Standard*, 7 February, p. 12.

Norman, N. (2002) 'The fatal side of attraction', *Evening Standard*, 6 June, p. 55.

Owens, C. (1985). 'The discourse of others: Feminists and postmodernism', in Foster, H. (ed.), *Postmodern Culture*, London: Pluto Press, pp. 57–82.

Patterson, C. (2006). 'Family values don't stretch far enough', *The Independent*, 29 July, p. 16.

Patterson, J. (1999). '*The End of the Affair*', *Guardian*, Section 2, 10 December, p. 27.

Peachment, C. (1996). 'The soft core of the green-eyed monster', *Sunday Telegraph Review*, 18 February, p. 14.

Pearce, G. (2003) 'I made mistakes but I have finally grown up', *Evening Standard*, p. 21.

Pearce, L. (1996). 'Review: engaging characters, fiction, emotion and the cinema: Murray Smith', *Screen*, **4**, winter, 415–18.

Penley, C. (1985). 'Feminism, film theory and the bachelor machines', *MLF*, 10, 39–59.

Phillips, M. (1999). 'Genre, star and auteur', in Nelmes, J. (ed.), *An Introduction to Film Studies*, 2nd edn, London: Routledge, pp. 161–207.

Pickering, P. (1988). 'Son of Spartacus in the reptile pit', *Sunday Times*, 1 May, pp. 18–19.

Pihama, L. (2000). 'Ebony and ivory: Constructions of Maori in *The Piano*', in Margolis, H. (ed.), *Jane Campion's 'The Piano'*, Cambridge: Cambridge University Press Film Handbooks, pp. 114–34.

Polan, D. (2001). *Jane Campion*, London: British Film Institute.

Potter, L. (1999). 'Unhappy for I am white: Questions of identity and identification when Othello goes to the movies', *Times Literary Supplement*, 5 March, 18–19.

Powrie, P. Davies, A. and Babington, B. (2004). *The Trouble With Men: Masculinities in European and Hollywood Cinema*, London: Wallflower Press.

Price, R. (1982) 'Richard Gere', *Rolling Stone*, 30 September, pp. 13–16.

Prigge, M. (1998). Available at: http://www.rec.arts.movies.reviews. Accessed 9 July 2000.

Proust, M. (1913) 'Swann's way', in Proust, M., *Remembrance of Things Past*, trans. C. K. Moncrieff (1981 revised edition), London: Penguin Books, pp. 1–462.

Queenan, J. (1998). 'Twist again', *Guardian Guide*, 10 October, pp. 16–17.

Quirke, A. (2000). 'Love in a damp climate', *Independent On Sunday*, 13 February, p. 3.

Radstone, S. (1995a). '"Too straight a drive to the tollbooth": Masculinity, mortality and Al Pacino', in Kirkham, P. and Thumim, J. (eds), *Me Jane: Masculinity, Movies And Women*. London: Lawrence & Wishart, pp. 148–65.

Radstone, S. (1995b). 'Cinema/memory/history', *Screen*, 36(1), 34–47.

Radstone, S. (1996). 'Heroes for our times: Tommy Cooper', *Soundings*, 3 (Summer), 191–209.

Radstone, S. (2007) 'Clinical and academic psychoanalytic criticism: Differences that matter', in Bainbridge, C., Radstone, S. Rustin, M. andYates, C. (2007), *Culture and the Unconscious*, Basingstoke: Palgrave Macmillan.

Rice, J. C. (1976). 'Transcendental pornography and *Taxi Driver*', *Journal of Popular Film*, 5(2), 109–23.

Richards, J. (1997) 'Obsessions: Richard Gere', *Guardian*, 9 May, p. 16.

Riviere, J. (1929). 'Womanliness as masquerade', in Burgin, V., Donald, J. and Kaplan, C. (eds) (1986), *Formations of Fantasy*, London: Routledge, pp. 35–44.

Riviere, J. (1932). 'Jealousy as a mechanism of defence', *International Journal of Psychoanalysis*, 13, 414–24.

Robey, T. (2002) 'Seductively sleazy', *Daily Telegraph*, 7 June, p. 23.

Robinson, N. (1999). 'With choices like these, who needs enemies? *The Piano*, women's articulations, melodrama and the woman's film', in Coombs, F and Gemmel, S. (eds), *Piano Lessons: Approaches to The Piano*, Sydney, Australia: John Libbey, pp. 19–43.

Rodowick, D. N. (1982). 'Madness, Authority and Ideology in the Domestic Melodrama of the 1950s', *Velvet Light Trap*, 19, 40–5. Reprinted in Gledhill C. (ed.) (1987). *Home Is Where the Heart Is: Studies in Melodrama and the Woman's Film*, London: British Film Institute, pp. 268–80.

Romney, J. (1993). 'Cinema appasionata', *New Statesman and Society*, 29 October, pp. 33–4.

Rook, J. (1983). 'How they turned shy Sam into a sexy superspy', *Daily Express*, 23 August, pp. 16–17.

Rose, J. (1987). 'Femininity and its discontents', in *Feminist Review* (eds), *Sexuality: A Reader*, London: Virago Press, pp. 177–90.

Rose, J. (2003). 'The cult of celebrity', in *On Not Being Able to Sleep: Psychoanalysis and the Modern World*, London: Chatto & Windus, pp. 201–15.

Rowe, K. (1995). 'Melodrama and men in post-classical romantic comedy', in Kirkham, P. and Thumim, J. (eds), *Me Jane: Masculinity, Movies and Women*, London: Wishart & Lawrence, pp. 184–93.

Sandler, K. (2000). 'Mighty Fiennes', *DC*, April, p. 9.

Sands, S. (2006). 'Brown Vs Cameron: May the best dad win', *The Independent On Sunday*, 20 August, p. 11.

Sayers, J. (1991). *Mothering Psychoanalysis: Helene Deutsch, Karen Horney, Anna Freud and Melanie Klein*, London: Penguin.

Sayers, J. (1997). *Freudian Tales About Imagined Men*, London: Vintage.

Schatz, T. (1993). 'The new Hollywood', in Turner, G. (ed.) (2002), *The Film Cultures Reader*, London: Routledge, pp. 184–205.

Schickle, R. (1976), 'Pot holes', *Time Magazine*, 16 February, pp. 62–3.

Schmideberg, M. (1953). 'Some aspects of jealousy and of feeling hurt', *Psychoanalytic Review*, 40(1), 1–16.

Schrader, P. (1990). *Taxi Driver*, London: Faber and Faber, reprinted 2000.

Segal, H. (1988). *Introduction to the Work of Melanie Klein*, London: Karnac Books.

Segal, L. (1990). *Slow Motion: Changing Masculinities, Changing Men*, London: Virago.

Segal, L. (1999). *Why Feminism?* Cambridge: Polity Press.

Seidenberg, R. (1952). 'Jealousy: The wish', *Psychoanalytic Review*, 42, 345–53.

Shepherd, M. (1961). 'Morbid jealousy: Some clinical and social aspects of a psychiatric symptom', *Journal of Mental Science*, 107, 687–753.

Shiware, S. (2002) 'Sex, lies and regret', *Asian Age*, 27 September, p. 9.

Shone, T. (1996). 'More is less', *Sunday Times, Section 10*, 18 February, pp. 6–7.

Shone, T. (1998). 'One hitch after another', *Sunday Times, Section 11*, 18 October, p. 7.

Shorter, E. (1976). 'Take a taxi-ride to Grand Guignol', *Daily Telegraph*, 20 August, p. 11.

Silverman, K. (1980). 'Masochism and subjectivity', *Framework*, 12 (4), 2–9.

Silverman, K. (1988). *The Acoustic Mirror: The Female Voice in Psychoanalysis and Cinema*, Bloomington: Indiana University Press.

Silverman, K. (1990). 'Historical trauma and male subjectivity', in Kaplan, E. A. (ed.), *Psychoanalysis and Cinema*, London: Routledge, pp. 110–27.

Smurthwaite, N. (1992). 'Ralph Fiennes: The star whose time has come', *Ms London*, 12 October, p. 9.

Spicer, A. (2003). *Typical Men: The Representation of Masculinity in Popular British Cinema*, London: I. B. Tauris.

Staiger, J. (1992). *Interpreting Films: Studies in the Historical Reception of American Cinema*, Princeton: Princeton University Press.

Staiger, J. (1993). 'Taboos and totems: Cultural meanings of "The Silence of the Lambs"', in Collins, J., Radner, H. and Collins, A. P. (eds), *Film Theory Goes to the Movies*, London: Routledge, pp. 142–54.

Staiger, J. (2005). *Media Reception Studies*, London and New York: New York University Press.

Stanbrook, A. (1988). 'Star sign of the times', *Daily Telegraph*, 11 May, p. 18.

Stearns, P. N. (1988). 'Anger and American work: A twentieth-century turning point', in Stearns, C. Z. and Stearns, P. N. (eds), *Emotion and Social Change: Towards a New Psychohistory*, New York: Holmes & Meier, pp. 123–49.

Stearns, P. N. (1989). *Jealousy: The Evolution of an Emotion in American History*, New York: New York University Press.

Stenner, P. (1992). 'Discoursing jealousy', in Burman, E. and Parker, I. (eds), *Discourse Analytic Research*, London: Routledge.

Steyn, M. (1993). 'Pulling faces', *Spectator*, 30 October, p. 46.

Steyn, M. (1998). '*A Perfect Murder*', *Asian Age*, 27 October, p. 14.

Stoddart, H. (1995). 'I don't know whether to look at him or read him: *Cape Fear* and male scarification', in Kirkham, P. and Thumim, J. (eds), *Me Jane: Masculinity, Movies and Women*, London: Wishart & Lawrence, pp. 194–202.

Storey, J. (1996). *Cultural Studies and the Study of Popular Culture: Theories and Methods*, Edinburgh: Edinburgh University Press.

Storey, J. (1999). *Cultural Consumption and Everyday Life*, London: Arnold.

Studlar, G. (1985). 'Masochism and the perverse pleasures of the cinema', in Nichols, B. (ed.), *Movies and Methods*, Volume 2, Berkley and Los Angeles: University of California Press, pp. 602–22.

Summerskill, B. (2002). 'Good news for British men: They have never been happier', *The Observer*, 25 August, p. 6.

Sutcliffe, T. (2000). 'The heart of darkness', *Independent Review*, 12 February, p. 5.

Sweet, M. (1998). 'How I learnt to love Michael Douglas', *Independent on Sunday, Culture*, 18 October, p. 5.

Tabakoff, J. (1993). 'An indecent living in Hollywood', *Daily Telegraph*, 17 May, p. 17.

Taubin, A. (1992). 'Invading bodies: *Alien3* and the Trilogy', *Sight and Sound*, 2, July, 3.

Taubin, A. (1993). 'Mirror, mirror', *Village Voice*, 20 July, 57.

Taubin, A. (2000). *Taxi Driver*, London: British Film Institute.

Taylor, J. (1989). '20 facts we're Abel to tell on Whiz-Kid Kane', *The Sun*, 14 January, p. 19.

Thomson, D. (1993). 'The face to watch', *Independent on Sunday*, 26 September, p. 20.

Thomson, D. (1995). 'The Michael Douglas thing', *Independent on Sunday*, 3 December, pp. 22–3.

Thomson, D. (1998b). 'Robert De Niro is feeling better', *Independent Review*, 12 November, p. 12.

Time Out (eds) (2002). *Time Out Film Guide, 2002*, 10th edn, London: Penguin Books.

Tolstoy, L. (1890). *The Kreutzer Sonata and Other Stories*, London: Penguin Books, 1984.

Tookey, C. (1993). 'Here's a film which is out of tune with its time, and has no rhyme or reason', *Daily Mail*, 29 October, pp. 40–1.

Turner, G. (ed.) (2002). *The Film Cultures Reader*, London: Routledge.

Turner, G. (2004). *Understanding Celebrity*, London: Sage.

Van Sommers, P. (1988). *Jealousy*, London: Penguin Books.

Vaughan, V. M. (1996). *Othello: A Contextual History*, Cambridge: Cambridge University Press.

Walker, A. (1976). 'Hellish', *Evening Standard*, 19 August, pp. 18–19.

Walker, A. (1993). 'Mutual release in the key of lust', *Evening Standard*, 28 October, p. 41.

Walker, A. (1996). 'The wrong shade of black', *Evening Standard*, 15 February, p. 32.

Walker, A. (1998). '*A Perfect Murder*', *Evening Standard*, 15 October, p. 26.

Walker, A. (2000). 'Sex and the third man', *Evening Standard*, 10 February, p. 29.

Walker, A. (2001). 'It's the word of mouth that counts, not the words of critics', *Evening Standard*, 26 June, p. 13.

Walster, E. H. and Rapson, R. L. (1996). *Love and Sex: Cross Cultural Perspectives*, Boston, MA: Allyn & Bacon.

Watson, S. (2000). 'Exit macho man: Are men the new women?', *Evening Standard*, 14 February, p. 27.

Weeks, J. (1985). *Sexuality and its Discontents: Meanings, Myths and Modern Sexualities*, London: Routledge.

Weeks, J. (1992). 'Homosexuality', in Wright, E. (ed.), *Feminism and Psychoanalysis: A Critical Dictionary*, Oxford: Basil Blackwell, pp. 157–61.

Wenn (2006) 'Gere fails to see eye-to-eye with director', *Movie/TV News*, available at: http://www.imdb.com/news/wenn/2002-05-13. Accessed 20 July 2006.

Westerbeck, C. L. Jnr. (1976). 'Beauties and the beast', *Sight and Sound*, 45(3), 134–40.

White, T. H. (1939) *Once and Future King*, London: Book Club Associates, 1973 Edition].

Whitefait, W. (1954). 'The movies; "Dial M for Murder" at Warner's', *New Statesman*, 5 March, BFI Press Cuttings Pack, London: British Film Institute.

Wieland, C. (2000). *The Undead Mother: Psychoanalytic Explorations of Masculinity, Femininity and Matricide*, London: Rebus Press.

Wilkinson, H. and Mulgan, T. (1995). *Freedom's Children*, London: Demos.

Williams, L. (1991). 'Film bodies: Gender, genre and excess', in Baudry, L. and Cohen, M. (eds) (1999), *Film Theory and Criticism*, 5th edn, Oxford: Oxford University Press, pp. 701–15.

Williams, R. (1998). '*A Perfect Murder*', *Guardian Section 2*, 16 October, p. 9.

Winnicott, D. W. (1971). *Playing and Reality*, London: Routledge.

Worrall, S. (1997). 'The Dalai luvvie', *Independent on Sunday*, 2 November, p. 3.

Wrathall, J. (1998). '*A Perfect Murder*', *Independent Review*, 15 October, p. 11.

Wyatt, J. (1998). 'The formation of the "major independent": Miramax, new line and the new Hollywood', in Neale, S. and Smith, M. (eds), *Contemporary Hollywood Cinema*, London: Routledge, pp. 74–90.

Yates, C. (2000). 'Masculinity and good enough jealousy', *Psychoanalytic Studies*, 2(1), 77–88.

Yates, C. (2001). 'Teaching psychoanalytic studies: Towards a new culture of learning in higher education', *Psychoanalytic Studies*, 3(3–4), 333–47.

Yates, C. (2006). 'Masculine jealousy and the struggle for possession in *The End Of The Affair* (N. Jordan, US/Ger.1999)', *Journal For Cultural Research*, 10(3), 219–35.

Yates, C. and Day Sclater, S. (2000). 'Culture, psychology and transitional space', in Squire, C. (ed.), *Culture in Psychology*, London: Routledge, pp. 135–47.

Zacharek, S. (2005) 'Have you seen this man?', *Guardian Review*, 28 January, p. 7.

Index